FUTURE CHURCH

FUTURE CHURCH

Ralph W. Neighbour, Jr.
Compiler

BROADMAN PRESS
Nashville, Tennessee

All Scripture references marked NIV are from the HOLY BIBLE *New International Version*, copyright© 1978, New York Bible Society. Used by permission.

All Scripture references marked NASB are from The New American Standard Bible. Copyright © The Lockman Foundation, 1960, 1962, 1963, 1971, 1972, 1973, 1975. Used by permission.

All Scripture references marked NEB are from *The New English Bible*. Copyright © The Delegates of the Oxford University Press and the Syndics of the Cambridge University Press, 1961, 1970. Reprinted by permission.

Dewey Decimal Classification: 252
Subject heading: SERMONS—COLLECTIONS
Library of Congress Catalog Card Number: 79-50338

Printed in the United States of America

Preface

The Second Conference on Church Renewal was held April 22-27, 1979, at the West Memorial Baptist Church in Houston, Texas. Its theme was "Future Church." Five hundred seventy eight delegates from a score of evangelical denominations and fellowships attended. From videotapes of some speakers, delivered messages have been edited and prepared for use in this volume.

The Conference looked toward the church in the coming years of this century. Os Guinness and Cal Thomas dealt with the entrapments the church will face, and John Newport dealt with the religions she will encounter. Roy Edgemon, Ray Stedman, Jack Taylor, Charles Aranyas, and I spoke of the tasks and gifts to be exercised in the emerging cultures. Tom Wolf, Eugene Kerr, Charles Solomon, and Larry Richards dealt with other facets of the strategy and training potentials available to the "Future Church." In a sense, each chapter stands alone. In another sense, each one is like a piece of a tapestry, which, when completed, gives unique insights into the work of the church in the coming generations.

Each writer accepts responsibility only for the views of his *own* words. *All,* however, accept responsibility for the testing of their words by the inspired authority of Holy Scripture. On that point, there is no variation among any of the speakers!

We who have contributed chapters have relinquished royalties to Touch Productions, a ministry within the body life of the West Memorial Baptist Church. They will be used for the further development of strategies for penetrating our world with the gospel of Christ. All of us share a common desire to be free from profiteering out of the ministry our Lord has given us. Ours is a gift of love!

The publisher had suggested we use our pictures on the front cover of the book to help generate sales. Os Guinness' response was quickly accepted by all of us: We would much prefer to be known by our words than our faces! We pray this volume will stir your heart, mind, and mouth to be better prepared to penetrate the world *you* live in with the gospel of Christ.

RALPH W. NEIGHBOUR, JR.

Contents

1. The Urbanization of the Earth

Ralph W. Neighbour, Jr.

Ralph W. Neighbour, Jr., is pastor of the West Memorial Baptist Church, a congregation deeply involved in church renewal. He has served as a missionary in Vietnam and Singapore. He is the author of eight books.

Fasten your seat belts for a jolting statement! In twenty-two years, the existing population of earth will live in urban centers! To fully comprehend that fact, we must first consider the world's . . .

POPULATION EXPLOSION

The human race is growing so fast that it will double in about twenty-five years. It required the entire history of man to give birth to the first billion people, by 1830. It took only 100 years to add the second billion. The third billion came in thirty years. In fourteen more years, we added the fourth billion. By 2000 A.D., we will add three billion more! Demographers are conservatively forecasting 7.2 billion by the end of the century.

The world is now bracing itself for the task of housing, clothing, and feeding these billions, most of whom will be too young to work. Unfortunately, the largest birthrate is going to take place in the nations which can least afford the costs of the new people. Zambia, for example, had a growth rate of 3 percent in 1970—meaning that it will double in only twenty-four years—with a per capita gross national product of $220. Incidentally, that same year, 600,000 died in a Pakistan cyclone. It took only sixty days for that nation to replace the dead with 600,000 babies!

YOUTH EXPLOSION

Next, consider the youth explosion we are currently experiencing. In Southeast Asia, there are nations where 63 percent of the entire population is under twenty-one years of age. Rhodesia and Kenya have the highest rates of population increase in the African continent. If birthrates such as these continue in these two countries their population will double in only twenty-one years. One of the forgotten facts for the Christian strategists is the *youthfulness* of our earth! Consider the amount of budget, of personnel, of activity, of *discussion* you have participated in regarding this crucial matter. If we do not give direction to these youth before they leave their teens, their value system is shaped. It is virtually ten times harder to win a person at 26 than at 16! When we realize that the *present* group under 21 is monstrous in size, we face a *fact of urgency:* We cannot dawdle four or five years preparing to reach them . . . they will be harder to reach!

Critical, too, is the need for *rapid discipling* of the existing youth in our churches. They are our greatest asset for evangelizing other youth. Too often we think that married or middle-aged Christians are the only ones who can undertake great tasks. We must destroy that idea. The young people are the pilots, the soldiers, the "risk takers" of the world. Singapore has shown that its young men can develop an urban center rapidly and efficiently and in a fraction of the time that older city planners had forecast. To reach the cities, we must train *young* men and women with the spiritual and practical tools, to cut new patterns to reach their generation for Christ.

In developing an urban strategy, much attention must be given to the ways youth congregate. In the Shinjuku district of Tokyo in 1972, for example, I watched 20,000 young men and women milling in the streets and shops, long past the hour of midnight. Not one evangelistic thrust had been attempted in that area of pleasure! Hundreds were simply "there," with nothing to do. They were available—yet, not one of the nearby church buildings ever opened her doors when the streets were crowded. They opened for "worship" when the streets were empty caverns!

NEW PATTERNS NEEDED

To keep pace with this expanding population, the Christian community will have to add 62,500,000 converts a year from now to the end of the century! The alternative to such evangelism is frightening. At our present snail pace of evangelism, some missiologists forecast a world Christian community of less than 1 percent of the total population by the end of the century.

While we rejoice that Africa's spiritual birthrate is about five times greater than its physical birthrate, we must face another fact of the future which may well put a halt to that . . . I refer to the . . .

POPULATION IMPLOSION

The urbanizing of the earth is a new phenomenon in the history of man. In 1800, only 5 percent of the earth's people lived in cities. Presently, 51 percent live in cities . . . and by 2000 A.D., 73 percent of the people will live in them! Africa itself will grow from 400 million to 813 million by then. Imagine Nairobi, four times larger than at present, with 3⅓ million people . . . Mombasa, growing from 331,000 to 1,296,000; Kampala multiplying fivefold to 2,777,000 people.

This world urbanization will require the equivalent of 5,000 new cities of a half-million residents each. City growth will move from the 172 cities of one million people in 1975, to 300 cities of one million or more by 2000 . . . and 200 of those cities will be in third world countries! Even today, Mexico City's residential poverty pockets number over four million people. These people live without official recognition of their existence because their government throws up its hands at the impossible task of providing water, sewer, streets, and amenities for these desperately poor urban dwellers.

East Africa gave birth to its first million-resident city in 1975. It will contain thirteen cities that large by the end of the century. Africa, as a whole, had only thirteen million people living in cities of 100,000 or more in 1950. Today, sixty-one million live in them . . . and in 2000 A.D., there will be 226 million. Imagine an Africa, for centuries rural, where one out of four live in cities! This brings us to still another harbinger of desperate things to come . . .

THE RURAL-TO-URBAN PUSH-PULL SYNDROME

Migrating into the city is a *worldwide* phenomenon. It is false to believe that the city attracts by its glamour and excitement. In over 80 percent of the cases, there is one purpose for people coming to the city: money! Jobs are available, and cash is needed.

In Jakarta, the rural poor pour in. That city "officially" claims to have 4½ million residents, but the real figures are *actually* closer to 7½ million . . . and it is projected to become twenty million or more by 2000 A.D. It will be a 120-mile-long "strip city."

Manila will also surpass the twenty million mark, and will extend itself from the China Sea to the Pacific Ocean! Immigration inevitably occurs at a rate breathtakingly faster than local and national government agencies can accommodate.

Unlike most of the rest of the world's cities, however, East Africa's migration pattern is unique. It is referred to by sociologists as the *"shuttle migration."* This term refers to men who spend their lives shuttling back and forth between the city and the village. They do not *plan* to live permanently in the city. These men first come to the city to earn the price, for example, of a bride. They marry and live for a while in the village. Later, they return to earn money to build houses—*in the village*. They next return to the city with their sons, who live with them during the school year. Finally, these men return to the village to care for their aged parents, and live out their years there.

In Nairobi, the mass of the people of Kikuyu, Luyia, Luo, and Kamba do not regard it as their city to the extent that they will commit themselves and their families to it. Their interests, goals, and identifications are only partially urban. One sociologist interviewed men in Nairobi who lived 200 miles away. He then interviewed men in the distant village. Matching the two groups exactly by age, education, and family status, he discovered the average number of years spent in Nairobi by the two groups was practically identical!

Van Velsen did a similar survey in Malawi. He learned that, far from breaking down social forms, labor migration to the city is an important factor in insuring the tribal society of the Tonga. Absent villagers maintain an active role in the social and political structure of Tongaland. It is the exception, not the rule, for them to settle permanently in the towns. The influence of an effective urban strategy in Africa, therefore, will spread continually to the most remote hamlet!

It is usually the *educated* who plan to *settle* in the city, for their training makes it impractical for them to return to the rural area. The semiliterate or semiskilled are the ones who cause the "planned backflow" from the city to the village, and return. These people behave in predictable ways in the city. Housing, social contacts, voluntary participation in church activities, and use of savings are all determined by their plans to return to the country.

Stable migration is reflected by Santiago, Chile, where there are eighty-four males per 100 females migrating. In Mexico City, the figure is ninety-two males per 100 females; in Lima, Peru, ninety-four per 100; in Seoul, Korea, ninety-nine per 100. Contrast this with Nairobi: *187 men per 100 women migrate into the city!* This is the highest ratio of any city on earth. Close behind are Kinshasa, Congo, with 172 per 100, and Karachi, Pakistan, with 147 per 100. In such cities, the families remain behind in the villages. Evangelism in such cities must be adjusted to this influx of men.

A patchwork pattern will emerge over the next decades, with migrants from certain rural areas becoming more and more committed to the city, while other groups will cling to temporary residence there. An effective world urban strategy must give serious consideration to this matter. When the Luhya tribesmen from the Kisa district come to Nairobi, where do they live? Where do they work while supplementing low agricultural income? *How can they be penetrated while in the city?*

Another factor of the city migration is the "outcast" group who arrive, never to return to the villages. These people are the social outcasts, the fugitives. Barren women find no place in the country. Widows face the same problem. Blood feuds send others to the city, along with those accused of witchcraft. Losers in local political contests may also flee. The prostitutes, the hurting outcasts, who often have the greatest need when they arrive in the metropolis come from these groups. They make money from their only available sources: prostitution and scavenging. Can they be reached apart from a self-help plan, which equips them to support themselves in a more dignified manner? I do not personally think so! Evangelism must penetrate *all* of these groups!

The migrants in the throes of social upheaval are unusually susceptible to an urban witness. They are *literally* ships without rudders. The happy-go-luck life of the rural area is gone. Unless Christ is presented quickly to the migrant, secularism—*the religion of the city*—replaces earlier beliefs. Once firmed, the next generation in the city will follow the trend set by the parents.

Unfortunately, one of the most neglected segments of the earth is the poverty-stricken city dwellers. After a full week of teaching and pleading with pastors in a Southeast Asia metroplex, during which time I walked through cardboard shacks which housed over a half-million souls, one pastor concluded: "God did not equip me to work with such people. I am unable to understand them. I must continue to work with the educated." He was telling the truth! Unfortunately, we price the gospel too high for the urban poor. They are literally condemned by their poverty for time and eternity! We cannot consider the city's evangelism patterns without considering the poor. *Rural patterns of evangelism do not fit the slums.* We must find the answer to this problem . . . and find it quickly!

Reaching migrants is one of the oldest successful strategies for evangelism! Migrants took the gospel to the Roman empire. Paul went to a minority group when he went evangelizing. The seed of the Word of God was not scattered everywhere in equal measure. It was sown specifically among the *diaspora,* the migrants. Think of those converted in the book of Acts while they were migrants: the eunuch from Ethiopia, Barnabas from Cyprus, Saul from Tarsus, Cornelius the Italian, Lydia from Thyatira, Apollos from Alexandria.

Migrant groups are often more responsive in the city than in the village. Being away from home creates conditions favorable to evangelism. The traditional guardians of customs and ideas do not exist in the city. People away from home are "off balance"— impressed by what they would have considered unthinkable or strange back home. As Ed Dayton points out, the migrant is forced to be a "learner" in the city. New ways are accepted out of necessity.

Ed Dayton points to 1 percent of Japanese who are Christian in Japan, compared to 43 percent of the 700,000 Japanese in Brazil who have been Christianized! That's a story repeated by the Chinese—less than 1 percent of the mainland was Christian after 10,000 missionaries worked among them . . . but 5 to 7 percent of the forty million Chinese migrants in the world today are Christian. Much attention must be given to the immigrating city dwellers as urban patterns of evangelism are developed.

THE CURSE OF CHURCH BUILDINGS

Twenty thousand stone, thatch, or other types of church buildings dot the countryside in Kenya. They often serve as prisons in which the good news is locked up, insulating it from the teeming masses who live nearby. As land values skyrocket, thought must be given to the significance of buildings in urban areas. Alternate forms of buildings, which can provide weekday space for evangelistic endeavors, are required. Church auditoriums sitting empty except for one or two hours on Sunday are not nearly as practical as all-purpose rooms which can provide weekday ministries. This challenge must be met in time for the youth of our cities, who could be reached through them during the week days. How can they better be used to reach the migrant masses? What do they mean to the prostitutes who walk past them or, to the hungry children or, the sick? We need answers to this problem.

THE CAPTIVITY OF THE LAITY

Consider the millions of urbanities without Christ, and consider the potential task force needed to reach them with the gospel. The Holy Spirit has sealed every believer, and has endowed them with spiritual capacities for ministry. Every member of the church must find their place in the evangelizing of a city! More and more of God's finest pastors are resigning the role of *director of the Church,* to become the *equipper of the ministers.* This is the highest task God can call a man to do! Those who shepherd their flocks with the spirit of John, saying, "they must increase, but I must decrease," see rapid growth in their churches.

The entire earth is being exposed to the power of the released laity. The explosion of Pentecostalism in South America has little to do with their doctrine, for other groups who are not Pentecostal have grown just as fast after adopting their simple pattern. Their growth stems from church members who have been trained to lead small Bible Study groups in their homes. They penetrate their own neighborhoods through visitation and witnessing. Imagine a congregation of 25,000! In Korea, one church now has 70,000 members, composed of over 2,000 "Shepherds" of as many home Bible Study groups. When Presbyterians copied this pattern, they grew just as rapidly. A church in Dallas, Texas, pastored by Dr. Gene Getz, grew from 38 to nearly 5,000 in only five years. More and more, we are recognizing that *Christ's greatest untapped resources are church members who have never been adequately discipled, trained, or challenged* to become evangels of the gospel in their own neighborhoods. Important, indeed, to an effective urban strategy, is the plan to train large numbers of the laity.

CHRISTIAN DILEMMA: "DOUBLE-CULTURE SHOCK!"

The rush of people to urban centers in the world today has a special problem for Southern Baptists. William Matheny pointed out, "Big cities remain a mystery to us generally. Baptists are a rural people as a whole, by history and by temperament. The city ghetto is as foreign to our people as any foreign country. We are not at home in the city. Our sermons and our literature are full of rural illustrations and small-town stories." Matheny's words, delivered to the 1970 Conference for Furloughing Missionaries, affirms what one Foreign Mission Board member has pointed out: that *over 90 percent of the present missionaries grew up in rural or village contexts,* never fully exposed to the urban milieu prior to overseas assignment! Matheny continued: "We are a rural-oriented people, and even in the cities we tend to move to the suburban areas and maintain rural-oriented values and attitudes. This is not good or bad in itself, but it does reflect who and what we are."

Therefore, many pastors and missionaries face a "double-culture shock." They must not only relate to a second culture and language, but also face transition from the childhood country patterns to the unknown city patterns of life. To have to do this without any assistance is one of the saddest dilemmas facing many a missionary today. At the very time when the people of the earth are moving to the cities, those responding to missions are ill-equipped to work in them.

Many existing pastors and missionaries were born into an economic, social, physical, and cultural environment which differs enormously from the one they grew up in. They were taught churchmanship by teachers who were raised in a world whose features are now fading rapidly. They are called on to instruct a new generation whose future living conditions are still shrouded in curtains of rapid, shattering change. Few mortals are overcharged with creativity. Most people feel confident doing what they have done before, or at least copying what they have seen others do in the past.

But this pattern will not work for the cities of today and tomorrow. Rural models—1955 models—evangelism patterns of the past, which centered around revivals, buildings, and "pack-the-pew" campaigns, are a disappointment today. *What are the alternatives?* These ideas are challenging to a few, but frightening to most. Nevertheless, church leaders *must think in new patterns*— the urgent need of the masses demands discarding that which worked at another place, another time, and which does not work now!

Fear of the city has caused a worrldwide phenomenon: direc^t

evangelism takes place for the most part in the country. Missionaries, who live in the cities, relate to management, teaching, bookstores, printing, and so forth, and often attend English-speaking churches with their families on Sunday. Today, the metropolitan areas are virtually abandoned, or contain token missionary activities.

Missionaries assigned to church planting in the city are often at a loss to know what to do. Surely the time is not too far off when men will be given specialized training to minister in the cities! Surely it will be soon—very soon—that precious workers in the cities will be provided help for their overwhelming tasks!

2. Future Church

Ralph W. Neighbour, Jr.

I would like to coin two terms—admittedly artificial—to make a point: *present church* and *future church*. The first refers to a type of organized religious body which lives in the *present,* without enough spiritual power to birth another generation of Christians. I am not referring to all *present* churches, but rather to a form of church which has only three dimensions: breadth, length, and depth. By "Future Church" I refer to churches both past and present which have an added dimension . . . *height.* That is, they live both in the physical world and in that spiritual environment where "principalities and powers of the air" are dealt with daily. *Present Churches* clutter the pages of history like wreckage left after a battle. Future Churches shape history, generation to generation! They are described in the following verses:

> That he would grant you, according to the riches of his glory, to be strengthened with might by his Spirit in the inner man; that Christ may dwell in your hearts by faith; that you, being rooted and grounded in love, may be able to comprehend with all the saints what is the breadth, and length, and depth, and height; and to know the love of Christ, which passeth knowledge, that you may be filled with all the fulness of God. Now unto him that is able to do exceeding abundantly above all that we ask or think, according to the power that worketh in us, unto him be glory in the church by Christ Jesus throughout all ages, world without end. Amen (Eph. 3:16-21).

It is depressing to view Present Churches in history. For example, it is not surprising to know that from 1550 to 1800 A.D., Protestants taught that the Great Commission had expired with the apostles?

18

Those were dark ages in Protestantism, following centuries which were called the dark ages of Catholicism. Imagine . . . a century and a half *lost* as the church *deliberately* ignored the task of evangelizing the earth! You may ask, "What were they *doing* for 150 years?" The Christians of that day were trying to *reform* the church. No thought was given to *planting* churches, or preaching the gospel to the lost.

That was an era of the Present Church. It left generations lost! Those interested in church renewal must learn from this, or again many years may be lost attempting to "straighten out" segments of today's church that need reforming. God does not send us to debate, but to find his power, "TOUCH" receptive people, and bring them to his cross.

God's way of renewing the church is best. He desires that we "may be filled with all the fulness of God." F. B. Meyer was a successful pastor, conducting a Present Church ministry. Then, youthful C. T. Studd arrived to preach in his pulpit for a week. As Studd lived his victorious Christian life, Meyer finally swallowed his pride and asked, "Studd, you have something I do not have, and I want it! What is the source of victory and power in your ministry?" Humbly, Studd replied, "Ah, sir, there is nothing I have which you may not have . . . *if you are filled up to all the fulness of God!*" In the days which followed, Meyer wrestled with areas in his personal life which had not been surrendered to the Lord Jesus. Out of that powerful period of confession and yielding came an anointed man. *That is God's way of renewing his church!*

Consider a special form of the body of Christ, which is called "Future Church." The term does not refer to a certain type of revolutionary building, or to the use of sophisticated electronic equipment for Christian education. Nor does the term "Future Church" describe a unique structured model which will fit more effectively into the noisy, busy world of cities we shall see in the next 20 years. Rather, the term "Future Church" refers to a special kind of body of Christ. It will be the church God sends into the next generation! It will contain the elements of all the churches of past centuries which have been built by God, not men. It will be a church which effectively penetrates its culture for Christ.

Consider the characteristics of this Future Church:

1. *The "Resident" Holy Spirit is the "President" of its members.*

When people let him be President, all his power flows through them. That is precisely what Paul prayed for the church in Ephesians 3:16. The church in the future must be a church made up of persons having the powerful work of Christ in their lives. It is not because of what a church *has* that makes it significant, but because the church is used by the Holy Spirit for the work of the Father. Future Churches learn to rely upon the presence and power of God's Spirit for their work. Through them, God is going to penetrate the slums of the Third World cities, high-rise apartments, and all of the other factors influencing a world of cities. Apart from this Resident President, the church is nothing but a hollow organization. Therefore, the Holy Spirit must be a most welcomed, *invited* guest in the Future Church.

2. *The Future Church will live in the "Fourth Dimension."*

While humans are *three*-dimensional objects, composed of length, breadth, and width, the Fourth Dimension is spiritual. The life of the church is in it. If it becomes preoccupied with three-dimensional buildings, organs, and institutions, it loses touch with reality. In the Fourth Dimension the power of God is known, and the power of Satan is overcome. There, warfare takes place. There, spiritual victory is gained. There, men are called by the voice of God to follow Jesus Christ, and to declare him Lord of their lives.

This Fourth Dimension was alluded to by Jesus in John 1:3, when he said the kingdom (reign) of God cannot even be *seen* unless one is born again. Paul describes it in Ephesians 3:18-19. He explains that this Fourth Dimension has the features of "breadth and length and height and depth." It is in this *Fourth* Dimension that "the love of Christ which passeth knowledge" is discovered. The Fourth Dimension is real!

In each generation, God raises up a new, lovely body of Christ—his church. How will he structure it in the future? While it is most wise to consider the many alternate forms it may take in the urban world during the next 20 years, one thing is certain: *it will be a spiritual, "Fourth-Dimensional" entity, not a three-dimensional one!*

What is the difference between churches which explode and grow, and those which struggle along, with pastors working from morning to night with no results? It is precisely this: some congregations live in the *Fourth* Dimension, and some live in the *third*.

John wrote from Patmos to churches who had—or were about to—slip out of the fourth into the third. He warned them that if they intended to remain alive, they should return to the Fourth Dimension. Sad to say, each of them died! *Future Churches live in the Fourth Dimension.*

When a church becomes overbalanced by people who want a sermon, good social fellowship, and a quality religious education for their children . . . but want nothing to do with a life of prayer and ministering to others, that church lives in the third dimension. It may go on paying its building debt and its pastor, but it will have no real life, no real destiny in touching the world for God. Its leadership will continually make excuses for not getting down to actually seeking God, cultivating the lost, and ministering to those in need.

One certain assurance that a church *is* a Future Church is the evidence that the body is being directed by the Holy Spirit to work in the Fourth Dimension. Its members will be ready and willing to storm the gates of hell, confident that nothing is too hard for God. From all indications, the challenge of calling out unbelievers from the world of unbelievers will be more formidable than ever before.

Those who are most aware of the lightning-speed changes taking place in our world today are the most cynical of all people. Isaac Asimov, author of 172 books, suggests that the big slogan of the 21st century will be: "No More Twentieth Centuries!" Buckminster Fuller, inventor of the geodesic dome, has said, "For the past 20 years, we have had the nations of the earth getting ready for Armageddon, taking the highest capabilities of man and focusing them on waste." Aurelio Peccei, founder and president of the Club of Rome—an organization made up of some of the most brilliant minds on earth who gather to deal with the future—has written, "Ten years ago, the mood was still one of great expectations. Now . . . it appears not only that the world situations have substantially deteriorated but also that adverse trends are steadily gaining ground."

Man, living in rebellion against God, can be accurately forecast to make a bigger and bigger mess of our planet. As people are crammed into smaller and smaller islands of human life, crime can be expected to increase. Is it a time to throw up hands in defeat? Not at all! The same God who led Joshua to supernatural victory at Jericho is in charge of the Future Church's invasion of the future world. New paths for the gospel to penetrate the unbeliever's world must be found, but those who live in the Fourth Dimension know that nothing has changed *there!* Christ is victor; Satan is defeated; the church is his living body on the earth. ". . . to live is Christ, and to die is gain" (Phil. 1:21).

To these two characteristics, a third one can now be added. It builds on the first two.

   3. *Leadership in the Future Church is made up of those who have had God's miracles take place in their personal lives.*

Recently, I had the honor of spending a few hours in the company of Chuck Colson. His hard-hitting life had made him the prime target of the press during the Watergate scandals. When he was at the edge of despair, a Christian friend put C. S Lewis' *Mere Christianity* in his hands. He was, as he says, "born again." Soon after, he found himself behind prison bars. Others in prison threatened to murder him. He found God's protection in every situation. God met every one of his needs!

I was left with a deep sense of awe when I let him out of my car in front of his hotel. He had a sharp edge on his testimony. His religion was not picked up secondhand as a "church brat," sitting in the back of the church writing notes as a teenager . . . nor had he joined the church to accomodate his wife! Chuck Colson had met God face to face . . . and he knew him to be adequate for *any* situation.

When a man has had the power of God touch him, he does not have to be *prodded* to believe that all things are possible through Jesus Christ. It is easier to explain to a man what has happened *after* it has happened, than to try to convince him that something is *going* to happen! People whose Christianity is tradition-bound are never part of Future Churches.

Not long ago, a pastor of a true Future Church said, "I have learned an important truth from Acts 2:17. When the Holy Spirit is poured out on young men, they see visions. When he touches old men, they dream dreams. But unless that occurs, old men will collect gold watches, middle-aged men will fight to preserve the status quo, and young men will flit from one diversion to the next." *Nothing will put greater fire in a man's bones than to have seen God face to face.*

What many of God's children need is a fresh touch of the Spirit of God upon their lives. One of the most thrilling prayers to ever pray is, "Oh, Holy Spirit of God, you are welcome in my life. I joyfully ask you to enter all the facets of my life."

What can a leader like *this* do that Present Church men cannot do? First of all, this Future Church leader will be able to *love*. He will not be bound by fears, mistrust, and skepticism. Love requires a pure heart, not one motivated by self-preservation. Secondly, a leader who has seen God do miracles in his own life will be able to give *hope* to others. The person who has found victory over a stronghold of Satan in his own life will be able to encourage others. Those who have not known such power cannot offer hope. Third, he will be able to impart *faith* to others. Those who have low self-images, who have lost faith in themselves, who have trouble placing faith in others, are helped most readily by those who can build their faith in a God who has shown his mighty power.

I have been watching for several years the astonishing growth of the Yoido Island Full Gospel Central Church. It is located on a sandy island in the middle of the Han River in Seoul, Korea. This church, which numbered 27,000 members in April of 1976, has now passed the 70,000 membership mark . . . and by the end of 1980, they project a membership of 100,000. It is unfortunate that some Christians refuse to examine such amazing growth, simply because they reject Pentecostal teachings. One need not be a Pentecostal to agree with Peter Wagner, who wrote: "I have simply looked at what God is doing through my Pentecostal brethren, and I can do nothing but praise him for it." Presbyterians in Korea have recognized that church growth is not based on Pentecostal teachings, but upon the power of God working through a flock of deeply committed believers. Catching the pattern, Korean Presbyterians are now patterning congregations after Yoido Island, and finding the same explosive growth potential now possible.

The key to the growth is really quite simple. Every person in the body of Christ who has discovered God's power is encouraged to gather a group of people into their home. There, they share the Word of God with them. Literally thousands of these small groups now meet all over Seoul. Any means used to make friends with unbelievers is considered valid. Those who are sick are prayed for. Those who are hungry are fed. Those who seek friendship are nurtured.

God is now calling up the members of his Future Church. The Future Church will face the challenge of bringing the gospel to a world in which 50 percent of its people go to bed hungry every night, and 25 percent are starving. They will know that for the 500,000 persons behind bars at all times in the U.S., eleven million other known offenders are not yet arrested. Future Church will live in a society in which 1.6 billion people will be too poor to "afford" the gospel. The leadership of Future Church will be called on to develop a new strategy, a new breed of missionary, and a new work in slums which stagger the imagination of those who have not visited the Third World countries.

It is shocking to realize that all those who will be over fifteen years of age in 1994 *have already been born,* and that they will represent the greatest challenge for youth evangelism the world has ever known. For the most part helpless to speak politically about their world, this new generation of young people will, by the end of the century, reach the age to parent another wave of astonishing population growth. Will they be reached for Christ?

They will not be reached with the Present Church. Not with, for example, an average baptismal rate among Southern Baptists of perhaps *one* person baptized for *thirty or more* church members. Not when that *one* is usually a child of one of the members. We must see the "Future Church" born quickly. You and I cannot delay becoming a part of it! The alternatives are eternally unacceptable . . . not thousands, but *millions,* living their lifetimes without the sound of the gospel penetrating the little cell of twenty people that composes their "world."

We must take advantage of radio and television, of all forms of media. We must use drama to reach those that sermons cannot reach. We must share our faith with an unprecedented boldness. We must come to know the power of prayer firsthand, instead of avoiding our places of prayer, the way a timid fox might circle a beam of light in the darkness of night.

How will the Future Church be born? By an act of *metanoia,* an act of repentance, in each one of us. By facing the stark reality that our present relationship to Christ is not adequate, and that we *can* be, as young Studd said to Meyer, "filled up to all the fulness of God." The Future Church will be born in the same way Jacob's name was changed to Israel . . . by squarely facing spiritual bankruptcy, by wrestling with the angel of Jehovah, crying, "I will not let thee go, except thou bless me" (Gen. 32:26). Out of such powerful periods of confession and yielding will come anointed men and women. They will become the Future Church.

The Future Church needs old men to dream. It needs young people to move off the back pews to the front ones; to exchange their notes for notebooks, to see visions of a world which needs to be loved, given hope, and pointed to faith. It needs middle-aged men, who have the courage to move into the new age, and penetrate a generation of unbelief. It needs men who consider this more important than keeping up an image. Future Church needs people who dare, who will deliberately leave the comfortable ruts of dead activities. It needs men who discard methods which are deadly because they only *add* converts, instead of *multiplying* them. The future is upon us!

Like most Vietnamese, the pastor who came to hear me teach about the "house church" stood no taller than my shoulder. The Saigon room was hot, and one fan was broken. He had a cold, and constantly wiped his nose all day long as I taught him and four other Baptist pastors. Sam James, my interpreter, earnestly put into their mother tongue all my knowledge of how cells could penetrate neighborhoods. At the end of the day, he asked for an appraisal from the group. With deep emotion, this fine pastor of the Grace Baptist Church said, "Missionaries came here many years ago. You brought us money and built us buildings. You trained us in seminary to pastor *in the buildings*. But one day our country may not be free. Why have you waited so long to tell us about house churches? We must begin to train our people to meet in this way at once. But why did you wait so long?"

Only a few short weeks later, Earl Bengs and Gene Tunnell slipped out of Singapore and returned to Saigon in the midst of the confusion of evacuations as the South Vietnamese government collapsed. They slipped into the services at Grace, already in progress. The dear pastor was teaching his flock what he had heard in that room with the broken fan. "If I am taken away," he said, "continue to meet in your homes. Take the Bibles and hymnals from the pews, and keep them in safe places. I know God will preserve you. His church will not die."

I have often prayed for those precious sons of God! I pray for their safety in a Communist country. Later, we heard that the new government had taken over the church building as headquarters for a "puppet church" controlled by the government, propagating Communist doctrine. Future Church came to Saigon without warning. In a matter of hours, all vestiges of Present Churches were erased. Those who had a loose cultural attachment to the Christian religion disappeared. Only those who had seen the power of God in their personal lives would remain.

I can guarantee that the members of those secret Future Church cells have made the resident Holy Spirit *president* in their lives. They are living in the Fourth Dimension, where they fight not against earthly powers, but against the prince of darkness and all his armies of devils. For them, there can be no Third Dimension church. Do you doubt for an instant that *their* leaders are composed of men and women who have seen miracles take place in their lives? Apart from knowing firsthand of God's power, not one would risk death by leading a Christian cell.

If you are ready for it, a place in the Future Church is yours. But, before you decide to transfer your membership into it, count the cost. It will cost you . . . your life!

3. The Way Up Is Down:
The Servant Ministry of the Church

Roy Edgemon

Dr. Roy Edgemon directs the Church Training Department of the Sunday School Board of the Southern Baptist Convention. Previous to this responsibility, he served as a missionary in Japan and Okinawa and then with the Evangelism Commission of the Home Mission Board.

INTRODUCTION

God speaks to us in John 13 about a direction for our churches—a direction of renewal, a direction of evangelism, a direction that can bring this world to a knowledge of Christ. Churches today are not growing. I cannot speak concerning other denominations; I am limited in the sense that I only know and understand in an intimate way Southern Baptists and what's happening to us. I know that in this past year we've had the lowest number of baptisms in 28 years. At a time when there are more churches and more opportunities of reaching people through the media, we have had our weakest year in trying to bring people into a knowledge of Christ. As far as America is concerned, we're "losing" it. Gallup and other polls indicate that America is fast developing into a pagan nation. We are not reaching people for Christ. America today is the largest nation in the western world without Christ. The lostness is phenomenal. It is estimated that only one out of every four homes knows anything about a regular Bible study. The attitude, behavior, and value system of the millions of lost people in America is contrary to the teachings of the traditional church as we know it today.

Recent studies tell us some strange things that are happening to the behavioral attitudes and the value systems of the people in America today. There is a tremendous interest in religion. Some of the latest statistics indicate 79 percent of unchurched Americans believe that Jesus is the Son of God and have a real interest in him. Yet these same people are looking for a religion without spiritual commitment and sacrifice, and the behaviorists tell us that this is the trend of the future. People want a religion that sounds good and gives them a warm feeling, but one without any kind of ethical teaching that brings about a sacrifice and commitment of life.

There is a trend in America today to reject the concept of discipline. It is seen in the work ethic as we know it and have known it in the past. This ethic is being rejected, and there's a new term coming on the scene. This term is "entitlement." Our whole society is saying, "Give me what I've got coming. There is something that is owed to me, and I'm here to take it." A research report from a national training organization describes the attitudes of working people 35 years and younger. Here are some of the results of that report: (1) A concern for meaningful work—only 13 percent of the labor force today think that what they're doing is meaningful and fulfilling. (2) A shift of energy and attention to leisure-time activities. (3) A renewed focus on money. (4) A strange combination of fear and super-confidence—a realization by young people that they have been judged by a standard that is lower and less rigorous than generations in the past. (5) An apparent indifference to traditional penalties for poor performance. (6) An intense need for feedback on every performance that they do. (7) A stepped-up sense of time that comes out in a motto "Live for today, now is all important." (8) A receptivity to excitement at work and a wider range of self-expression and life-style. These factors are evidenced in every area of human life today.

A monitoring system reporting on the values of Americans indicates that there is a lessening of the value of having children in the traditional home. Today the traditional home comprises less than 6 percent of the 77,000,000 households in our country. Less than 6 percent of the households have what we would normally, in days past, call a traditional home with the father working, two children in the home, and the mother staying at home. A new term is popping up in social reports that speaks to the behavior and the value system of our country, "child-free" homes. It means not just to be childless but to be child-free.

There is a movement toward private religion. The media or

electronic church is a part of this movement. This movement says that you do not have to be identified with anybody, but you can be a part of an invisible group. In Japan the no-church movement has existed for years. Every time a census asks the Japanese people about Christianity it comes up to about a 10 percent positive response. Only 1 percent of these are identified with any church. The other 9 percent are in that group which prefers Christianity, but is not identified with a visible congregation.

This particular media concept feeds off the community church and gets its total life's blood from the community church. Since the media churches produce their own products, there is no accountability to judge or to correct themselves. They can do just as they want to do without accountability. But the media church does provide private religion that people seem to be hungry for. Private religion turns on itself and ignores a hurting world that Jesus came to seek and save. It simply enjoys itself within the solitude of the home.

It seems as though we're regressing to the 18th century emphasis on naturalism. In that century there were attempts made to substitute a new cosmology for the one taught by Christianity. It was called the period of enlightenment. During that period of time people were saying that a church was not really necessary. It was probably the darkest moral period in the history of America. We need to read J. Edwin Orr's description of the terrible decay of the 1700's that prompted the beginning of the revivals at the turn of the century. During that period of time Tom Paine was saying, "My mind is my church. My own mind is my church. I do not need a local community and a local church of believers." William James said: "Religion is that in which the individual can find meaning." Alfred North Whitehead said: "Religion is what a person does in his solitariedness."

America seems to be reverting back to those days, the blackest days in the moral and ethical history of our country. It is a retreat into private religion. The trends today run counter to the teachings of our Lord. In contrast to these current trends, he chose for us and gave us the example of servanthood. In Matthew 20:28 he said, "Just as the Son of Man did not come to be served, but to serve, and to give His life a ransom for many" (NASB). Jesus' model of servanthood runs against the sociological and behavioral trends of our American culture.

We may not want to think that society is moving one way and

Christian faith is moving another. But we might see the greatest day for our churches if we can be identified with Jesus as the servant of God. Jesus announced a new formula for greatness. Society claims that the great are to be served—that one's power and prestige are measured by the quantity and quality of service that can be demanded from others. Jesus turned that formula around and declared that true greatness is in the lives of those who are willing to serve others. Jesus said in Matthew 10:39, "He who has found his life shall lose it, and he who has lost his life for My sake shall find it" (NASB). In Mark 9:35 we read: "And sitting down, He called the twelve and said to them, 'If any one wants to be first, he shall be last of all, and servant of all' " (NASB). In Mark 10:42 he said, "And calling them to Himself, Jesus said to them, 'You know that those who are recognized as rulers of the Gentiles lord it over them; and their great men exercise authority over them. But it is not so among you, but whosoever wishes to become great among you shall be your servant; and whoever wishes to be first among you shall be slave of all' " (NASB). We read in Luke 13:30: "And behold, some are last who will be first and some are first who will be last" (NASB). And in Luke 14:11 "For everyone who exalts himself shall be humbled, and he who humbles himself shall be exalted" (NASB). The role of the servant responding to the will of his master is repeatedly present in the model for the Christian life presented to us by Jesus. In Matthew 18, 20, and 22; Luke 12, 16, and 17, Jesus gives one parable after another about servanthood, a commitment to a life of service.

The church can affect this generation if it's willing to follow the way to success. Jesus taught, through servanthood, that the way to success is down and not up. The way to success is commitment and a willingness to be a servant.

The disciples were going to that last Passover with Jesus. As they walked along the way there was strife in their midst. Jesus had been trying for weeks to prepare them for his death. Somehow they had ignored it and worried about who was going to be the greatest in the kingdom of God. Luke 22:24 says, "And there was also strife among them, which of them should be accounted the greatest."

There are three areas mentioned in John 13 that speak to the call to the church today in the area of servanthood. First, the motivation for servanthood is love. Love is the only thing that can call us to be different from the world, and it is that commitment to love that is like unto Christ. Second, the model for leadership in the church is servanthood. Third, the measure of judgment is service.

THE MOTIVATION FOR SERVICE IS LOVE

"Now before the feast of the Passover, Jesus knowing that His hour had come that He should depart out of this world to the Father, having loved His own who were in the world, He loved them to the end" (John 13:1, NASB).

When I realize what Jesus was facing on that particular night, the word "love" chokes in my throat. I can't help but feel a burning in my eyes as I think about Jesus when he said "He loved them to the end." It is difficult for us to imagine the commitment of love that he had for those men, even though they were doing something that was little, trite, and hurtful. Jesus was saying that he was extending himself beyond any single act of love. His whole life had encompassed that love for his disciples and he was going to love them until he died on the cross. His last thought would be for them. He had an undying love for them.

The time of the departure would unite him with his Father. The Scripture says, "Jesus, knowing that the Father had given all things into His hand, and that He had come forth from God, and was going back to God" (v. 3, NASB). I imagine there was a great deal of homesickness as he realized that he was going back to the glory that he had left thirty years before. And yet William Barclay says something striking about Jesus. He says the wonderful thing about Jesus was that in his nearness to God, instead of being separated from men, he was brought nearer to men than ever before. The closer he got to the cross the more sensitive, the more loving, the more caring he was with those men. One incident talks about that very thing.

The disciples and Jesus had walked from Bethany to Jerusalem. As they traveled those roads in Judea, oftentimes in the dryness of the year the road would be serveral inches thick in dust. If rain should fall upon it, they would have to wade through mud. Their sandals were just leather soles with a few straps around their feet. When they arrived at a place for a meal there was always someone ready with a water pot. A servant with a basin of cool water would wash and dry their feet. This simple servant act would bring refreshment from the heat of the day's journey.

When they arrived in Jerusalem, everything was in order. Jesus would never have used this illustration if the pot had not been prepared, if the basin had not been available, if the towel had not been provided. There had been a discussion going on which was recorded in Luke 22:24. The nature of the discussion centered on greatness. "And there arose also a dispute among them as to which one of them was regarded to be greatest. And He said to them, 'The kings of the Gentiles lord it over them; and those who have authority over them are called 'Benefactors.' But not so with you, but let him who is the greatest among you become as the youngest, and the leader as the servant. For who is greater, the one who reclines at table, or the one who serves? Is it not the one who reclines at table? But I am among you as one who serves. And you are those who stood by Me in My trials; and just as My Father has granted Me a kingdom, I grant you may eat and drink at My table in My kingdom, and you will sit on thrones judging the twelve tribes of Israel' " (NASB). That was the nature of the conversation. But immediately they began to quarrel among themselves as to who was going to be the greatest in this kingdom, who was going to have the highest judgeship, who was going to be the ruler over the most. It was in that attitude they arrived at the setting for the Last Supper. As they arrived I can see them walking past the waterpot. I think I know enough about myself and about human nature to see them in their sullenness walk by that waterpot. Here was a group of peers walking together and no one was willing to say, "I'll do the task today."

They go in and have supper. In the midst of that supper Jesus takes off his robe and puts on a towel, the dress of a servant. He takes the basin of water and begins to wash their feet in an act of servanthood. Jesus made it clear that the practical consequence of love is always service. He was trying to help them understand that he was there to serve and he loved them enough to do what they refused to do.

If you want to understand the theme of Jesus in those last hours look closely at John 13-17. Look at how many times Jesus used the word "love" and commands his disciples to love one another. John 13:34, "A new commandment I give to you, that you love one another, even as I have loved you, that you also love one another. By this all men shall know that you are My disciples, if you have love for one another" (NASB).

John 14:15, "If you love Me, you will keep My commandments." (NASB). John 14:21, "He who has My commandments, and keeps them, it is he who loves Me" (NASB). Then he goes on to talk about it more in John 14:23. "Jesus answered and said to him, 'If anyone loves Me, he will keep My word; and My Father will love him, and We will come to him, and make Our abode with him. He who does not love Me does not keep My words; and the word that you hear is not Mine, but the Father's who sent Me" (NASB). John 15:9-10, "Just as the Father has loved Me, I have also loved you; abide in My love (live in my love). If you keep My commandments, you will abide in My love; just as I have kept My Father's commandments, and abide in His love" (NASB). John 15:12-14, "This is My commandment, that you love one another, just as I have loved you. Greater love has no one than this, that one lay down his life for his friends. You are My friends, if you do what I command you" (NASB). John 15:17, "This I command you, that you love one another" (NASB). And that great priestly prayer in John 17:26, "And I have made Thy name known to them, and will make it known; that the love wherewith Thou didst love Me may be in them, and I in them" (NASB).

Jesus says that the motivation for servanthood is love. Without love we will never take responsibility for being the kind of church that will penetrate the secularism of our day. The willingness to love is the motivation for servanthood.

John 21 describes Jesus' several resurrection appearances to his disciples. The disciples were fishing from a small boat and Jesus called to them from the shore. They rowed the little boat in and Jesus had breakfast ready for them. After the meal he called Peter aside. He said, "Peter, I just want to ask you one thing—do you love me?" And Peter said, "You know everything, Lord. You know that I've got a great deal of affection for you." Jesus then gave him the command to feed his lambs. Then he asked him again, "Peter, lovest thou me?" and Simon Peter said, "Lord, you know all things, you know that I have affection for you." But Jesus said, "Peter if you love me, shepherd my sheep." Then the third time he asked him, "Peter, do you really love me?" Peter said, "Lord (and it expresses the fact that he was hurt) you know all things, you know I love you." Then Jesus replied, "Shepherd, or tend my sheep." Everytime Jesus asked Peter if he loved him, he was asking, "Peter, what are you doing to serve others?" The motivation of service and of the servanthood church is the motivation of love. Jesus Christ has called his church to be the servant people in a lost and dying world. The motivation is love.

THE MODEL FOR LEADERSHIP IS SERVANTHOOD

Examine verses 6-11 of John 13: "And so He came to Simon Peter. He said to Him, 'Lord, do You wash my feet?' " Jesus answered and said to him, 'What I do you do not realize now; but you shall understand hereafter.' Peter said to Him, 'Never shall You wash my feet!' Jesus answered him, 'If I do not wash you, you have no part with Me.'' Simon Peter said to him, 'Lord, not my feet only, but also my hands and my head.' Jesus said to him, "He who has bathed needs only to wash his feet, but is completely clean; and you are clean, but not all of you." For He knew the one who was betraying Him; for this reason He said, "Not all of you are clean" (NASB).

When the Lord finally knelt at Peter's feet, Peter did not want Christ to wash his feet. Have you ever wondered why? It was inconsistent with Peter's image of what lordship ought to be about. He was saying "Lord, never!" He uses the strongest of Greek words. Literally, he says, "Never in eons will I let you do it." If you want to bring it into our vernacular he said, "never in a thousand lifetimes will you ever touch me." That's strong speaking! Peter was offended by an act of servanthood, although Jesus had taught him many times that servanthood was the call of God. Peter still had the world's standard of greatness and leadership in his life-style even though Jesus had sowed the seed of commitment and service over and over again. Jesus had strongly condemned the leadership style of the religionists of his day.

In Matthew 23:1-39 Jesus pronounced the seven woes on the scribes and Pharisees. He said "Don't be like them, that's not what I have called you to be and do. I've called you as a different kind of people." In Matthew 23:8-12 he said, "But do not be called Rabbi: for One is your Teacher, and you are all brothers. And do not call anyone on earth your father; for One is your Father, He who is in heaven. And do not be called leaders; for One is your Leader, that is, Christ. But the greatest among you shall be your servant. And whoever exalts himself shall be humbled; and whoever humbles himself shall be exalted" (NASB). Jesus told these disciples to reject the style of the religious leaders of their day. "Do not allow yourselves to be called Rabbi." You do not get your authority and ability to lead others from a superiority of knowledge or education.

Authority comes from service and not from degrees, status, or position. Don't allow anyone to call you "Father." Father assumes superiority by authority of age, experience, or relationship.

I have been reminded as never before of the attack on our doctrinal belief in the priesthood of the believer. There is a movement in our churches to set up authority figures. Some church leaders say, "If you disagree with me or my program, you are under the leadership of Satan because I alone know the will of God for this church." That runs contrary to what the Bible says about the priesthood of the believer and the ministry of the laity. Another church leader has said that God speaks to him and through him and when God wants to; God will share his will through him alone. Others say God speaks with a woman only through the husband. Others say that children only can know the will of God through parents.

I was a lost boy who was not raised in a Christian home. I thank God that he saved me and then helped me to lead my family to Christ. I thank God that I wasn't waiting for a lost dad or a lost mother to bring me to a knowledge of Christ.

The idea of authority is not New Testament in the sense of Jesus' model of servanthood. Jesus was saying to his disciples, "Don't let anyone call you master or leader because that authority is given on the basis of position, status, or delegation. He said, "If you want to lead, be the servant." Be willing to give of yourself.

We are becoming a secular society caring less and less about the institutional church. Seventy-nine percent of the unchurched Americans in Gallup's 1978 poll believed that Jesus is the Son of God. Eighty-four percent said they prayed. But 60 percent said they didn't see a need for an institutional church. This is a tremendous number of people who say that they're being turned off by what they see of the church's role in our world.

Jesus said to Peter, "If you do not choose to be my disciple and follow my example, you can have no part in me." Impulsively Peter said, "Lord, if that's the case, then, wash all of me." But Jesus said that it's not the washing that is important. It is the act that's important. It is the commitment to be a servant that will change the world's image of the church.

THE MEASURE OF JUDGMENT IS SERVICE

Finally, the Scriptures tell us in John 13:12-17 that the measure of judgment on all Christian ministry is service. "And so when He had washed their feet, and taken His garments, and reclined at the table again, He said to them, 'Do you know what I have done to you? You call Me Teacher, and Lord; and you are right; for so I am. If I then, the Lord and the Teacher, washed your feet, you also ought to wash one another's feet. For I gave you an example that you also should do as I did to you. Truly, truly, I say to you, a slave is not greater than his master; neither one who is sent greater than one who sent him. If you know these things, you are blessed if you do them" (NASB).

Jesus confronted the disciples with the meaning of his act. "Do you understand what I did this day? Do you understand the meaning of this act? Tell me, can you understand what I'm trying to say?" This act of Jesus was free and voluntary, an act chosen by him to teach his disciples. In this act he is saying to us, "Greatness to the world is linked to power, authority, position and prestige, but greatness in the kingdom of God is linked to servanthood and ministry and self-denial." John 13:16 says, "Truly, truly, I say to you, a slave is not greater than his master; neither one who is sent greater than one who sent him" (NASB). Jesus was saying, "I try to demonstrate and model the example that I want you to have in your life." Since you know these things, he said in John 12:17, "If you know these things, you are blessed if you do them" (NASB). The word "do" is emphatic. The present subjunctive mood points to duration—keep on doing them. Always do these on every occasion. Make this a part of your character. Do these things that I have shared with you that you be servant of all.

Our Lord's summary statement on servanthood is found in Matthew 25:31-40.

"But when the Son of Man comes in His glory, and all of the angels with Him, then shall He sit on His glorious throne. And all the nations will be gathered before Him; and He will separate them one from another, as the shepherd separates the sheep from the goats; and He will put the sheep on His right, and the goats on the left. Then the King will say to those on His right, 'Come, you blessed of My Father, inherit the kingdom prepared for you from the foundation of the world. For I was hungry and you gave Me something to eat; I was thirsty, and you gave Me drink; I was a stranger, and you invited Me in; naked, and you clothed Me; I was sick, and you visited Me; I was in prison, and you came unto Me.' Then the righteous will answer Him, saying, 'Lord, when did we see You hungry, and feed You, or thirsty, and give You drink? And when did we see You a stranger, and invite You in, or naked, and clothe You? And when did we see You sick, or in prison, and come to You?' And the king will answer and say to them, 'Truly I say to you, to the extent that you did it to one of these brothers of Mine, even the least of them, you did it to Me' '' (NASB).

This is the kind of church that will make an impact on a secular world. This is the kind of church that will run right against the stream of humanity in speaking and performing a servant ministry. It is a giving church. If one values power, he acts to enhance that power. If one values his love of God and neighbor, he'll find a way to serve them. The righteous serve without reward and authentic greatness comes to those who do not seek it.

Salvation may be personal, but it is never private. We have been saved to serve. Every person who is saved has a responsibility to the community of faith. The church of the Lord Jesus Christ is called to servanthood, and the church has never had a better time to stand up as a loving, serving, caring people as in this generation.

4. Touch Ministries

Charles Aranyas

Charles Aranyas, a former computer management specialist, is the traveling expositor of the TOUCH approach to building ministering churches. He is Director of TOUCH Productions, a ministry within the Body of the West Memorial Baptist Church.

In America today, church programs have little or no appeal to 41 percent of the population. That is an important fact! Examine your own church field. Knock on the doors of 100 homes or apartments. Present the plan of salvation to those who will permit you to do so. Further, invite *all* to attend Sunday School, a worship service, a special event, or even a home Bible study. Of the 100 you visit in a typical urban setting, *from 60 percent to 85 percent will not respond to these invitations:*

Few people seem to recognize that our current methods of evangelism are designed to minister to an unbeliever only after he is already more than 50 percent of the way toward making a decision for Christ. What can we be doing to reach the rest of America! Shall we continually consign men to eternity without Christ, simply because we use a limited strategy of evangelism? This is a question which the Future Church must answer. How can we who are Christians impact the lives of those who will not attend any of the activities which take place in church buildings? Let me suggest an answer: TOUCH ministries:

The answer is not simplistic, mainly because TOUCH ministries are not "canned" programs. They are, primarily, the *servant work* of Christians who have made a commitment of their lives to reach outsiders. TOUCH is a relationship between believers who contain the living Christ, and outsiders who are filled with self. The word "TOUCH" stands for *T*ransforming *O*thers *U*nder *C*hrist's *H*and.

In Acts 17:24-27 we read:

> The God who created the world and everything in it, and who is Lord of heaven and earth, does not live in shrines made by men. It is not because he lacks anything that he accepts service at men's hands, for he is himself the universal giver of life and breath and all else. He created every race of men of one stock, to inhabit the whole earth's surface. He fixed the epochs of their history and the limits of their territory. They were to seek God, and, it might be, *touch* and find him; though indeed he is not far from each one of us, for in him we live and move, in him we exist . . . (NEB).

TOUCH is a relationship, not a program. Therefore, the first question to ask about it is not what methods does it use to reach people, but how does an unbeliever "fall in love" with the Lord Jesus?

This is God's ultimate desire for outsiders! Christians are to help unbelievers fall so deeply in love with Jesus Christ, that they will surrender all of life to Him. The Christian provides the outsider with a "TOUCH POINT" with Christ. Later, when he knows Christ better, the outsider may trust Him as Lord and Savior.

Two years before I married, if someone had walked up to me and had given me four reasons why I should fall in love and marry the girl who was to become my wife, I would have said, "No, thank you! I don't *know* this girl you recommend so highly. I haven's even met her." First of all, I had to have a "TOUCH POINT," a way to *meet* her.

Then, two years before our marriage, I was working for one bank, she for another. These two banks merged: that was our "TOUCH POINT." We started dating. Thirteen months later, I knew her well enough that I wanted to trust myself to her, and she trusted herself to me. We were married.

An individual comes to Jesus Christ in the same way. Why should a person who knows nothing *about* Jesus Christ trust himself to Him? We do not trust ourselves to people we do not know. Too often, we try to persuade outsiders to trust Jesus Christ when he is still a stranger to them. There must be a TOUCH POINT, followed by a growing relationship. Later, a point of *total* trusting may be expected, and another outsider will be born again.

TARGET GROUPS

The target groups for TOUCH ministries are not church-oriented people who can be reached by Sunday School or other church-building related meetings. TOUCH's target group are people who will *never* become involved with the activities of the church. As we allow the indwelling Holy Spirit to express Himself through us, we ourselves become TOUCH POINTS. This means a personal commitment to the Lordship of Christ in our lives. By becoming TOUCH POINTS, others will have opportunity to know and trust Him.

Where does a ministry like this begin? It begins with a *theology* that breeds a *methodology*. The proper theology will provide a methodology which is fluid, adapting itself to any person, any culture. There are three important points to this theology.

1. THE CALL TO SALVATION IS A CALL TO MINISTRY. God has a purpose for each Christian. He places each believer in the body. He puts each of us exactly where He wants us to be. Paul refers to "spiritual gifts," which cause us to be hands, feet, inward parts, and so forth. We are to perform by the function God has given us. A call to salvation is a call to ministry.

2. ALL CHRISTIANS ARE MINISTERS. To belong to the Lord Jesus—regardless of age—is to be a part of His plan to redeem the world. Christ has a *body* on this earth, the Church. When our Lord Jesus Christ prayed at his birth: "I have come, O God, to do thy will!" (Hebrews 10:5-7), He projected the words of the prayer from the *present* body of Christ, the Church. Through a virgin, God caused a unique body to come into being for His Son. No less miraculous than that virgin birth is the miracle of God forming the present body of Christ, the Church. Each part of that body is functional. *All* of its members are to become TOUCH POINTS.

3. PASTORS ARE EQUIPPERS: THE LAITY ARE MINIS-TERS. While pastors are also ministers, they are not the *exclusive* ministers of the church. Trueblood has called pastors "Player Coaches." Someone has said: "Christianity began as a little company of lay ministers serving each other, and ministering to the world. Christianity has now deteriorated into professional pul-piteers, financed by lay spectators. The lay spectators hire full time staffs of professionals to do all the work of the church, and the laity sits and watches them do it." The greatest hindrance to the spread of the gospel today is the difference we have made by using the words clergy and laity!"

"ONE-NATURED" AND "TWO-NATURED" PEOPLE

Christians need to understand outsiders. Unbelievers are "one-natured" individuals. They have only one nature, the *old* nature! On a trip to Mexico, I was travelling through a portion of the country covered with orange groves. The groves were all along the highway, as far as one could see. However, there were no oranges on the trees. I knew, however, that at a later time, when the season was right, there *would* be oranges on them! How could I be sure? Well, I knew that orange *trees* have an orange *nature*. The fruit of a tree which has an orange *nature* is called "oranges." Apples will never come forth from an "orange nature" tree.

An unbeliver has one nature, and the Bible calls it a "sin nature." What fruit can a sin-natured person produce? *Sins*. That is all he can be *expected* to produce. Man is not a sinner because he commits sins; he commits sins because of his nature. His problem is a "nature problem." All world religions attempt to take a one-natured man and train him to produce fruit other than *sins*. It can't be done! We must always keep this in mind as we deal with people.

On the other hand, Christians have *two* natures. Although the old sin nature is not yet eliminated in the life of the believer, Jesus Christ comes to live within the Christian at salvation. From then on, the Christian possesses the *new* nature, the *Christ* nature. A one-nature life is based on *discipline*. The person does the best he can, and adheres to a set of rules. A two-nature life functions in obedience to the indwelling Christ.

Here is a fantastic truth: *we cannot live the Christ-life!* Discovering this frees us from the bondage of trying to be "like Jesus." Trying to live the Christian life by observing ethical principles is aptly described in this poem:

> They said it was a job that couldn't be done;
> So, with all his might, he went to it.
> He tackled the job that couldn't be done;
> *They were right . . . he couldn't do it!*

Trying to live the Christ-life can't be done in the strength of human discipline. Rather, it occurs as we begin to understand the impact of Christ living His life in us. By being obedient to the work of the indwelling Christ, we learn that God does things in our lives which could not have taken place by self-discipline alone. That is important to understand!

Unbelievers we shall be dealing with are all one-natured individuals. They have one nature, a Sin Nature, and the only fruit they can produce is *sins*. Since Christians have *two* natures, they have an abundant life which confronts the one-natured unbeliever. In that confrontation, the unbeliever finds his own eternal hope. "If God can do it for my friend, he can do it for me!" says the unbeliever. The whole concept of TOUCH is based upon this premise; whenever, wherever a Christian shares his two-natured life with a one-natured unbeliever, a very special form of evangelism begins to happen.

THE TOUCH CYCLE

First, we must discover the needs and interests of the one-natured outsider. *Second,* we build a relationship with him. *Third,* through this relationship we establish enrichment groups, where we have ample opportunity to share Christ with several unbelievers. *Fourth,* some of those involved in Enrichment Groups may be motivated to enter Search Groups, where the Bible is studied in a way that helps unbelievers learn about being born again. *Fifth,* some unbelievers make the decision to accept Christ. *Sixth,* the new Christian is then discipled, using *Survival Kit for New Christians,** and enters the Body of Christ, the church. *Seventh,* converts are equipped, and go out to discover the needs and interests of one-natured persons. In this way, the cycle continues!

The first step, then, is to discover needs and interests in the life of the unbeliever. This leads to building relationships. Most Christians have such opportunities built into their lifestyles. One lady, a champion baton twirler in high school, had a TOUCH ministry built right into her life. She invited young girls in her community to come to her home one day a week. She would teach baton twirling. She served refreshments, and used a time of Bible study to share what God means in her own life. Another man, a former addict, related to others still trapped in drug addiction. He also had a

---

*Available from Convention Press, Nashville, Tennessee.

TOUCH CYCLE

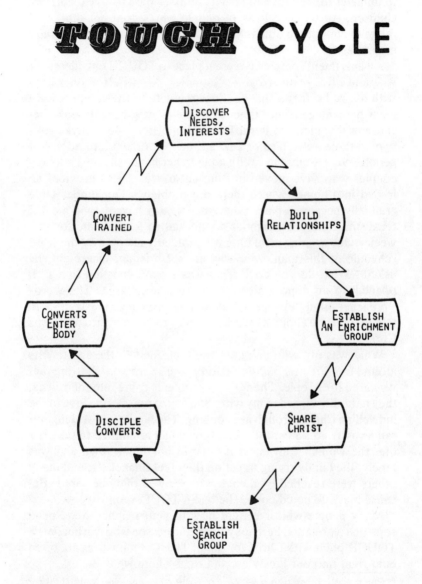

TOUCH ministry. Another couple with an exceptional child began to minister to the hurts and needs of other parents of exceptional children. All touched lives of people who would not otherwise relate to church programs. Many became Christians through their ministries.**

An apartment complex is a great place to TOUCH outsiders! My wife and I live in an apartment complex. My wife's mother lives with us, bed-ridden. This confines my wife to the complex for a great percentage of her time. My wife is an excellent cook. Because of that fact, she has a TOUCH ministry. She always cooks two or three extra pies or cakes. She takes them into homes of people living around us. With a pie in her hand, she meets lonely couples who have moved in from out of state. This provides an inroad into homes where there are problems. Our dinner table gradually became a place where people can have a good meal. I recall the time one neighbor's wife had to leave home for two weeks. Our evening meal time was suddenly dictated by the work schedule of this man, who was not a Christian. One night, he asked "What do you do?" That was a good question to ask; it opened up an opportunity for me to share Christ. The words "preacher" and "evangelist" do not describe my ministry. So, in telling someone about my work, it is easy to insert my trust in Jesus Christ.

What was my wife doing as she took food to the apartments around us? *She was building relationships;* she was showing that we cared for people. Then, when problems came into their lives, they naturally turned to my wife. She had expressed the love of the indwelling Christ through her cooking! The family whose daughter ran away from home, the woman who had attempted to take her life, the woman who knew no one in our home town and was lonely, the family trying to get on their feet financially, and many others were reached by a cook who showed that she cared. Because my wife could cook, she had a TOUCH ministry.

Many people who live right now in your neighborhood need someone who cares. Perhaps *you* are the person who can become a TOUCH point with Christ for them! TOUCH ministries are often built right into our lifestyles, and right where we live.

**For more information, see *Target Group Evangelism*, published by Broadman Press (1975).

The Way People Come To Christ...

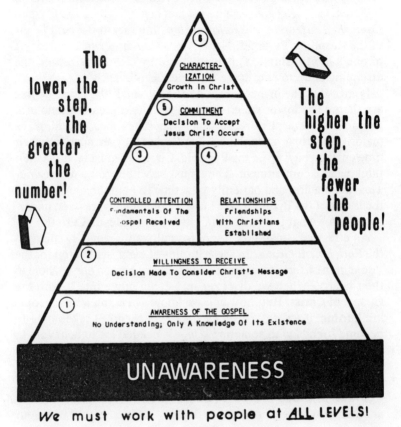

The lower the step, the greater the number!

The higher the step, the fewer the people!

6
CHARACTER-
IZATION
Growth In Christ

5 COMMITMENT
Decision To Accept
Jesus Christ Occurs

3
CONTROLLED ATTENTION
Fundamentals Of The
Gospel Received

4
RELATIONSHIPS
Friendships
With Christians
Established

2
WILLINGNESS TO RECEIVE
Decision Made To Consider Christ's Message

1
AWARENESS OF THE GOSPEL
No Understanding; Only A Knowledge Of Its Existence

UNAWARENESS

We must work with people at **ALL** LEVELS!

THE RESPONSE PYRAMID

How do people come to Christ? Consider the Response Pyramid. The base of the pyramid is the vast level of *Unawareness.* Many people are totally unaware of the Gospel. Houston, my home town, is now an international city. A recent study revealed that in our local school district a total of 97 different languages are spoken in the homes of students! People from all over the world are living in my home town. The majority of internationals living in Houston are unaware of the Gospel. Those who fit the category of

Unawareness are to be brought by us to the next level, the *Awareness Of The Gospel*. Next, we are to guide them to the level of *Willingness To Receive*, where we can begin to share the Gospel. *Controlled Attention* and *Relationships* interact at the next levels of the Response Pyramid. Next comes *Commitment:* the trusting of one's life to Christ. This is followed by *Characterization*, the discipling and growing stage for a new Christian.

Notice that the higher we go on the Pyramid, the fewer people are there. The lower we go on the Pyramid, a greater number of people are there. The reason most churches miss reaching the majority of people around them is that what they are spending their time on it too high up on the Pyramid. Churches must readjust their thinking and commitment. They must be willing to go where *unaware* people are, and patiently take time to help them up through the levels of the Pyramid. We must *bring* unbelievers to an understanding of what it means to fall in love with Jesus Christ!

An effective, small-group tool for cultivating non-Christians is the *Enrichment Group*. In these groups of eight, we search for the "hole in the heart" of each outsider. Every person *has* a "hole in their heart;" when we discover it, we can move into it with the Gospel of Christ. But, how can we know *when* and *where* people are hurting, *if we do not spend time with them?* It takes time to become friends with someone. *Time* is needed for unbelievers to see Christ's love in our lives.

TOUCH EVANGELISM

Evangelism has been defined as "one hungry beggar telling another hungry beggar where to find food." I remember when our country was just coming out of the Great Depression, in the 1930's. Men were constantly coming to our back door to beg for food. My precious grandmother never turned away a man. I recall one day in particular: I can still see the man's face in my memory. My grandmother gave him a sandwich. A short time later, three other men, one at a time, came to our door. They came because the first man told them about a gracious woman who would give them something to eat.

TOUCH evangelism produces the same multiplication process. We, as hungry beggars, have found food; we must share that food with the world. It takes *love* to do that, and our homes are one of the greatest places to share love. Real impact and interaction take place in the home. Whenever I travel away from home for a conference, I always ask to be placed in a home rather than a motel. The best visitation program which churches can develop is an invitation by members to "come to my home!" When we have people in our homes, they are more willing to accept the fact that we want them in heaven.

Two weeks after I had conducted a seminar in Louisiana, I received a phone call. It came from the pastor of the sponsoring church. He shared with me that the church had just baptized ten people. Most of the ten were reached by one lady, who had baked some pies and opened her home to neighbors. After all, her home was as much part of the church as the sanctuary!

All this *really* cost her was two ingredients: *love,* and *time.* It takes time to prove to someone that you love them. It takes *time* to "love the *hell* out of people." It starts with Christians becoming TOUCH POINTS.

SPECIAL INTERESTS

Did you ever stop to realize that the non-Christian is not interested in Jesus Christ? He is only interested in himself. Our task is to discover how a non-Christian thinks about himself. Here again, we are talking about *time.* We also must see in the non-Christian the potential of what he will become after Christ enters his life.

I met a remarkable man a few years back; he was from Nairobi, Kenya. As a child, he was prepared to become the witch doctor in his village. He developed a fantastic capacity to memorize. One day, he found Christ. Christ now uses his ability to memorize. This man can quote most of the first five books of the Bible. Jesus Christ changes lives and transforms people. Because a person may seem to be unreachable, we must not limit God. We must always see the potential way God will use them after they have received Christ.

Communication is important in developing relationships with non-Christians. To have an effective one-on-one relationship, the Christian must understand that all his words are important. Since the non-Christian does not have our "churchly" vocabulary, we must be selective of the words we use; they must be words the non-Christian comprehends.

Then, too, the non-Christian *mindset* is different from the Christian mindset. In today's world, we work "cross-culturally" with non-Christians. Their values are different; their priorities are different. In short, the non-Christian has a culture at variance with the Christian culture. It is an area we must study! Our words and actions must not be cultural barriers in reaching non-Christians.

Enrichment Groups give us opportunity to develop such "cross-cultural" relationships. There are many activities of interest to unbelievers which can become Enrichment Group opportunities. Teaching guitar playing, music appreciation, photography, crafts, swimming, all kinds of recreation activities, how to study more effectively, first-aid, interior decorating, flower arranging, sewing, cooking, personality development, English, and hobbies, are but a few. There are many ways we can create Enrichment Groups to meet needs.

Enrichment Groups usually meet for ten weeks. This gives time to help individuals move up the levels of the Pyramid. In ten weeks, we share Christ in a non-threatening way. Individuals will come from these groups who will be willing to enter a *Search Group,* which is a special kind of Bible study. Searching people are now involved in studying God's Word. Our task then is to help them make a commitment of their lives to Christ.

The first four weeks of the Search Group deals with questions about the Christian lifestyle. The latter part of the ten week Search Group is more directed toward making a decision to accept Jesus Christ. It is then that searchers are confronted with: "What are you going to do about Jesus Christ? What will Christ mean to you?" Each person is helped to move up the Pyramid, until they come to the point of surrendering their life to Christ.

After a person accepts Christ, he is brought to the level called *Characterization.* He is discipled until the *character* of Christ controls his life. At this point he studies *Survival Kit for New Christians* for eleven weeks. The convert is taught about . . . *One Body*—At salvation, the Christian is baptized into the Body of Christ. *Two Natures*—The old Sin nature and the new Christ nature now both reside within his life. *Three Aspects of Salvation* —There is *Salvation Past:* that moment when a person becomes a Christian. There is *Salvation Future:* the moment when the Christian will be with Christ forever. There is *Salvation Present:* the process between the two points, where by the power of the indwelling Christ the Christian has freedom from the *power of sin.*

I recall a Wednesday night Bible study in a home, where God used the teaching of my pastor, Dr. Ralph Neighbour, to bring a truth into my life. The verse was Colossians 1:27; "Christ in you, the hope of glory.'' My life began to change. I discovered that night that *I* could not live the Christian life, but that Christ *could* and *would* live it through me. I needed only to commit myself to Him. The reason you are reading this right now, dear friend, is because of what God began to do in my life that night! *Salvation present* for me was first explained in that Bible study. I wish I had been given a *Survival Kit for New Christians* when I first accepted Christ. Many wasted years might have been saved.

Next, *Survival Kit for New Christians* deals with *four sources of authority* for determining Christian truth. They are *intellect, experience, tradition* and *scripture. Scripture,* God's word, is the only reliable source. Intellect, experience, and tradition that cannot be verified by God's word are *wrong!* The Bible is the ultimate authority for determining Christian truth.

Finally, *Survival Kit for New Christians* explains the *"Five and Five Principle."* This principal represents five people to whom the new converts is witnessing. It represents five others for whom he is praying daily because they are not open to his witness.

After the searcher becomes a Christian, he is led to enter a local expression of the body of Christ. In the church, he can be trained to start his own TOUCH cycle and involve himself with the unchurched. Keep in mind that the job of discipling is not completed until the person being discipled can *himself* disciple *another* convert. Teaching new Christians is not merely passing on information to them, but living a lifestyle before them. We can only *preach* what we *practice.*

COMMITMENT

What commitment does TOUCH call for? I believe it takes *total Christianity,* and nothing less! Consider for a moment the battle of the Alamo. For the handful of defenders, all hope was gone. There remained the possibility that by acting quickly they might be able to escape. Colonel Travis drew a line on the ground with his sword. He asked all the men who would make a *total commitment* of their lives to defend the Alamo to step across the line. We are told that all but one man made that type of commitment. The men knew when they stepped across the line that *they were giving their lives.* This is what I mean when I use the phrase total Christianity. If we commit anything less, we are back to programs. TOUCH is not a program. TOUCH is *commitment.*

Where do we start? We begin with the journey inward, to discover the biblical meaning of being a Christian who ministers, and what the church is to be in our world. Why do we need total Christianity? Because if we do not *love* a non-Christian, he will not hear us. When we prove to someone that we *do* love them, they will listen.

It is costly to love! Look at the price God paid to love us. It will also cost us to love; not all will respond by accepting Christ. Some will take advantage of us but, if we *don't* love them, *they will never hear of Christ.* If they do hear us, and our message is without *content,* what good has it done for them to hear? Our message must never be just religious words without content! Our message must come forth from the Word of God. This means we must spend time in study and prayer. This means a Christian lifestyle, dictated by the Bible, regardless of public opinion. There must be love and content. Love, flowing as rivers of living water; content, Christ dwells in us, and is our hope of glory.

As a two-natured person, the Christ nature in us must be touched by the one-natured individual. By being obedient to Christ, His indwelling life can express itself through us. We are then involved in true evangelism. As we create relationships, outsiders begin to see a value system they do not possess. As they wonder what the difference is between us and them, we can begin to share Jesus Christ with them. We are to do this in our homes, in their homes, in apartment complexes, all over the community, wherever we can get people to gather together. We do it with people who will not enter our church buildings, but who *will* enter our homes. This is what Christ has commissioned us to do. Let us be about the task! This is TOUCH, a theology that leads to a methodology; pouring ourselves into others so they, too, can fall in love with Jesus Christ.

When you discover the ministry that God has for *you,* as *you* begin to *T*ransform *O*thers *U*nder *C*hrist's *H*and, people will discover that Jesus Christ lives!

5. Beware the Boa!
Reflections on the constricting of Christian discipleship in the modern world

Os Guinness

Os Guinness is a free-lance writer, currently completing his doctoral research at Oxford University, England. Born in China, where his parents served as missionaries, he worked for several years with Dr. Francis Schaeffer at the L'Abri Fellowship in Switzerland. He is the author of The Dust of Death, *a Christian critique of the counter culture, and* In Two Minds, *which deals with the dilemma of doubt.*

"If you want to know what water is, a fish is the last thing to ask."

This old Chinese saying is an appropriate picture for Christian discipleship. It reminds us that discipleship is not in a vacuum, its context is never neutral, and the worst dangers are often those which are least obvious. One of the root meanings of the Hebrew for faith is tautness or tension, again relating to the social and cultural dualism which characterises discipleship. "In" the world, we are "not of" it; "no longer" what we were, we are "not yet" what we will be, and the critical distancing inherent in this space-time tension means that our involvement in the world should never lead to complete identification with it, and our commitment to the world should never lead to our captivity in it. As the Hartford Manifesto put it, we are "Against the world for the world."

One implication of this is the importance of prophetic analysis, not as a periodic necessity or a supplementary option, but as a constant and fundamental prerequisite for faithfulness in Christian life and witness. If we must watch as well as pray, if discernment is basic to discipleship and understanding of our context to the practice of our calling, then we must be constantly aware of the question:

What are the forces surrounding and shaping the church?

In which ways are they helpful, and in which ways are they harmful? Thus, the danger of "worldliness" is a main impetus [along with a desire for "mission"] behind the recent stress on the more fashionable-sounding concerns of "contextualization" which is now a vital feature of current theology [e.g. the spate of new studies such as "Gospel in Context" or the Willowbank Report, or strong warnings such as the recent Reith lectures by Edward Norman or Richard Quebedaux's book *The Worldly Evangelicals*].

There are three main types of contextual analysis currently being used by Christians. The first uses the history of ideas, the second cultural anthropology, and the third sociology and the analysis of social experience. While each of these is complementary and not contradictory to the other two, the merit of the third—in this decade anyway—is that it is perhaps least used and most useful. By contrast the first and second, though much better covered in Evangelical circles, have striking deficiencies: the history of ideas approach, though crucial, rarely manages to translate its insights to the ordinary person in the pew, and the best work of cultural anthropology has tended to deal with non-Western cultures and therefore to be more used if not more useful to those "on the mission field." An analysis of social experience, on the other hand, while intrinsically no more important than the other two, has the special attraction of being both relevant to ordinary life and also to modern Western experience.

This third approach, known technically as the sociology of knowledge, and best developed by Peter L. Berger (whose work I am following closely in this chapter) seeks to analyse the social location of knowledge. Accepting as fundamental whatever *passes* for knowledge, without passing judgment on its truth or falsity, it seeks to relate it to the wider social context which is its interpretative background. [The technical theory behind this is irrelevant here, though it is important to stress that its method is "dialectical," and not "deterministic," and "interpretative" and not "reductionist"—ideas are interpreted according to their social context, not explained by social causes.] For our purposes, then, as disciples in 20th century Europe, as compared with, say, 17th century Europe or 20th century Asia, there would be at least three questions basic to any analysis of the social experience which may be shaping our discipleship:

1. What do we mean by 'modernity,' 'modernisation,' and 'modern consciousness'?
2. What are the pressures of modernity which particularly affect religion in general?
3. What effect are they having on our Christian faith?

I. THE PROCESSES OF "MODERNITY"

What do we mean by modernity and modern consciousness? To follow the interesting and important directions indicated by this question would lead into far-off and fascinating fields, but since our focus of concern is the limited one of the impact of modernity on religion [so that modernisation in its widest sense is only of background importance] the central point can be put briefly: modern "culture" and modern "consciousness" [the subjective and inter-subjective awareness of those living in this culture] are the result of human interaction with the "carriers" of modernity. [The word is Max Weber's.] The two primary carriers are the capitalist market economy and the centralised bureaucratic state, and among "secondary carriers" the new industrial technology, rapid urbanisation, population growth, and the mass media are the most important.

In some ways these things are so obvious that for our purpose just to specify them is sufficient [and I will do no more] but remember that their very obviousness is itself a danger. The history of the discussion shows that two simple pitfalls need always to be borne in mind:

1. *A false presumption:* it is sometimes presumed that because we are modern we obviously know what modernity is; but that is precisely the error at root in the Chinese saying, or the biblical seriousness about worldliness. The deceptiveness of modernity may be in its very familiarity. We do not see it because we see with it. This is probably why foreigners are so shocked not only by our "cultural captivity" in Western Christendom but by our unconcern or inability to see it.

2. *A false assumption:* it is sometimes assumed that, if we know what "modernity" is, we also automatically know whether it is good or bad. Put differently, the conflation of "description" and "evaluation" while not necessarily wrong, is often too hasty and can be a bar to good communication. The history of the shift in labels from "backward" to "underdeveloped" to "less developed" to "developing" [in describing other coun-

tries] is an example rooted in this confusion, and Christian thinking, in its aptness to descry before it has described, is prone to similar errors. To insist on an absolute purity of distinction between description and evaluation is both impossible and pedantic but much unnecessary confusion is cleared up when, at least in principle, speakers are prepared to make the difference.

This then [modern culture, brought by its "carriers," producing its own "consciousness," exacting its own "costs," etc.] is the broadest background of context for our discussion, though to the commonplace understanding of the devastating impact of modernisation on traditional human life should be added the biblical insistence on the power of the world and of the Prince of this World. "Modernisation," writes Peter Berger, "operates like a gigantic steel hammer, smashing both traditional institutions and traditional structures of meaning." Other images of power and impact have been used, such as a steel press, or pressure cooker, or boa constrictor, but what they have in common are the themes of power, pervasiveness and pressure. As such, they highlight starkly our second question: what are the pressures of modernity which particularly affect religion?

II. THE PRESSURES OF MODERNITY ON RELIGION

At the risk of distorting a vast field of discussion and debate it may be safely said that there are three particular features of modernisation which are basic to understanding religion in modern society. These are "secularisation," "pluralisation" and "privatisation" [all technical words, and as such ugly and liable to become jargon, yet worth using: (1) because technically precise; (2) because they may all soon become as common as the first already is]. These, while not the causes of our problems, are the contexts in which they can be much more easily understood.

1. *Secularisation*

Secularisation, which is undoubtedly the central problem of the sociology of religion today, may be defined as the process by which religious ideas and institutions are losing their social significance, the ideas becoming less meaningful and the institutions more marginal [a good picture of the process is Julian Huxley's cheshire cat—the cat disappears but the grin lingers on]. First used in a narrow and descriptive sense [transferring property from the Church to the State after the Thirty Years War], it has now become both broader [covering subjective consciousness as well as objective institutions] and more emotive [e.g., "National Secular Society" in contrast to a preacher's "the secular world"].

Secularisation is best seen when contrasted with the more normal human experience, in which some sense of transcendence, however interpreted, is nearly universal. As far back as records go, human beings have reported instances of occurrences, forces, and beings that differ radically from those in ordinary life. Certainly most of life was occupied with "ordinary reality" [the "seven to eleven waking world"] and not all experiences of transcending this world were religious [e.g., dreams of ecstasy]. But religious experiences were held to be the deepest of all ["sacred," "other," "transcendent"], calling ordinary life in question, and putting a cosmic frame of reference around human existence, so that even things as human or mundane as business, sex, agriculture, and kingship were given religious interpretation and support.

Seen this way, the impact of secularization may be simply described: "Ordinary reality" has become the "official reality" and is for many people in modern society the "only reality." What G. K. Chesterton wrote of empiricist philosophers—they "have the same conception of reality as that held by a slightly drowsy, middle-aged business man right after lunch"—is now true of thousands of ordinary modern people. With transcendence denied, modern secular consciousness is a "world without windows." (Peter Berger)

Lack of time precludes an adequate discussion of the lively debate over secularisation although in this case parts of it would be crucial to our discussion. A telegraphic summary of certain of the main points of discussion might be as follows:

1. Over the roots of secularisation: two main sources are suggested, one from the history of ideas (growth of scientific rationalism, rise of protestant spirit, latent biblical secularity, etc.) and the other from material and social factors such as industrialisation and urbanisation.

2. Over the definition of religion: some (such as Bryan Wilson) take a narrower substantive definition (in terms of belief in God, gods, or the supernatural) and conclude for the evidence for secularization that religion is in overall decline; others (such as

Jacques Ellul, Daniel Bell, Thomas Luckmann) who take a broader, functional definition (in terms of what it does and how it functions for people) see a shift taking place rather than a decline (Marxism, nationalism, etc. being as 'religious' as either Christianity or Hinduism).

3. Differences over diagnosis of current religious resurgence (i.e. the swing to Eastern religions, the occult, the Jesus Movement and the charismatic movement, etc.): those who follow the substantive definition see it only as a reaction. In other words, secularization, the decline of the old faiths, and sectarianism, the rise of new cults, are two sides of the same coin. On the other hand, those who follow the functional definition see the resurgence as part reaction and part reversal, e.g. Jacques Ellul who says that 'post-Christian' is not to be confused with 'secular.' What we call secularisation is only the temporary period between one form of sacred and the next.

The important point to grasp, however, is that while secularisation is not universal (since modernisation is a process, countries are *more* or *less* modernised, no one country is totally modernised) nor uniform (its spread and distribution differ according to continents, classes, age, profession, religion, etc.) its power and impact are such that there are certain broad agreements despite the differences. Namely, a) that religions are adversely affected by secularisation to the extent that the area is dominated by heavy industry; b) that they are more adversely affected still if the decline proportionately with the size of an urban concentration; d) that the more a society is differentiated the more an individual's religion is cut off from other areas of his life and encouraged to become compartmentalised or make personal only.

2. *Pluralization*

Pluralization is the process by which modern societies have come to have an increasing number of world and world-views available for their members. (If the vanishing cat pictures the secularization process perhaps the best picture here might be of a "religious supermarket"—choice to the point of surfeit). There is a variety of world-views, within *one* society and no *one* world view is in control.

Unlike secularization, pluralization is not radically new (one example is the first century A.D. with a pluralism resulting from the breakdown of the classical gods) but the present situation is very different from the recent past, and it is occurring at an unprecedented rate. Once again the more normal situation in human history provides an illuminating contrast. While there have always been differences within society (resulting from division of labour or social tensions, such as slave revolts) there was at the same time a very high degree of unity and integration and the strongest integrating force has always been religion. Whether for an individual or a tribe or a nation religion was like a "sacred canopy" defining the limits of meaning, and foreclosing on the possibility of alternatives. The strongest religions of all were "monopolies" providing overarching structures and symbols to all within it. (e.g. Christianity of Mediaeval Europe, despite Jews, Infidels, heretics, or Hinduism in India despite Muslims or Buddhists). It is this situation and its attendance sense of "givenness" and solidity which pluralization has undermined.

The road to the present situation can be traced back to two main sources. The first is religion. Some, like David Martin, say that Christianity itself is "inherently pluralistic and voluntaristic." Since its truth transcends and criticises every given situation, every established status quo (social or religious) it inevitably becomes an agency of choice and change. Others would rather join with his second point that if choice is inherent in Christianity, it is rampant in Protestantism. It may even be said that the Protestant principle stresses choice to a degree that is "sociologically unrealistic" (David Martin). Seen this way there are three crucial stages to the present moment. Stage 1: the emergence of the pluralistic potential following the Wars of Religion (the combined effect of the fragmentation of Christendom and the disillusionment with religious bigotry). Stage 2: the acceptance of denominationalism in principle (coming to terms with the permanent presence and competition of other churches within the same territory). Stage 3: secularization (for the first time the strongest rivals were not within the church but outside).

The second source is social, and a moment's reflection on the consequences of such things as urbanization, role specialization, economic surplus, mass communication, popular travel, social and geographical mobility, the knowledge explosion, etc. will show that whatever other consequences they also have, one of their main effects, especially when combined together, is to increase the consciousness of choice and change. Put simply, modern people are aware of two things as never before: the "presence of others" (from their cuisines to their customs to their convictions, etc.) and the "possibilities for ourselves." We have the means, we have the time, so following the crucial shift from "givenness" to "choice" we are presented with a proliferating variety of options—hobbies, holidays, therapies, life-styles, religions—many of them replete with their own "little worlds" or accompanying subcultures. The problem this creates can be seen in the relating of variety to relativity. Pluralization eats into "givenness" like a relativising acid until it becomes choice. Obligation becomes option, a "fact of life" becomes a "fashion for the moment." Put differently, the more choice and change there is the less commitment and continuity there will be. On the level of possessions the effect is psychologically trivial (if you lose a silk handkerchief you look for it, but a tissue is made to be disposable) but pluralization bites deeper as it touches homes, marriages, and supremely faith. Yet without exaggeration we might say that many modern people's relation to marriage partners or their faith is in a way closer to the tissue model than to that of the silk handkerchief. (I have so far resisted applying these points to Christianity but it is easy to see why pluralization is reckoned to have rendered modern man "conversion prone.")

3. *Privatisation*

The third important feature of modernisation is 'privatisation,' which may be defined as the process by which a cleavage is made between the private and public spheres of modern life and there is a crystallisation of the importance of the private as the unique sphere of individual freedom and fulfilment. (The picture I suggest here is of a "religious zoo"—an extraordinary variety of wild life but in captivity).

Privatisation is not to be confused with notions such as "privacy" or "pietism"—one result of the confusion is the bad press each now suffers. These are older and different ideas, although not unrelated. (We could say that privatisation is a partial consequence of the simultaneous "democratisation" and devaluation of privacy, while pietism is undoubtedly one of the theological slipways from which privatisation was more easily launched). Privatisation, far from being in the nature of things, is an unintended consequence of modernisation, and centres around the modern cleavage between the private and public spheres.

While there must always have been some distinction between a person's private and public lives, the relationship has more normally been characterized by a continuum rather than a cleavage. For example, in traditional societies the family, though deeply personal, also had a key part not only in religion but also in economic production, education, and sometimes even the army and even medicine. Today it is separated from all of these except religion. This represents both a "shrinkage" in the sense of a loss of its former scope and functions, and a "shift," in the sense of a discovery of new functions; its primary concern is now the individual and his needs, expectations and fulfilment.

On one side is the public sphere or "macro-world," the world of the state, big business, the trade unions and bureaucracy. Highly rationalised, well organised, it represents the epitome of "functional rationality" and as such is at the heart of modern society. But, for that very reason, to many individuals it is a large and impersonal world, anonymous in its character, incomprehensible in its inner working, alien and Kafkaesque to a degree. On the other side is the private sphere or "micro-world," the world of the family, leisure pursuits, voluntary associations, youth and the church, all areas outside the sphere of modern work activity.

What are the consequences of privatisation? Any attempt to draw up a balance sheet at once shows that privatisation is double-edged, a mixed blessing; it may be experienced as either positive or negative, as opportunity or as oppression. On the positive side, the privatised world has two great advantages. First, it represents genuine freedom. Compared with the past more people have more chance to do more than ever before, while compared with totalitarian countries it is enough to say that there *is* a private world. Second, it offers a degree of compensation for whatever is not available in the public world, so it serves as a kind of safety value or balancing mechanism. "Out there" a person may wear a uniform, play a role, be identified by a number but "here is one place" where he can "get out of those things," be himself or "do his own thing." Public relationships must inevitably be partial, functional and superficial to some degree but private relationships can make up for it by being deep, personal and whole.

But while the privatised world works well for many, providing a heyday for hedonists especially) it also has its negative side, and certain in-built weaknesses are evident—all of which become crucial to Christian discipleship. First, the privatised world is strictly limited and limiting. If any identities can be adopted, any life-styles or value systems practised (yoga? wife swapping? pigeon fancying? praying in tongues?—all are possible) this is true *only* of the privatised world. But the public world, the world of GM, ICI, The Pentagon or Whitehall, and so forth, is a very different world with very different ways. As Peter Berger puts it: "The narrow enclave of the nuclear family serves as a macro-socially innocuous play area in which the individual can safely exercise his world-building proclivities without upsetting any of the important social, economic and political applecarts."

Second, the privatised world represents fragmentation, and therefore to some degree compartmentalisation and dislocation. The corollary of greater freedom than ever before *within* each world is greater difference than ever before *between* each world. The boundaries, for instance, between the worlds of youth and business and Church are sharper than ever before. As Karl Mannheim says of the bureaucrat, "He lives in two worlds, and he must therefore, so to speak, have two souls." The implications of this for ethics are obvious.

Third, the privatised world is unstable, being simultaneously over-sold (e.g. the expectations for fulfilment stirred up by either advertising or movements such as the Human Potentials Movements) and under-structured (the decline of religion and the disappearance of extended family removing two basic ways of ordering private life). So while the surface impression gained of the privatised world is one of freedom, the truer picture also includes its fragility. D-I-Y identities, values and life-styles are all very well for the successful or the fortunate but for many people the liberty of privatisation very easily becomes anxiety if not crisis and breakdown (e.g. divorce strikes in, children drop out, the neighbourhood changes, business dictates a move, sickness strikes) and the precariousness of the privatised world is easily exposed.

Fourth, the privatised world is highly vulnerable to this infiltration or manipulation of outside forces. Once again, its ostensible freedom is counterbalanced in practice by various problems, which each gain entry because of what the privatised world means to modern individuals, as the prime sphere of their individual fulfilment and economic consumption. The combination of these two factors explains why the inhabitants of the privatised world are the easy prey if not the deliberate target of such forces as political propaganda (the appeal of the "Quiet Life Vote"), commercial advertising (privatised man is a champion consumer), religious cults and sects ("Jonestown" or the JWs are too easily dismissed without understanding the "hunger for home" they represent) and the therapeutic agencies ("How to" publishing, counselling techniques, self-awareness courses, and so forth.)

In short, size and impersonality are the two most anathematised features of modern society, yet privatisation means that "small is beautiful" and may not only be a welcome return to the humanly scaled, but a weak-retreat from the challenge of modern living.

These three pressures—secularisation, pluralization, privatisation—should not be seen as separate, unrelated forces, one or other of which may cause problems to a particular religion. Their challenge lies, rather, in their combined interacting power and it is little wonder that while no religions remain unaffected, those which stress such things as truth, objectivity, or historicity are the hardest hit of all. So we turn now to the third main question: What are the problems these pressures have created for Christianity?

III. THE PROBLEMS CREATED FOR CHRISTIANITY

That such forces have contributed in some way to the Christian credibility crisis is hardly surprising. As the very shallowest level, if all this is "modern" anything different is bound to appear "old-fashioned." If secularization, pluralisation are facts to any degree, Christianity is bound to appear at least to outsiders, "unreal" just "one among many" or a "private preference" respectively. But we need to look closer and examine more carefully the links between the pressures and the problems they create. Only then will we be in a position to make positive and practical recommendations about a Christian response. Before we do this, though, two preliminary points need to be made.

1. The problems are not unique to Christianity. This again is obvious, but needs to be borne in mind or the overall picture will be both distorted and discouraging. It is certainly true that Christianity has been the first major religion to bear the full brunt of modernity and the damage done is plain to see for friend

and foe alike. But the very reasons it hit Christianity earlier and with greater intensity turn out on examination to be both complimentary in terms of the past and encouraging in terms of the future, though both of these are beside the point here. What I would stress, though only in passing, is that other religions and other institutions (including the state itself) have been as badly, if not worse, hit and only now is the toll on millions of individual lives being taken seriously into account. Bryan Wilson's comment on modern society may be taken as typical of the problem at a national level: "Contemporary society is less legitimated than any previously existing social system. . . . We know no moral order to give meaning to our social order."

2. The general problem is one of "plausibility crisis." (This point is the only technical one in the paper and may be skipped without loss of the thread of argument). Ideally the credibility of any belief should be related ultimately only to its truth or falsehood. But it doesn't take a cynic to recognise that many things are in fact believed or disbelieved without any relation at all to their being true or false. Psychology, for instance, points to one level of non-rational motivation for belief and disbelief, and while the charge of "rationalising" may be hotly rejected in a particular situation it is rarely disputed today as a general possibility. Sociology of knowledge adds a further dimension of non-rational motivation for belief and disbelief, and while the charge of "rational motivation, when it points out that the plausibility of any belief *in practice* is related to the strength of its supporting structure. Put simply, in a world of other people it is extremely difficult to believe something by oneself. *Sociologically speaking,* then, a belief needs a stable social psychological base, or "plausibility structure" (Peter Berger). This provides a supportive community, co-inhabitants of the same world whose presence is therefore a constant reiteration and confirmation of what is believed, whether true or false. In this sense, *regardless* of their respective truth-claims, the Party is the plausibility structure for the Marxist, the university world to the liberal humanist and the church to the Christian. (Paul's reference to the Church in 1 Timothy 3:15 as "the pillar and bulwark of the truth" is probably to be understood in this context, though in this case the belief is also true epistemologically speaking!)

This becomes practically relevant when its implications are followed through. First, the stronger the plausibility structure the "more true" the belief will *seem* to be to those who believe it (the "Catholic world" is stronger in Ireland than in England, just as the "Mormon world" is stronger in Utah than in the USSR, and the "Christian Arts world" is stronger in London because of the ACG, than in some provincial churches where art is considered "worldly"). In fact the strongest plausibility structures of all are those which have a monopoly in their area (such as Christianity in Europe down to the eighteenth century). Second, there is inevitably a crisis of confidence for any religion that is "de-monopolized" especially from one that shrinks from being a "monopoly" to being a "majority" to being a "minority." This is exactly the fate which Christianity has suffered. If the expansion of the early church (the movement from "minority" to "majority" to "monopoly") meant that some people must have believed for the wrong reasons, it is not hard to see that the numerical and social decline of the church means that others will also disbelieve and defect for the wrong reasons. This is what is meant by a plausibility crisis, and its import is usually seen in at least two ways— objectively the group becomes more and more of a minority, and subjectively its faith becomes less and less of a certainty.

Perhaps the best way of analysing the plausibility crisis facing Christianity is to examine the impact of modernity on three specific levels—that of Christian institutions (the impact on the church's structures), that of Christian ideas (the impact on the substance of the faith) and that of Christian involvement (or the impact on the church's stance in the world.)

1. *Effects on the Level of Christian "Institutions"*

Among various possible effects, four may be selected as specially important or interesting, the first from the viewpoint of wider society and the others from the viewpoint of the Church.

(a) *The exclusion and polarisation of Christianity:* seen from the point of view of society at large the influence and distribution of religion in general and Christianity in particular is marginal and peripheral. There are two discernible parts in this reduction of influence. The first is exclusion. Modernisation has produced a centrally located sector which is something like "liberated territory" with respect to religion. In this central area all the main components of modernity (economics, science, technology, business, and so forth) operate in a world freed of religious influence. The second is polarisation. Religion, banned from the centre, is pushed to one of the two extremes, either the most private areas of life or the most public.

In the most public areas (such as state occasion) Christianity becomes largely "public rhetoric." Peter Berger puts it, "At a time when everyone takes for granted that 'religion stops at the factory gate,' it may nevertheless also be taken for granted that one does not inaugurate either a war or a marriage without the traditional religious symbolisation." This has two particular dangers for the faith. One is that the powerful pull of the State's priorities makes of Christianity a 'civic religion' with the twin consequences of theological idolatry and cultural captivity. The other is that Christianity becomes unnecessarily exposed to the anti-formalist feelings of today, and with the twentieth century firmly on the side of the small boy against the Emperor, Christianity is needlessly dismissed as hollow or hypocritical in the general reaction against the ritual clothes. Thus, excluded from the centre, or pushed to the most public areas as "public rhetoric," religion in general and Christianity in particular have only one area left—the most private, and here typically they represent no more than 'private religiosity' (a point worth taking up on its own).

(b) *The Privatisation of Christianity:* It must be stressed that these trends are only that—trends and general tendencies. They are neither universal nor inevitable and that is particularly relevant as we see in the next two points how different parts of the Church have responded differently to different parts of the modern world.

Nothing is more characteristic of the church's modern captivity than the privatisation of the Christian faith today, a direct and dramatic consequence of modernisation. On the surface, it might appear that the opposite is the case—that Christianity's recovery of the personal is its most encouraging sign of revival. Evidence for such a claim would be easy to find. Someone might point to growing lay participation, flourishing home groups for Bible study and fellowship, as well as a general emphasis on the personal, informal, extemporary and down-to-earth as against the institutional, the formal, the liturgical and the abstract. But all this suits privatisation only too well, which, remember, encourages and almost demands such personal freedom and fulfilment as essential to the private area. If this is so, much of the current "renewal" is not just a theological and spiritual revival—though this aspect need not be denied—but a movement with an easily observed sociological context, and, more to the point, with easily predicted sociological consequences. But simply, the renewal will show that its motivation and dynamics are theological and spiritual (and not sociological) to the degree that it can transcend the limitations of privatisation.

Whether or not this is so, what can be said confidently is that many of the institutional expressions of contemporary Christianity show the same in-built weakness that characterise the privatised world in general. First, it is common for faith to be strictly limited to the private sphere (which includes, of course, the church). Lord Melbourne's remark in the early nineteenth century after listening to an evangelical sermon—"Things have come to a pretty pass when religion is allowed to invade the private sphere"—is in striking contrast to a late twentieth century comment on the church: "privately engaging, if socially irrelevant." (Theodore Roszak). Seen theoretically in terms of meaning the sacred canopy of Christian truth, once coextensive with the horizons of knowledge and experience, has now shrunk to the size of a folding umbrella, while in terms of morals total life norms have become part-time values. Seen practically, in terms of life-style, the experience is one of compartmentalisation. A Christian businessman or politician, for example, may adhere faithfully to the Christian norm of family life or even personal relationships at work while at the same time conducting his activities in the public sphere without any reference to Christian values of any kind. What Islam is refusing to succumb to, and the Bible explicitly calls us against, is being accepted by many contemporary Christians with a smile and a song.

Second, there is a marked instability to the different expressions of privatised Christian world, hardly surprising since their basic plausibility structure is often no stronger or more lasting then the nuclear family or the home fellowship group. Being smaller they are both shakier and more short lived. Easier to join, they are easier to leave. Fear of discipline and disdain for tradition mean that the emphasis on being free and personal may have a heavy toll.

Third, the privatised Christian world shows a decided vulnerability to the infiltration if not manipulation of alien external forces. This is more marked in the United States than in Europe, since religion in general is more highly regarded there, but the danger of alliances compromising to the church's mission is a real one. Drawn by the power of the state, privatised Christianity easily becomes "civic religion"; attracted by the blandishments of business, privatised Christianity borders on "commercial religion" (as secular salesmen have been quick to see) and pulled down to the level of popular opinions and needs, privatised Christianity easily becomes "common religion" (the broad amalgam of hope, fatalism and superstition which is not so much post-Christian as pre-Christian and pagan).

The central issues of privatisation should be clear. It is all about space and sovereignty—whose is the sovereignty? Over how much space? As such it strikes at the heart of Christian discipleship. Christ's Lordship is confined to the personal and the private, and under the impact of privatisation Christianity is so shorn of its intellectual and ethical implications that it is reduced to technological society's equivalent of a harmless folk-religion.

(c) *The bureaucratization of Christianity:* If privatisation is most visible at the level of ordinary Christian experience it clearly does not apply to the greater part of Christian leadership, where a countervailing movement may be noted—that of bureaucratization.

I am personally less well acquainted and therefore more tentative about this point, though from my limited experience it at least "rings true" to an uneasiness I already feel. So the comments are worth including for the sake of completeness or for their value in raising questions.

Bureaucracy is notoriously difficult to define, easier to describe (a separate organisation with a full-time staff, orderly hierarchies, fixed areas of jurisdiction, a rational system of training and expertise, and so forth) and easier still to illustrate ("the Pentagon", "Whitehall", and so forth). But it is now held to be spreading to all areas of institutional life as the most rational and effective form of organisation and administration. It would be, therefore, far from surprising if it did not affect the church at its more organised levels, and this is the charge now being made. Put simply, the same procedures which have proved effective in landing men on the moon or marketing a new perfume are being applied in planning stewardship campaigns or running a denomination.

This is not entirely new, of course. As David Martin says,

"Henry VIII and Peter the Great in different ways converted—if that is the right word—churches into nationalised industries." But there, as he also points out, the similarity ends. Their take-over of the church was out of respect for its power. The modern take-over by contrast is from a position of Christian weakness out of respect for bureaucracy's power.

This does not mean that the consequences are necessarily or completely disastrous. Far from it. But it does mean that for all the obvious advantages it brings the alliance should be carefully monitored to check its unintended, even delayed, negative side-effects. These may be expected along one of two lines. First, where bureaucracy itself "fails." In other words, where it is not inherently dangerous in theory, but where its known "dysfunctions" make it counterproductive. For example, its tendency to forget its purpose, shifting its focus from ends to means and becoming fascinated with procedures, is already a weakness of parachurch movements over the course of time, so the prospect of increasingly bureaucratised para parachurch movements is sobering. Second, where bureaucracy itself "succeeds" but its very success has unforeseen consequences inherently dangerous for Christianity. In this connection the alleged relationship of bureaucracy to ecumenism might be mentioned, as well as its tendency to develop a type of personality which is a far cry from older categories such as prophet/priest or pastor/preacher. (This in my view was behind much of the non-rational, non-substantive suspicions against N.E.A.C. 1977, particularly from non-conformists. In effect they were reacting to a "new breed" of Anglican Evangelical).

(d) *The commercialization of Christianity:* Talcott Parsons describes the United States as "the lead society," by which he means, not that the direction is necessarily good or that others must necessarily follow, but simply that, for better or worse, the U.S.A. is the most modernised of any large society. Britain, by comparison, though the lead society in the nineteenth century— the crucial early era of modernisation—is both "behind," in terms of cultural lag, and different, in terms of its local characteristics, which both have a definite bearing on British development. Of course, to be behind may well be to be better off and the American tendency to commercialise Christianity, inhibited in Britain by various local factors, is a good example of this.

Much has been written recently on American "Civil Religion"

(Robert Bellah), the unholy alliance of faith and flag, but potentially just as dangerous is what might be called "Commercial Religion" the equally unholy alliance between doctrine and dollar. This tendency is most probably a direct consequence of the combined impact of both pluralisation and privatisation, and while a perennial problem in American Christianity it is assuming proportions of virulence as it coincides with the present resurgence of evangelicalism influence in North America (the celebrated "forty million evangelicals" are a sizeable market by any standards).

The best way to understand this 'Commercial Religion' apart from specifying its more striking or spectacular features (one million dollar Sunday collections, fourteen million dollar local churches, many single evangelical T.V. stations each bringing in more money annually than the entire Vatican budget, etc.) is to try to grasp the general context in which it arises. At least three factors are relevant here. First, the broader context is the long-established commitment to pluralism in American religion. A key feature of the "de-monopolisation of religion" (Peter Berger) in the modern world has been that the nation state has become emancipated from religious institutions or rationale. This has come slowly even in countries like Spain or Ireland, but in the U.S.A. the process was accelerated immeasurably by a separation of church/state and a commitment to religious egalitarianism *in principle* and *from the start*. (Britain is somewhat between these two extremes).

Thus whether by design or effect the state is no longer the enforcement agency for Christianity, and now stands as a general impartial guardian watching over freely competing religious groups, an analogous role to its position in *laissez-faire* capitalism. Individual churches are therefore 'out on their own' and it is entirely up to them to enlist and maintain voluntary adherents. Put differently, there has been a crucial shift in the churches' stance towards their people—from "coercion" to "competition;" from its being a 'monopolistic authority' to its becoming something of a 'marketing agency.' Christian institutions, in other words, whether on the level of local churches or large denominations, show signs of competitiveness, a pressure to produce results, and a marked "consumer orientation." In short, whatever the legitimations offered (and it is striking how evangelism—and especially, now, growth—is becoming an "institutional imperative" even for those with no theological or spiritual obligation). Christianity in a pluralistic society must 'sell itself'.

Second, a further fact is the relationship between leisure and consumption in the private world. With religion confined to the private sphere at the very time when the private sphere has become crucial to individual aspiration for freedom and fulfilment, it takes thought and effort to prevent two things combining into what Thorsten Veblen termed "conspicuous consumption" (consumption whose purpose is not to satisfy the particular needs of a consumer but to serve as a symbol of his identity and status). Veblen's term was coined to do justice to the era of the Great Gatsby, but its relevance in interpreting the motivation of grandiose church building schemes or the facile spuriousness of the theology of commercial religion is disturbing.

Third, an additional factor is the contemporary trend towards the commercialisation of communication systems, definitely present in Britain but rampant in the U.S.A. Raymond Williams sees four types of such systems—the authoritarian (Russian), the paternal (B.B.C.), the commercial (I.T.V., N.B.C., C.B.S., A.B.C.) and the democratic (an ideal, not yet in existence). He concludes "The main struggle, over the last generation, has been between the paternal and commercial systems, and it is clear that the commercial has been steadily winning." In the U.S.A., of course, there is virtually only the commercial system and it is on this level that the church has recently entered with some spectacular 'success'.

But for all its promise and early delivery of freedom, the commercial system has grave dangers both for democrats and for Christians, mostly due to its dependence on the market and commercial criteria. Without detailing these dangers, it is enough to say that its central assertion—"anything can be said, provided you can afford to say it and that you can say it profitably"—is no recipe for faithful evangelism. The much-vaunted 'Electric Church' (the multi-million dollar Christian television station) may be a major new force in American religion and society but its tendency to produce "clientele instead of congregations" (Martin Marty) may cause untold damage to the worship, fellowship and discipleship of the Body of Christ.

2. Effects on the Level of Christian "Ideas"

For various reasons less need be said about this point, especially because the crisis of faith is so well documented from a history of ideas viewpoint. But the sociology of knowledge is a gentle re-

minder that intellectual factors are not all—even for intellectuals—so to an analysis of the impact of "scepticism" on faith
(from the history of ideas) should be added an analysis of the
impact of "secularism" (from social experience). The latter is only
an additional, background factor, but an important one though the
points can be made quickly. Secularism, interacting with scepticism, of course, has probably affected the crisis of faith by con-
tributing to three main things.

(a) *The loss of certainty and a general "melting down" of faith:*
It would be impossible to apportion the blame between scepticism
and secularism but it is surely no accident that the contents of
much Christian faith are reflection of the consciousness of wider
modern society—secularized, pluralized and privatised. Three
areas of possible evidence are first, the breakdown of the traditional sense of disciplined obligation of faith (e.g. church going is
option rather than obligation; commitment is choice rather than
being chosen); second, the general, if misplaced, modesty about
convictions (what was once "known" is now "believed" if not
merely "felt"); and third, increasing moral divergence (even in
strong traditional Roman Catholic countries such as Poland or
Ireland over things such as divorce or abortion). Where there is
certainty, it often tends to be either subjective or sectarian (unconsciously depending on membership of a small, tight-knit group).

(b) *The loss of comprehensiveness and a general "miniaturiz-
ing" of the faith:* Once again it is surely no accident that the scope
of much Christian concern is no wider than the limits of the
privatised world, which represents a particularly drastic shrinkage
of Christian relevance. Sociologists are apt to point to such classic
examples as the contemporary evangelical view of sin (listen, say,
to an evangelist for ten sermons and see whether sin refers to more
than personal wrongs) but other evidence might be found in such
things as Christian book titles and sales or the well-known problem
of getting people to combine concern for the gospel and social
justice. It is much easier to "go with the grain" of privatisation.

(c) *The loss of compelling power and a general "maketing" of
the faith:* The commercialisation of ideas runs parallel to the commercialisation of institutions, though in this area it is even more a
matter of effect rather than design, and as such is perceived more
by non-Christians listening than by Christians speaking. Take, for
example, a recent statement by the futurologist, Herman Kahn:

"We're the only people who, for a while, claimed to have Moses, Jesus Christ and Buddha under contract but we looked at their product and changed our minds." Whatever our reaction to Kahn's comment, it is surely important, first, to examine the Christian communication which makes such a response far from rare; and second, to see its implications for the faith. At the very least, many modern methods of evangelism lead either to an inadequate perception of the gospel (seen less clearly it can be rejected more easily) or to an inadequate preparation for Christian discipleship (a gospel that is all invitation and no demand, all choice and no chosenness, is no basis for costly obedience).

3. *Effects on the Level of Christian "Involvement"*

If modernity is really as powerful and pervasive as is being suggested the question of the Church's stance towards it is central to any discussion of Christian mission and worldliness. What sociologists assert is that since the rise of the modern world and due to its impact on the Church, the Christian stance towards modern culture has been broadly characterized by a strong polarisation rather than by any balanced, credible Christian alternative.

This polarization can best be seen by identifying in principle the two polar extremes (the "conservative" and the "liberal") while recognising that no school or person exemplified them perfectly. They may be set out in tabular form (as below) but it should be stressed first, that they refer to general tendencies, not to individuals or schools; second, that they are sociological and not theological categories (e.g. while some evangelicals are "conservative" in

	Conservative Tendency	Liberal Tendency
Ideal	Resistance	Relevance
Characteristic	Defiance	Bargaining
Normal method	Deductive (from tradition)	Inductive (from experience)
Picture of itself	Speaking ("proclamation")	Listening ("dialogue")
Political tendency	Rightwards ("conserving")	Leftwards ("changing")
Common consequence	Containment	Compromise
End result	Sectarianism	Secularism
Image of theology presented	"Queen of sciences"— but in exile	"Fashion model"
Basic problem	How strong are the defences?	How far should one go?

theology they may also be very "liberal" in life-style, and vice versa); and third, that although many examples could be given—sometimes tragic, sometimes humourous ("fundies" versus the "trendies")—the issue of personal sincerity is *never* in question.

Such a tabulation is obviously a little stark if not simplistic but the dangers it highlights and the orientation it encourages are fundamental to the integrity of both our discipleship and our evangelism. One simple and overall lesson which emerges is that both tendencies have been tried and both have equal, if opposite, dangers. No stance Christians may make will ever be cost-free, but the perils are now sufficiently clear for there to be much excuse for blind repetition of past failures.

The next step is to look a little closer at certain aspects of the problems of each extreme.

(a) *The defensive stance of the Conservative:* The problems inherent in the conservative tendency can be seen by examining some of the potential dangers to which it can lead. These may be outlined (all too briefly) as follows:

(i) The danger of "eradication": This is a sobering if rare and extreme case. A small community can achieve a consistency and beauty in its alternative life-style, yet only at the price of almost total separation from wider society. Its problem, then, is not internal, because it can easily be eliminated by political decision. One example is the ease and severity with which the Russian Revolution dealt with utopian Christian communities, a sharp contrast to their inability to destroy Russian Orthodoxy without cutting off the greatest achievements of Russia's past.

(ii) The dangers of "exploitation": For reasons that are psychological as well as theological, conservative Christianity is ideal for use in justifying and legitimating 'cultures under stress', quite possibly in a manner that is an absolute contradiction to basic Christian convictions. Ulster, South Africa or the Southern United States are extreme examples today but milder versions are possible too. David Martin speaks of fundamentalism as "the cultural defence of a rural, small-town America." When such an identification takes place disengagement without disillusionment is well-nigh impossible, and what is 'success' for the future is inevitably "defeat" for the faith.

(iii) The danger of "ossification": if contamination is the price of contact with alien cultures, certain conservative communities and groups maintain their consistency by living in a closed world with only minimal contact with the outside world. Extraordinary consistency, strong loyalties and a powerful nostalgia are all possible, but sometimes at the price of becoming virtually "museums of religious history" (Peter Berger). Problems usually arise at one of two points—over keeping their children or gaining converts.

(iv) The danger of "domestication": The first three problems are all extreme. The fourth is less drastic but no less serious in terms of discipleship. It happens when conservative Christianity becomes an alternative world that is tolerated by the outside world but is given no chance of growing, in terms of real power, if that would pose a basic challenge or threat to the outside world. As Raymond Williams writes, "The idea of an alternative culture is radical but limited. It can very easily become a marginal culture; even at worst a tolerated play area. It is certainly always insufficient unless it is linked with effective opposition to the dominant culture." The privatisation of modern Christianity brings it perilously close to such a description.

(v) The danger of "oscillation": A recurring, if not general, feature of conservative Christianity is the curious tendency of some of its advocates to capitulate suddenly to the opposite extreme. As David Martin says, "Just as Catholics who cease to be conservatives often become Marxists, so those who cease to be Thomist easily embrace the most extreme existential fashion. They are experts at excluding the middle." But the same is true of Protestant conservatism too, as the biographical details of many theological liberals or political extremists will illustrate. "In religion, as in politics," writes Peter Berger, "if once one starts to clobber the opposition, one stops clobbering at one's peril."

(vi) The danger of "infiltration": Another of the dangers of conservatism is its tendency to be so conscious of one point of the battle that its entire attention and resources are concentrated on it to the neglect of other dangers. Massively defended where "the real battle is" held to be, it is carelessly exposed on other flanks. Conservatives, for instance, with noses sensitive to detect the slightest whiff of liberalism are often carelessly accommodating in life-style or business method, oblivious of the dangers of worldliness at these other points.

As an overall generalisation it might be said that conservatives often show sound sociological instincts, though because of their suspicion of sociological analysis they lose the chance to know why.

(b) *The accommodating stance of the liberal:* If the basic problem of conservative with his ideal of "resistance" is "How strong are the defences?" that of the liberal with his ideal of "relevance" is "How far should one go?" To the old problem of achieving "contact" without "contamination" is added a new element: the pursuit of relevance, with its corollary of the tactical necessity of making sense to the other personal culture, introduced an escalating factor into the engagement. Here lies the problem of liberalism. Tactical modifications all too easily become basic modifications to the point where the faith re-thought is a different faith altogether.

Peter Berger expresses it in a vivid picture: "To vary the image, he who sups with the devil had better have a long spoon. The devilry of modernity has its own magic: the theologian who sups with it will find his spoon getting shorter and shorter—until that last supper in which he is left alone at the table, with no spoon at all and with an empty plate. The devil, one may guess, will by then have gone away to more interesting company."

The built-in weaknesses of the liberal tendency may be seen in outlining two areas that are important.

(i) The basic procedures involved in surrendering: without in any way suggesting that many, let alone everyone, go to these extremes (any more than with the conservative case), it is helpful to identify the steps involved if anyone does go the whole way.

Step one: an assumption. Liberalism assumes the value or superiority of an aspect of some position other than Christianity (such as Marxism, secularism, or modern thought).

Step two: a reduction. Whatever in Christianity does not fit in with what is assumed to be superior is then removed or modified (such as Bultmann's tailoring of the New Testament to fit the world-view of "radio and electricity users").

Step three: a translation. Whatever remains of traditional beliefs or practices is translated into terms appropriate to the new frames of reference. Different "translation grammars" (Peter Berger) are used—such as psychoanalysis or Marxism—and different lengths are taken, some moderate, some extreme.

Step four: an accommodation. The end result of going all the way is the inevitable surrender of all that is distinctively Christian. "Dialogue," says Berger of this extreme, "is often a misleading term to describe the ensuing relationship. In many cases it would be more apt to speak of 'conversion' and I need hardly add that I don't mean anyone's conversion to Christianity)."

(ii) The basic problems involved in surrendering: For the sake of brevity I have completely ignored the positive qualities of either conservatism or liberalism, though it should be plain that being "in" the world but "not of it" entails a combination of the best of both—commitment without compromise, resistance *and* relevance. But since this paper focuses on the negative aspects of contextualisation, focusing on worldliness rather than mission, this omission is not crucial.

Equally the problems of extreme liberalism may be sketched quickly. First, there is often a deep inconsistency in its methodology. Its basic assumption of the superiority of some aspect of the modern over the traditional may be very uncritical. When the past is relativised but the present is absolutised, the method sets itself up to be criticised by its own tools.

Second, there is often a curious timidity in its desire for relevance. If everything odd, embarrassing, or unfashionable is to be modified or removed from the gospel the "Evangelistic modification" (in terms of tactics) will soon become an "epistemological modification" (in terms of truth) and the result will be a disembowelment of the faith.

Third, the short-term gains are transient at best. Relevance is a very fragile business. As Dean Inge warned: he who marries the spirit of the age soon finds himself a widower.

Fourth, the long-term results are self-defeating. The more extreme the accommodation the more likely it is that certain consequences follow—the distinctive contents of the faith are emptied, ordinary believers are bewildered and alienated, outsiders are unimpressed (after all, they believe it anyway without needing it dressed up in Christian language) and liberalism undermines its own effectiveness (often it cannot speak to the next "new wave," precisely because of what was surrendered as the price of being relevant to the previous one).

If this analysis which follows closely the approach of Peter Berger, David Martin and others, is correct to some degree then it raises significant questions in a number of important areas—posed here in the broadest terms.

First, in terms of Christian involvement in national affairs, it highlights the question of how to relate faith to socio-political issues while avoiding the scylla of "sociological idiocy" (a faith so "purist" or so "privatised" that it can contribute nothing to the crisis of national legitimation) and the charybdis of 'theological idolatry' (making faith captive to some viable non-Christian frame of reference for the sake of relevance or effectiveness).

Second, in terms of Christian concern for the untold number of individuals feeling the discontent of modernity, however dimly, it raises the question of what are the best means of reaching them and the best structures for helping them. If Christian methods and structures are too alien people will remain unreached, but if they are too similar, people will remain unhelped. "Jonestown" is not helped by the building of "Jesustown."

Third, in terms of evangelicalism as a movement, the main issues are quite clear though their resolution will not be simple. Will contemporary evangelicalism be able to break out of its continuing combination of privatisation and pietism and, if it does, will it be able to escape refuelling the liberal cycle all over again? Both parts of this question need to be stressed equally clearly. There are disquieting signs that,with the resurgence of evangelicalism in the sixties and seventies, many of the "new evangelicals" are aware only of the first question, and so are in danger of walking backwards towards the precipice represented by the second question. "Fundies" and "trendies" are in many ways the mirror image of each other, but in my own mind I have no doubt which is the greater danger at the moment.

6. Prayer . . . The Priority!

Jack Taylor

Jack Taylor is a free-lance writer and Bible teacher with an international ministry. The author of numerous books and magazine articles, his The Key to Triumphant Living *has already become a classic within deeper-life literature.*

There is a common flaw in most of our teaching. That is, we talk about concepts, necessities, and responsibilities, but not about the "how to." I remember being born into the kingdom with a conviction that I ought to pray. I do not remember anybody ever *telling* me that I ought to pray, and yet somehow I knew that prayer was a central responsibility. So, as a ten-year-old junior boy, I began to develop a prayer life. I did not know anything about how to spend the time, how to structure it, or what to do, but I do remember that my place of prayer was in our storm cellar. We lived in the buckle of the storm belt and we had a storm cellar with thick concrete walls. It was always warmer in the winter and cooler in the summer than any other place on my daddy's farm. That storm cellar is where I started praying and practicing my preaching.

I loved prayer. However, I got away from that love of prayer. Sadly, it has only been in recent years that I have returned to the same emphasis on prayer that I had as a junior boy. I knew prayer was important; yet, in the process of gaining a theological education, preparing to preach and to minister, I do not even remember being taught the "hows" of prayer.

If I were to pastor again, I would work with my people about specific ways to develop a time with God. We often talk about how a person ought to spend time alone with God. Yet, hundreds of people, a great percentage of Christians, get in the presence of God at their place of prayer, and do not know what to do. They pray out loud, but since they are not used to hearing their voices when they are all alone, it is uncomfortable and new to them.

When we first started our 24-hour prayer program in Castle Hills, many of our people took up the responsibility of prayer. They knew it was a pivotal ministry—an indispensable ministry—in a growing, ministering church. And yet, they told me: "I went to the place of prayer, and prayed over everything I could think of, until I *knew* I had been there for an hour. And then, I looked up at the clock on the wall, and discovered I had been there only ten minutes! Preacher, I don't know how to pray. Somebody needs to teach me how to pray!" It was then that we began to learn the many facets of prayer: how to confess sin in preparation to pray; how to confess the Word to set the atmosphere to pray; how to make petitions; how to praise and enjoy thanksgiving; how to engage in intercession; and so on. Our people began to learn to pray.

Do you know what we discovered? Few of our people had ever spent one solid, unbroken hour in the presence of God doing business with him in prayer! It would probably be shocking to us if we found out actually how few people had spent that amount of time in prayer.

In Matthew 22:36-40, Jesus and a lawyer were talking. The lawyer was tempting him and said:

> "Teacher, which is the great commandment in the law?" And he said to him, "You shall love the Lord your God with all your heart, and with all your soul, and with all your mind." This is the great and first commandment. And a second is like it, You shall love your neighbor as yourself. On these two commandments depend the law and the prophets" (RSV).

I confess to you that I do not know very much about loving God. I *want* to love God! I want to respond to God in a way that is pleasing to him. If I know my heart at all, I know that I want to be a pleasure to God. I have asked the Lord over and over again how can I love him better. I know I can love him by serving him. I know I can love him by talking about him. And I know I can love him by reading his Word.

But I *also* know that there is no exercise as vital to implementing a love relationship with God as the exercise of prayer. Without it in a pivotal position, we cannot really claim to love God. Love involves spending time with God; love involves expressing affection and praising God. We can *say* we love God with our *lips,* but do we truly love him? A basic quality in loving anything or anybody is allowing the one we love to consume our time without begrudging it. It is going to take *time* to develop a true love relationship with God. No amount of service or thinking will take the place of prayer. It is not a matter of these things conflicting with each other. Rather, it is allowing a love relationship to point the way to developing a deep relationship with God.

To tell the truth, I am not comfortable with this truth. I sometimes wish it were not true. I wish the implementation of the relationship with God involved something easier than prayer. I find it easier to *preach* on prayer than to *pray.* I find it easier to *write* on prayer than to *pray.* I find it easier to *talk* about Jesus than to *pray.* I find *anything* I do in my Christian life easier than *praying!* That ought to give a clue: the devil hates prayer as he hates few other things. In prayer, we are in fellowship with God; we are receiving strength from God. In prayer, our spirits are being united, implementing a love relationship. As a result, the devil will contest our prayer life more than any other thing. Let me give you seven basic facts which form some pivotal principles related to prayer by the church and by the individual.

The first principle is that *no believer's spiritual life will ever rise and stay above the level of his praying.* I am aware that we may have temporary spiritual "spurts," if you please . . . spiritual "hot flashes," every now and then. But we will always settle down afterward at the level of our praying.

Secondly, I also believe that *the level of discipleship is the level of prayer.* Somehow the impression is being left that a disciple can be developed by going through a book, by carrying out certain exercises, by going to seminary, or by putting one thing behind another. Prayer is the implementation of the relationship of a disciple. A disciple is someone willing to center the whole of life around the person of Jesus Christ. There is no implementation of discipleship apart from prayer. No believer's spiritual life will ever rise to stay above the level of his or her praying.

The third principle is that *no church's corporate prayer life will be greater than the prayer lives of those who make up its membership.* You will not be able to promote a program of prayer among a people who do not know how to pray. You can develop the skeletal designs of a great prayer program; you can have prayer chains; you can have 24-hour prayer programs; and you can have prayer meetings. But corporate prayer meetings or corporate prayer power within the church will *never be greater than the development of the individual prayer lives of those who make up its membership.* Therefore, we need to talk with individuals about their personal prayer life. We need to discuss the time they spend with God, how to spend that time, when to set aside quality time, how to use the Bible in prayer, and simply *how to pray*—just the "nuts and bolts" of how to pray!

The fourth principle is that *no individual's prayer life will be greater than the quality of his regular time set aside to meet God alone.* Now, I am for family prayer. I believe you ought to pray with your family. I believe you ought to pray anywhere, everywhere, by all means and every means. However, I have the conviction that no amount of praying with others, "snatch-time" praying, "driving-down-the-road" praying, or any other kind of praying, will take the place of time when an individual, alone with God and his Word, begins to develop a love relationship with God in prayer. No other amount of prayer will take the place of this quality time.

The fifth principle is that *your view of prayer will determine your practice of it.* Perhaps before we can establish prayer as a priority in our lives, we ought to do a biblical study on the prayer life. We may need to examine the prayer life of Abraham and Moses to learn what God thinks of prayer.

There are three instances of prayer that leave me open-mouthed and wide-eyed. The first is found in the book of Ezekiel, where God is recorded as looking upon the land. He saw that all the people, priests, and prophets were corrupt. They all had gone bad! There seemed to be no hope for the nation. Then, God said something about prayer: "And I searched for a man among them who should build up the wall and stand in the gap before Me for the land, that I should not destroy it; but I found no one" (Ezek. 22:30, NASB) What was God looking for? He was looking for someone who would interpose himself between a wicked, declining, rebellious nation and a holy God. God looked for a *man.* God took the initiative to look for a *praying man!* However, the sad words that end that verse are: "I found no one. Thus I have poured out My indignation on them" (v. 30).

The second instance is in the life of Abraham. God had made a covenant with Abraham. God heard the cries of Sodom and Gomorrah, and said: "I can't do anything about those cities until I talk with Abraham." So, God told Abraham what he was about to do: "I'm going down to see if their wickedness is as great as their cry, and if it is I am going to wipe them off the face of the earth!" Abraham then audaciously took it upon himself to question the proposed actions of God. He said: "God, will you destroy the righteous with the wicked? If there be 50 will you spare the cities?" Without equivocation or any further discussion, *a man in a prayer relationship with a holy, sovereign God of heaven,* stopped God! The amazing thing is that Abraham went from 50 people to 40, to 30, to 10 . . . and God was just as quick to agree that he would spare the cities for 10 just as he would for 50. What is amazing about this? Simply that a mere *man* could stand in the presence of *God,* and say: "God, will you destroy the righteous with the wicked, or will you postpone judgment upon the land?" *One man* was standing in the gap in prayer for two great wicked cities. The third instance deals with the case of Moses.

One day, God said: "I have had it with this crowd! I am going to wipe them out, start over with a new race!" Well, it would not have done for *me* to have been Moses. I would have said: "Lord, I think that's the best idea you've had today. Have at it! I'll find a high place and watch you wipe them out. That's the meanest, sorriest, gripingest bunch I have ever seen in my life."

Moses, however, was a "pray-er." He said, in effect (Taylor translation): "God, nothing doing! If you do this, the word will get back to Egypt that we have a God who couldn't finish what he started. Now, I understand that you are a God who visits the iniquity of the fathers unto the third and fourth generations of the children; God, I am asking you to pardon these people for my sake." One audacious man, and millions of people's lives in the balance. I would not have been surprised if, after he got that long utterance out of his mouth, God had said to him: "Who in this world do you think you *are?*" But do you know what God *really* said? He said: "I have pardoned them for your sake." Just like that! We need to adjust our idea concerning the audacity of prayer, the *greatness* of prayer, to God's view of it.

Sometimes we feel that prayer is a nice little exercise if you have time to waste trying to be *pious.* That is the way we treat it. It's a "good way to get into worship and out of worship," a "good way

to open a committee meeting and close a committee meeting."
This is the way we look at it! Pardon a note of cynicism: "Will you
lead us in prayer, so we can get on with the business?" I pray that
this is not true of *your* committee, but I imagine many committees
can be defined as: "A voting group of the unfit, substituting and
voting for the unwilling, voting to do the unnecessary; who get
together, read the minutes, and waste the hour." Somebody on the
church committee piously says: "Let's pray, so we can get on with
the business." After pooling their collective ignorance for an hour
or so, they will come up with a program that never saw heaven, and
never had heaven's stamp on it. Then somebody will say, "By the
way, before we go let us pray that God will bless this plan of ours."
Then the committee wonders why the power of God never falls on
their plans!

We need to develop a God-view of prayer! God delights in the
prayer of the righteous. God invites us to share in his sovereignty
through prayer: "Call unto me, and I will answer thee, and show
thee great and mighty things, which thou knowest not" (Jer. 33:3).

The sixth principle I want to share is that *praise is a vital and
indispensable factor in the prayer life, both private and public.* I
used to think that praise was limited to public exercises. I am
convinced that until our public worship becomes a meaningful
extension of *private* worship, it will continue to be inhibited,
formal, and largely inexpressive. If we ever get a congregation of
Christians together who have been in the presence of God *in
private* . . . and have learned how to respond to God *in private* . . .
we will have a true public worshipping unit.

The seventh principle is that *the only way to learn how to pray is
to pray.* We can go to school and study about it, but the only way to
learn how to pray is *to pray.* In Matthew 6, Jesus was teaching on
prayer. He assumed that the disciples would pray. Three times he
said: "when you pray . . ." Then, he taught:

> "And when you pray, you are not to be as the hypocrites; for
> they love to stand and pray in the synagogues and on the street
> corners, in order to be seen by men. Truly I say to you, they have
> their reward in full. But you, when you pray, go into your inner
> room, and when you have shut your door, pray to your Father
> who is in secret, and your Father who sees in secret will repay
> you. And when you are praying, do not use meaningless repeti-
> tion, as the Gentiles do, for they suppose that they will be heard
> for their many words" (Matt. 6:5-7, NASB)

Jesus answered three basic questions about prayer in that passage: *when* to pray, *where* to pray, and *how* to pray.

He told us *when* to pray. He used the adverb to indicate that prayer was to be *a regular part of their lives*. There is an overwhelming implication that it is to be *regular*. It is to be *continuous*. Jesus said in Luke 18:1 that: "Men ought always to pray, [always to be in prayer, to consistently pray] and not to faint."

Jesus taught about the *where* of prayer. He said: "Go into your inner room" (v. 6). Now there ought to be a *place* in our life—whether it is walking outside through the garden, or *wherever*—that is set aside for the exercise of prayer. It ought to be a set place, a secret place, a place where you feel alone with God. Do not make that place in the middle of traffic! It should be a private place.

During the great Welsh revival, F. B. Meyer went to Wales to visit the young champion of that revival, Evan Roberts. When he came to the place where Evan Roberts was staying, he introduced himself. Someone went to tell Mr. Roberts that the great Baptist preacher from England, F. B. Meyer, was waiting to see him. That young Welsh preacher responded: "Would you tell Mr. Meyer that I am in a very important meeting, and that I cannot see him now?"

He was at prayer! At first, Meyer was upset. Then, he realized that Roberts' prayer life was at least part of the secret of the Welsh revival. Here was a man who had ears and eyes for God. Here was a man who considered a meeting with God to be far more important than a meeting with a man!

Not only does Jesus tell us *when* to pray and *where* to pray, but he even tells us *how* to pray. The model prayer in Matthew 6 is not necessarily designed to be a publicly prayed prayer. I tend to view it as a checklist on whether you are *ready* to pray. What is the first word in the model prayer? "Our." That means I am acknowledging my position within the people of God. If I have unsettled anger with other Christians, if I have animosities that have not been dissolved, or if I have a hard place in my heart toward any of God's children, I cannot even *start* to pray.

The model prayer continues: "Our *Father*" (v. 9). If my daughter came to me after just having had a fight with her brother and piously said to me: "*Our* Father," do you know what I would say to her? I'd say, "Let's not have any of that '*Our* father' until you get right with your *brother*. *Then* you can say, '*Our* father' to me!" That is the reason why, when you come to pray, God will remind you of someone you have had an encounter with, and you will come away from prayer with a stirred heart and bothered soul. *"Our* Father!" Look to him as a Father, and discern the family.

The model prayer continues: "Thy kingdom come. They will be done" (v. 10). We do not have any business praying this phrase unless his will is *being* done, until the terms of his kingdom are already in motion, unless the lordship of Christ is a continuing reality in every province of life. We have no business praying "Thy kingdom come" unless every province of life is under his dominion. We cannot pray "Thy will be done" unless his will is being augmented in every part of our lives.

Once we understand these seven principles, *we also need a system of prayer.* Paul had a system of prayer. He told the Ephesians, Philippians, and Colossians, "I cease not making mention of you daily in my prayers . . . This I pray for you." He had many people on his prayer list. He prayed, and he prayed much. Some of the greatest prayers in the Bible are those in Paul's Epistles. I cannot believe that he relied on his memory for all those areas of prayer.

The first step in setting up a system of prayer is to make, or buy, a prayer notebook, and begin to use it. I have been using a prayer notebook for several years. As I fill up a page with prayer requests and answered prayer, I file it in my desk drawer. That drawer is now full of reports of answered prayer. Sometimes when my downcast heart tries to take over, I pull out that bottom drawer of my desk and flip through the prayers I have prayed in past years. What a joy it is to go back and see the answered prayers! It is amazing!

Here are some of the procedures I have found helpful. First of all, if I have thirty minutes to spend with God, I spend fifteen minutes in the Word conditioning my heart to be prepared to pray. I try not to read the Word as water goes through a pipe. Instead, I meditate upon the Word. I am not just reading red and black words on white pages, I am *fellowshipping* with the living Word, who by his Spirit makes this written Word alive to me. I try to read it with a hungry heart. Sometimes I read the Psalms, just to sense what it means to get into the presence of God in prayer. Or, for meditation I will read the Proverbs, or the Epistles of Paul. When my heart is set to seek the Lord through reading Scripture as an *in-breathing of life,* then I am prepared to pray.

After I have read the Word, I praise the Lord. I discovered a long time ago that you have to put your mind to work in order to praise the Lord. Nothing has helped me praise the Lord as much as memorizing the Psalms or other great passages of praise. Exodus 15, 1 Samuel 2, and 1 Chronicles 29 are all great chapters of praise. There are whole chapters of praise in the Psalms. One time, I went through the Bible and typed out about fifteen pages of praise. I find it is meaningful just to read them:

> "Unto thee, O God, do we give thanks, unto thee do we give thanks: for that thy name is near thy wondrous works declare" (Ps. 75:1). "For promotion cometh neither from the east, nor from the west, nor from the south. But God is the judge: he putteth down one, and setteth up another" (Ps. 75:6-7). "The heavens are thine, the earth also is thine: as for the world and the fulness thereof, thou hast founded them" (Ps. 89:11). "O satisfy us early with thy mercy; that we may rejoice and be glad all our days. Make us glad according to the days wherein thou hast afflicted us, and the years wherein we have seen evil. Let thy work appear unto thy servants, and thy glory unto their children. And let the beauty of the Lord our God be upon us: and establish thou the work of our hands upon us; yea, the work of our hands establish thou it" (Ps. 90:14-17). "The Lord reigneth, he is clothed with majesty; the Lord is clothed with strength, wherewith he hath girded himself: the world also is stablished, that it cannot be moved. Thy throne is established of old: thou art from everlasting. The floods have lifted up, O Lord, the floods have lifted up their voice . . ." (Ps. 93:1-3). "In God will I praise his word: in the Lord will I praise his word. In God have I put my trust: I will not be afraid what man can do unto me" (Ps. 56:10-11). "My heart is fixed, O God, my heart is fixed: I will sing and give praise" (Ps. 57:7). "I will praise thee, O Lord, among the people: I will sing unto thee among the nations" (Ps. 57:9). "My soul, wait thou only upon God; for my expectation is from him" (Ps. 62:5). "O sing unto the Lord a new song: sing unto the Lord, all the earth. Sing unto the Lord, bless his name; shew forth his salvation from day to day" (Ps. 96:1-2). "Make a joyful noise unto the Lord, all ye lands" (Ps. 100:1).

All these Scriptures are simply *praises* to the Lord!

Thanksgiving and *praise* differ from each other. Thanksgiving begins with where *we* are—with the physical things around us for which we thank him. While *thanks* is thing-oriented, praise is God-oriented. We are literally "bragging on God" to his face when we praise. We are valuing him in a vocal way. Praise in Scripture seems to be either visible, vocal, or audible. The psalmist said, "I will praise him with uplifted hands; I will praise him with a dance"—(visible); "I will praise him with my lips"—(vocal); and "I will praise him with cymbals and stringed instruments"—(audible). I find nothing as helpful as praise to get into the frame of prayer.

Then, of course, there is *petition*. In my prayer book, I have a growing list. I do not add to that list without thought and prayer, for it is my commitment to pray daily for a specific number of people. I may list a prayer request twelve or fifteen days out of the month. Or, I may just turn to that person's name in my prayer book, and pray briefly for them. Sometimes I wonder if my prayers are doing much good.

One night I was in the prayer chapel from 12:00 to 1:00 on Sunday morning. I had had a long hard day and it was one of those nights when I was tired. I was reading the names of those listed in my notebook, mentioning them to the Lord. I do not know whether it was the enemy or myself (we sound so much alike sometimes), but I began to wonder if this praying was doing any good. I was half-heartedly picking a name, calling that name to God. Some of the needs of these people I knew, and some I did not. About 12:30, when my doubt was at its peak, the door opened behind me. Now, I want to be a man of *faith*, but I also want to be a man of *caution!* I turned around to see who was coming in behind me at 12:30 in the morning. It was one of the couples in the church, accompanied by a very tall, distinguished-looking man. They introduced me, and this is what he said: "I wanted to come to the place where my name has been called, week after week, for five and one-half years. You see, I have just returned from being missing in action in Vietnam for five and one-half years!" After he left, I told that negative voice that had been talking to me to *go away*, because prayer *does* work!

In your prayer time, you may only call a person's *name* at the throne of God. I cannot help but feel that something happens *at the very call of a name*. Then pause a minute and say, "God, is there anything you want me to pray for this person?" You will find that when you later get together with this person and begin to hear what his needs have been, your praying has been right on target. I want to finish with one profound truth: You will never hear anything more profound than this statement: *God answers prayer!*

7. Ministering in the Future Church

Ray C. Stedman

Ray C. Stedman is part of a pastoral team, ministering at the Peninsula Bible Church in Palo Alto, California. He has authored over a score of expository treatments on scriptural books.

In 1912, a paperback book was published under the title, *The Minister as Shepherd*. It contained lectures on preaching delivered at Bangor Theological Seminary by Charles Edward Jefferson. He dealt with the pressures of preaching and the problems that arise out of a preacher's peculiar and unique relationship to both the Lord and the world. Here is the way Charles Jefferson dealt with two great temptations of a pastor. He referred to the danger of his succumbing to "covetousness and ambition; an inordinate desire to possess for personal gratification and an unlawful love of advancement, prominence and authority. Christian history makes it clear that these are the cardinal sins which ever lie like crouching beasts at the shepherd's door."

Then he went on to explain what this meant in terms of (especially the love of) rulership. He said:

> What liberty a minister enjoys in the disposition of his time! No other man but the retired millionaire is such a monarch of his day as is the minister. He can read on Monday morning, or write, or walk, or mingle all three, just as he deems best. On Tuesday morning he can attend to his correspondence, or catalogue his library, or eat the heart out of some new book, or meet a company of friends, just as he decides. The order of his going out and coming in is largely at his own discretion. Within wide limits he is the monarch of all the hours he surveys. Such liberty is dangerous, it has spoiled its thousands.

His dominion over his sermons is still more wonderful. He is free to say what the text shall be, the topic, the illustrations, the arguments, the conclusions, and no one can interfere. He can adopt any style of preaching that he likes, he can follow whatever line of thought he chooses. A merchant has to give his customers what they ask for, a hotel-keeper must supply what his guests desire, but a preacher can give what he thinks his hearers ought to want and ought to have, no matter what their needs and wishes really are. For half an hour or more every Sunday morning everything is silent while he speaks. This unparalleled immunity from the noises and interruptions and contradictions which other men are subject to, begets in certain types of men a tone of mind which says: "I am Sir Oracle, and when I open my lips, let no dog bark."

In social life a minister is ever at the front. He is the observed of all observers. Wherever he sits is the head of the table. He has his critics and detractors, but they are not visible at social functions. In social life, especially in small towns, there is a deference paid to ministers which no other man receives. This burning of incense before the minister has a tendency, in many cases, to turn his head, and to lead him to think more highly of himself than he ought to think. Is there a celebration in the town? The minister must attend it. Is the fitting word to be spoken on a state occasion? The minister must speak it. Here is a true description of ministers not a few: "They love the chief places at feasts and the chief seats in the synagogues, and the salutations in the marketplaces, and to be called of men, Rabbi [Doctor]." They love these things because they are human and because they are accustomed to them, and because they think they have a right to them. Constant deference and obedience have a tendency to beget in men of a certain grade a haughty and unlovely disposition.

But mightiest of all the forces working for the undoing of the minister's heart is the liberty he has in devising and shaping the policy of the church. Laymen, as a rule, are too busy to take continued interest in church affairs. [This is 1912, remember!] The result is that in many parishes almost everything is rolled upon the pastor's shoulders. Is a change to be made? He must make it. Is a new work to be undertaken. He must start it. Is there a fresh responsibility to be assumed? The pastor must shoulder it. In a multitude of parishes the minister must not only preach and conduct the prayer meeting, and make all the pastoral calls, but he must also superintend the Sunday School, manage the finances, map out the work of every organization, and possibly act even as leader of the singing. [As an aside we can add some new technological duties, such as running the mimeograph machine.] No wonder that ministers come to feel sometimes that they are of considerable importance.

It was in this way that church government blossomed into Romanism. The laity in the early Christian centuries were largely ignorant, incompetent, and indifferent, and the whole shaping and managing of the church fell inevitably into the hands of the pastor. This is bad for him, and it is bad also for the church. It makes it easier for the minister to build up in himself a dictatorial disposition and to nourish in his heart the love of autocratic power.

"A little Protestant despot, a petty parochial pope, is a sorry caricature of a minister of Jesus Christ. A minister who boasts under his breath that he proposes to run things and who chuckles at his adeptness in manipulating people, and who says by his manner that he is the boss of the parish, is a man who is a stumbling-block in the way of Christian progress.

I add another quotation from the pen of Dr. Earl Radmacher, president, Western Baptist Seminary, Portland, Oregon. This is his conclusion to Jefferson's remarks:

It is my conviction that God has provided a hedge against these powerful temptations by the concept of multiple elders. The check and balance that is provided by men of equal authority is most wholesome and helps to bring about the desired attitude expressed by Peter to the plurality of elders: ". . . shepherd the flock of God among you, not under compulsion, but voluntarily, according to the will of God; and not for sordid gain, but with eagerness; nor yet as lording it over those alloted to your charge, but proving to be examples to the flock." (1 Peter 5:2,3).

With this as an introduction, I would like to make an exploration of the theme of the pressures upon the preacher.

In 1 Corinthians 4, the apostle Paul deals with this subject. "This is how one should regard us, as servants of Christ and stewards of the mysteries of God. Moreover it is required of stewards that they be found trustworthy" (1 Cor. 4:1-2, RSV).

In verse 1, Paul describes how one should regard us: "as servants of Christ and stewards of the mysteries of God." I never utter those words without the feeling of awe settling upon my spirit. "Servants of Christ," "Stewards of the mysteries of God." They challenge me as no other words in the New Testament do.

Beginning with verse 3 the apostle proceeds to the subject of to whom a minister or preacher is accountable, or the problem of who evaluates the preacher. Paul says:

> But with me it is a very small thing that I should be judged by you or by any human court. I do not even judge myself. I am not aware of anything against myself, but I am not thereby acquitted. It is the Lord who judges me. Therefore do not profounce judgment before the time, before the Lord comes, who will bring to light the things now hidden in darkness and will disclose the purposes of the heart. Then every man will receive his commendation from God" (1 Cor. 4:3-5, RSV).

In these verses the apostle is facing the question of to whom a minister is accountable. Now, if you are a pastor, you know that there are hundreds of volunteers in this regard. Every congregation has people who want to get in on the act. That willingness to sit in judgment of the preacher, of his responsibilities, and especially of his delivery of sermons constitutes a very subtle pressure upon the one who ministers.

In this passage you will note that the apostle sees four sources of judgment in a minister's life. The first one is congregational evaluation. Paul's response to congregational evaluation is: "With me it is a very small thing that I should be judged by you" (v. 3). Now I can imagine that was one of the most popular verses in Corinth. People undoubtedly copied it and put it on their refrigerator to memorize. I am sure the apostle was looked upon with considerably less regard because he wrote this. It seems to put them down a bit. He obviously puts them at the bottom of his list of competent judges. "Congregational evaluation," he says, "is a very small thing."

Why is this true? Why is it that we should pay least attention, if I may put it in a relative way, to the evaluation of a congregation? Paul does not answer the question here, but if we look elsewhere in Scripture and at the implications of being the servant of Christ, we can understand why. Stuart Briscoe, pastor of Elmbrook Church in Milwaukee, gives a very helpful analysis of congregational pressure. He says: "There are three ways by which a congregation exhibits a degree of pressure upon the pastor. First, there is adulation; second, there is manipulation; and third, there is antagonism. *Adulation,* which swells the head. *Manipulation,* which ties the

hands; and *antagonism,* which breaks the heart. Those are the
pressures from a congregation." Now, what pastor has not felt
these very three potent forces upon himself?

Adulation, of course, is one of the subtlest and most enjoyable
forces and therefore one of the most difficult to defend against. As
Charles Jefferson pointed out, the minister is in a peculiarly unique
position in a community. He oftentimes is lionized at many social
functions, especially in the body of a congregation. His opinion is
listened to far beyond its intrinsic merit. He is often asked to
participate in ways that he perhaps is not prepared for, and people
too often hang upon his words. He is treated with undue adulation.
That is a very dangerous thing.

When I first came to a tiny congregation in Palo Alto, California,
we had a church member who was a marvelous woman with a
colorful personality. In the 25 years that I knew her she always
dressed in purple or in some shade of purple. So we called her
"Mrs. Purple," naturally. She drove a purple car; she lived in a
purple house; she even dyed her cat purple. She was also colorful
in other ways. She always introduced herself with, "I am a woman
of few words, but I use them all the time." And she did indeed.

When Mrs. Purple came to our congregation she did not know
the Lord. She had been a member of a church in Dallas for some
thirty or forty years but, at the age of 60, came to know the Lord in
our congregation. As a result, Mrs. Purple would meet me after a
message and speak in glowing terms of what I had said. She would
come up to me, her eyes brimming with tears, and say, "Oh, Mr.
Stedman, I can't believe that I could go sixty years to a church and
never know the Lord Jesus and never hear how to have my sins
forgiven!" She meant it from the depth of her heart. So, consequently, I was the one who had the privilege of introducing her to
the mysteries of God, the secret hidden wisdom of God, and the
secrets that would work toward her glorification (as Paul writes in 1
Corinthians 2). She loved it, and she would praise me after every
service. She would come up to me and say, "Oh, Mr. Stedman,
you can put it in such marvelous ways! You make everything so
simple! You have such a gift along this line!"

Well, that is a heady line for a young preacher to hear, but I
discovered there were certain things about the Scriptures Mrs.
Purple did not like. She was one of those people who did not like to
hear of any degree of suffering in the Christian life, any degree of

hardship to be endured, or any degree of cost in terms of discipleship. She also did not like to hear *anything* about death and
facing the problems of death. I soon discovered that there was a
subtle pressure exerted upon me to please Mrs. Purple, because
she was a wealthy woman. I found myself tempted to soften some
of the things of Scripture.

Now, *that* is the danger of adulation! It can destroy and has
destroyed many a young pastor who is unwilling to offend the
wealthy by causing any degree of confrontation with the unpleas-
ant or uncomfortable words of Scripture. "Adulation which swells
the head."

And, then there is the force of manipulation—a tendency to
control. Every pastor is subject to it. Today especially, as I travel
across the country and in other countries of the world, I am
meeting a lot of young men who have begun their ministry in great
expectation of accomplishment in the name of the Lord. They are
eager of heart and ready to throw themselves completely into a
ministry. Time after time I have met with them just a few years
after they have taken a pastorate in a church. As we have met, I
have found them discouraged and disillusioned. Many of them
were on the verge of resigning from the ministry and taking a
secular job and forgetting about the call to the full-time ministry
they once felt so strongly.

Why? Because they ran up against a tough, hardheaded, unyield-
ing power structure in their churches that refused to listen to the
Word of God. This power structure is in many, many churches.
Without exception, every church has its power structure. Whether
it is a God-given, Spirit-directed power structure depends upon the
degree to which those in leadership are willing to be instructed by
the Word of God. It also depends upon the degree to which the
leadership is willing to face the judgment of the Scripture upon the
exaltation of the flesh. However, in many places it is committed to
its own self-advancement and to the maintenance of a a comfortable religious club for the enjoyment of the membership. Such a
power structure is throttling, discouraging, and hampering the
work of the Spirit in thousands of churches across this country
today.

In all honesty, the greatest problem of the church today is the
leadership of the church as it is presently constituted. Men are
vested with authority and power and leadership as pastors and

officers. They then use their authority for their own advancement, and for the maintenance of an establishment that has long since drifted from the scriptural pattern. When a hapless young man should attempt to pastor that kind of a community he is met with a hard-nosed refusal to face any degree of change. The men of authority have a very subtle way of imposing their domain and tyranny upon him.

Recently I was talking with a man who was in this kind of situation. He said, "My struggle is to retain an identity in the denomination to which I belong and yet make any possible change in it." He found it almost impossible to do so. That is manipulation! "Manipulation which ties the hands."

Then, of course, there is the force of antagonism. "Antagonism which breaks the heart." A few months ago, a young pastor shared with me that his board had called him in and told him: "You have been here as pastor of this church for over a year and in many ways you have done very well. However, there are two things we want to make very clear to you. First, this is *our* church! It is *not* yours! We were here first. We were operating as a church for a long time before you came, and we will be operating as a church a long time after you leave. This is our church, and we don't want you to forget it! Secondly, we have hired you to do a certain job here for us. We have given you the job description and it is up to you to fulfill it. If you are not willing to do so then we will have to make other arrangements!" This young man asked me, "What shall I do?" That's clear cut antagonism, isn't it? It was breaking his heart. I told him what I would do if I were in his shoes. I told him I would go back to the church and take a stack of Bibles to the next board meeting. I would say to them: "Brothers, we have come together and you have invited me to minister here to you in your midst. I have been here for a year and there are many things about this congregation that I have come to love. I love you men. I love your families. I love the opportunity. I love the community. I want to be a part of you. But, in order to function as a servant of Christ and a steward of the mysteries of God there are certain theological errors I believe you are suffering from that we need to clear up. The only ground of appeal for any of us is the Word of God." I would then pass out the Bibles and say: "Now, let's look at some things together. I want you to face this question. Where in the Word of God does it ever say that the church belongs to the people? Jesus says, 'On this rock I will build my church; and the gates of hell shall not prevail against it' (Matt. 16:18). He is the Lord of the church. He is the head of the body. Therefore, the ultimate decision as to what occurs in a church never resides with any human body or individual but with the Lord of the church himself. I want to see this truth threshed out in the Scriptures and thoroughly understood.''

Secondly, I would ask them: ''Where in the New Testament do you ever find any arrangement to hire someone to carry out the work of the ministry? Preachers are not hired. They enter into a mutual agreement with a congregation to serve together as brothers and sisters in the Lord—as laborers together. Now, a support arrangement is arrived at by mutual consent, but it is never to be regarded as an employer-employee relationship.''

I told this young man he should as simply and as graciously as he could seek to reason this out with them. But, if they could not reach an agreement on those two points, I would go someplace else. No one, no servant of Christ, can labor under those conditions—under a petty tyranny that replaces the lordship of Christ, seeks to take his place, and exercises his prerogatives in a local body! So much for pressure from the congregation. This is why Paul says: ''It is a very small thing with me what you think about me.'' Now we may not like it, but that is what the Scripture says.

Paul now turns to another matter—the pressure of evaluation from society. ''But with me it is a very small thing that I should be judged by you or by any human court.'' Literally, it is ''by man's day.'' That is, this is the judgment of society, non-Christian society, outside the church. Paul says that society's evaluation is not very much higher on the list. He says, ''I don't listen a lot to that. I am not too interested in what society says.''

Os Guinness asks the question, ''What does the thinking non-Christian think about Christian thinking?'' His answer was quite accurately, ''Not very much. They do not think very highly of Christian thought.'' We often feed the world sloppy or shallow Christian thinking that deals merely with aphorisms and slogans and offers shallow judgment and shallow remedies. If the non-Christian's evaluation is based on this kind of thinking it is a fully warranted conclusion that Christian thinking is not worth bothering about.

However, true Christian thinking contains deep, penetrative

insights which are arrived at within the framework of the Word of God and the biblical revelation. It is deeply investigative of the phenomena of the day in which we live and explains from the biblical framework what is going on in history and in this world at the present time. If the non-Christian's evaluation is based on true Christian thinking, and they still judge it as foolishness (as it was judged in the days of the apostles and our Lord), then they are wrong. If it is based on true Christian thinking, we are perfectly warranted in putting their evaluation very low on our list of the influences to which we give heed today.

I think it is important for us to recognize that the Word of God teaches us that human *wisdom* is faulted. However, it never puts down human *knowledge*. There is no discipline or area of research into which a Christian is not permitted to enter. There is no body of knowledge that he cannot investigate. Everywhere in the Word of God there is an encouragement to explore the mysteries that God has hidden in nature, in humanity, and in the whole of the universe. There is *no* area in which a Christian is forbidden to participate. He can explore in any direction, and he is invited to do so. In these areas, human knowledge can add tremendously to our grasp of what we are up against, where we are, and what God has worked out in the marvelous mystery of the universe.

But what we *are* warned against is human *wisdom*. Wisdom is the true use of knowledge. Wisdom is applying knowledge to specific situations. This is where humanly everything goes wrong. To deduce certain philosophical conclusions from the research and investigation of humanity almost invariably results in ideas that are narrow and incomplete, shutting out the whole range of reality that needs to be considered. Human wisdom in this area is always untrustworthy and ought to be suspect. We need to understand this.

I find many people and many pastors turning away from the insights and the revelation of the Word of God because they are so impressed by the conclusions of secular thinkers. Now, I am impressed by the conclusions of secular thinkers in many ways. But when it comes to conclusions which are directly opposed and contradictory to the insights of the Lord Jesus Christ and the apostles and the prophets, however, I infinitely prefer the biblical insights. I find it necessary to correct the conclusions of the secular writers in the light of the revelation of the Word of God. Therefore,

Paul puts this rather low on his list again. He says, "Whether the world's view of us is contemptuous or patronizing it is not very high on the list of things that influence me."

Then Paul comes to a third area—personal evaluation. "I do not even judge myself. I am not aware of anything against myself, but I am not thereby acquitted." Now that is a very helpful word. Once again we must face a universal result of the fall of man, even in the believer—a tendency to be blind to our own errors. Paul says, "I am not aware of anything against myself." But he suggests very clearly that it is quite possible that he might be very, very wrong in some area. At the moment he is writing, he is not aware of any area where he might be wrong. Of course, if he did become aware of an area, he would immediately face it, judge it, and deal with it. I am sure this is true of him all through his life. He dealt with that which was troubling him. He dealt quickly and positively with whatever it was that he saw to be wrong. But he also recognized what we must all recognize—that there is a blind spot in us and we cannot often see our own errors.

A very revealing statement at the close of the book of Judges summarized the whole history of that book. It says: "Every man did that which was right in his own eyes" (Judg. 21:25). The people were not doing what was *wrong* in their own eyes. They were doing what was *right* in their own eyes. Yet what was being done was terribly hurtful and destructively wrong. The people were unaware that their actions were wrong because they were unwilling to use the value or standard of measurement which the Word of God provides. They were doing what they all thought was *right*. But their actions were far from the continuing revelation of the Word of God! This is what always happens! If you trust yourself to walk in the light of your own conscience, uninstructed or little instructed by the Word of God, you *will* end up doing things that you are deeply and sincerely convinced are right. But, they may be terribly hurtful and destructive within the church.

So, Paul says, "I am not aware of anything against myself, but I am not thereby acquitted." Here is where the Lord was provided a particularly helpful means of seeing yourself. It comes in the openness we are to have with one another and the willingness we are to have to listen to one another and to evaluate one another. Part of the command to us from the Lord Jesus is "confess your sins to one another, and pray for one another that you may be healed" (Jas. 5:16, RSV). If you see your brother committing a fault, go to him and tell him his fault in private. Throughout the Scriptures we have this continual admonishment to be willing to listen to someone else's evaluation of where we are. Our church has found this to be one of the most neglected but one of the most significant and important aspects of carrying on a harmonious church relationship and staff relationship. Every year we conduct a mutual evaluation process. All the elders are evaluated by one another and all the pastors are evaluated by the elders. I believe that the Scriptures are clearly telling us that we have a responsibility to mutually help one another in these areas. This is the only way I know how to overcome some of our blind spots.

Even reading the Word of God does not often touch us in our blind spots, because we tend to run everything through our own grid and read the Word of God with minds that are blind and clouded. The words that would judge us otherwise are read in terms of some support or encouragement. The very things that the words are condemning we cannot see in ourselves. That is why God has provided the rest of the body for our needs. Every man or woman who teaches ought to be open to the evaluation of those who are being taught. We try to practice this in a close, intimate, loving, mutual evaluation process.

Next Paul comes to the final and supreme point: "It is the Lord who judges me." How does he do it? One way is by the study of the Scriptures. Our church staff of fourteen pastors meets every Wednesday morning for an hour and a half of Bible study together. No one teaches the others but everyone takes the passage of Scripture before us and shares what they see in it. We compare it to what we see going on in our personal lives and in the life of the congregation and in the life of the world. *We sit under the judgment of the Word of God every week.* Nothing is more helpful to us than that. It is the very key to our functioning as a staff. Calvin called it the "magisterium of the scripture." We are constantly being corrected by the Word of God and the insights that come from Him.

The Lord also judges us through the mutual ministry of brothers and sisters, one to another. This is one means provided by the Lord to make us aware of our accountability and to correct the things that are wrong. And, ultimately, the Lord judges through the continual inner voice of the Spirit. Paul goes on to say: "Therefore do not pronounce judgment before the time, before the Lord comes, who will bring to light the things now hidden in darkness and will disclose the purposes of the heart. Then every man will receive his commendation [not condemnation] from God" (1 Cor. 4:5, RSV).

There is coming in every one of our lives an ultimate time of accountability. A time when the Lord, in his graciousness, will walk with us back through our life and point out the true meaning of all that was said and all that was done. It will not be to condemn us. Rather, like his actions with his own disciples, it will be a time when he and I together will look back at what I have done. I think there will be times when he will just be silent and I will know what he means. Other times he will say, "Well done! That was good!" Perhaps I will be surprised because I did not think it was well done at the time. Perhaps I will be eager to show him something and he will look at it and shake his head. At the end of our walk, however, there will be commendation from him because what I have done that is worthwhile is the result of what he has done through me. He cannot deny himself. He will remain faithful to himself at work in me. Scripture calls this "the judgment seat of Christ."

In a sense, this process goes on all the time. Since we are living in eternity in our spirits and souls, we are already subject to the judgment of the Lord. We have all experienced these moments when the Lord, in sometimes the most unexpected ways, puts a finger of appraisal upon something we are doing or have done, and we know exactly what he means. This is what Paul says is the ultimate judgment. It deeply affected him. He sought continually for that to be the source of correction for the things that were wrong in his life.

There is never a day, or even hardly a portion of a day, in which I am not in some way, either consciously or unconsciously, reminding myself of Christ's coming, the time of judgment and accountability when all that I am and all that I have done will be made visible before all, including the Lord. Paul speaks of "the judgment seat of Christ." I do not look at it with fear, even though I know things of which I will be ashamed will be revealed. John speaks of being ashamed before the Lord at his coming. Paul speaks of it as receiving the things which are done in the body, whether they be good or bad. But I do not look at it with fear because I know that it will be seen through the loving appraisal of my loving Lord. One of the great hungers of my life has always been to be real, not to be phony or hypocritical, and to see things as they really are. The day of judgment will be my great opportunity to see my life as it really was. I look forward to this. But I am also aware that every moment I live I have an opportunity to correct things. So in that day of appraisal there may be much more that will merit his "well done" than would be otherwise.

I spent the summer of 1950 in the company of a dear and beloved servant of God, Dr. Harry A. Ironside, former pastor of the Moody Memorial Church. He was like a father in the faith to me. We traveled together all summer. I was his chauffeur, his secretary, and his personal friend. He used to tell me delightful experiences out of his own life that have left an indelible imprint upon my life.

I have not checked *The Guinness Book of World Records,* but Dr. Ironside probably holds the record for the fastest eater. We would sit down in a restaurant together and be served at the same time. By the time I had arranged my knife and fork, he would be finished. He inhaled his food! Then, while I ate, he would regale me with the most amazing stories and humorous incidents. He would quote from memory whole passages out of *Mark Twain's* writings. We had delightful times.

One of the stories he told me about his own experiences made an unforgettable impression on me. At the age of fourteen he lived in Los Angeles with his widowed mother. In those days all shoes were made by hand and were repaired by hand in cobbler shops. To help with the finances, he got a job working for a cobbler—a dear Christian brother named Dan. It was Ironside's task to put the leather which had been soaked in water to soften it, on an anvil, and pound the water out of it with a hammer. This process made the leather permanently flexible. It was a tedious task, onerous, and routine. Ironside would get weary of the endless pounding of the leather until it was dry.

Down the street, about three or four doors, was another cobbler shop run by a very ungodly man. Every time young Ironside would go by his shop, he would see the man cutting the leather and nailing in on the shoe with the water splashing every which way.

One day Ironside stopped and said to him, "Sir, I noticed that you don't pound the water out of your leather. Why is that?"

The man looked at him, gave him a leering wink, and said, "They come back quicker thi. way."

So Harry Ironside went back to his boss and said to him, "Sir, I wonder if we really have to pound all this water out of the leather. The man down the street doesn't pound the water out like we do. He says that the customers come back all the quicker that way."

Dan did not say a word. He took off his apron and, taking young Harry Ironside by the hand, sat down with him on the bench. He said, "Harry, I apologize to you for not having explained my reasoning. You see, Harry, leather that doesn't have the water pounded out of it dries out by itself. Then it becomes very brittle and wears out quickly. That is why they come back all the quicker. But, Harry, I am a Christian and one of these days I am going to appear before the judgment seat of Christ. I believe that every pair of shoes I have ever made is going to be piled up in a great pile beside the Lord. He is going to take them, one by one, and run his eye down them and look them over. After he looks at some of them, perhaps he will look at me and say, 'Dan, you did a terrible job here.' But the hunger of my heart is that I will make shoes so that when the Lord looks at them he will say, 'Dan, that was a fine pair of shoes!' I hope you will remember this, Harry."

Harry Ironside went back to his work. He said he never forgot it and he never complained again about pounding the water out of the leather.

I do not think there is ever a time that I sit down to prepare a sermon or stand up to preach one that I do not remind myself that every message I ever preach and every word I ever utter in the name of Jesus Christ is going to be reviewed at the judgment seat of Christ. I want to hear him say to me, "That was a masterful, workman-like job."

That is the true judgment. We are servants of Christ, and we must ultimately be accountable to him.

8. Preaching in the Future Church

Ray C. Stedman

I heard a story about a young man who was being ordained to the Presbyterian ministry; he was meeting with the Ordination Committee. One rather rugged Calvinist on the committee asked him, "Young man, would you be willing to be damned for the glory of God?" The young man thought for a moment and said, "Yes, I think I would. In fact, I think I would be willing to have this whole presbytery damned for the glory of God."

I don't feel that way. I want to share some of the things God has shown me in the course of some thirty years in ministry. I do not want to appear as any kind of a model of a preacher. I consider myself a very mediocre preacher. I stumble. I falter. I grope for words. I say things the wrong way. Many, many times I feel ineffective, and in no sense am I putting myself up as a model of a preacher.

But, I believe in preaching! In our church, we call preaching "The Big Burner Concept." Preaching is the thing which keeps the fire going under everything else, the thing that keeps our church hot and reaching out to the world around us. We fully believe that.

In my estimation preaching is intended to be the key element of education in a church. It establishes the parameters of truth within which a church will live and function.

I believe, therefore, that preaching is as powerful a tool in the hands of God today as it *ever* was, despite all of the other methods of communication that we hear about today.

As you know, the Word of God says a great deal about preaching being God's appointed tool. Through it, he seeks to communicate the truth unto a darkened world by means of an enlightened people. It is the enlightenment of people that makes possible the reaching

102

of the darkened world. That is why preaching is so central to the ministry of any church.

There are a number of passages of Scripture that have helped me to understand the work of preaching. The first one is found in the fourth chapter of Paul's first letter to the Corinthians. Recently, I have been preaching through Corinthians. I have been so struck by the parallel between the conditions in Corinth and the conditions of the churches in California, that I have repeatedly referred to these letters as "First and Second Californians."

In First Corinthians 4:1, Paul says: "This is how one should regard us." He means Apollos, Peter, himself, along with other leaders who had been the center of controversy in the church. Around these personalities, factions were gathering in the church of Corinth. Some were saying, "I am of Paul," others were saying, "I am of Apollos." Others said, "I am of Cephas," *i.e.* "I am of Peter," and so forth. In correcting that error, Paul said: "This is how one should regard us, as servants of Christ and stewards of the mysteries of God. Moreover it is required of stewards that they be found trustworthy (or, I prefer the King James at this point: *"faithful"*) in the discharge of their stewardship." By this stewardship he is referring to preaching.

I want to say a brief word, which I think necessary, about the definition of *preaching*. I find when I use this term many people have a mental image that differs widely. In the South, if a man takes flight in passages of oratorical rhetoric, waving his arms as though he is fighting bees, shouting with a loud voice as though he is arguing with his wife, he is said to be *preaching*. Often, only that *style* of delivery is called "preaching."

I discover in the Word of God, however, that there is no emphasis made whatsoever on the *style* of delivery. Paul speaks of going about in the Gentile world, "preaching and teaching" everywhere he goes. He obviously, therefore, makes a distinction between *preaching* and *teaching;* but he also combines the two together.

If we turn to the New Testament for a definition of preaching, we find that the major component is not the *style* of delivery, but *the content of what is preached* that constitutes preaching.

It is very difficult to tell, when the Apostles stood up to preach, just what style they used. How did Peter sound on the day of Pentecost? Did he thunder at people? Did he wave his arms and shout and yell? Or, did he speak in a conversational tone of voice that could carry out over the multitudes? Was he rather quiet?

It is difficult to tell Paul's style of preaching from Paul's letters. We gather that he did not have a very powerful delivery. Some of his enemies charged that his preaching was faltering and stumbling; that it lacked a commanding presence; that he did not use oratorical flights of human wisdom. It is clear, therefore, that *style* is certainly not what constitutes preaching! What does? As I have suggested, it is *content*.

Preaching is the declaration of the hidden truths which only God can give. It is the proclamation of those truths which makes up preaching. In contrast, *teaching is the explanation of those truths as they touch human life as lived in any generation.* Preaching, as we think of it today, is largely made up of a *combination* of both those elements. It is the proclamation of unique truth, revealed by God, and applied to normal daily human situations. It is also an explanation of the implications of those truths as they touch human life. That description would make up what we ordinarily would think of as *pastoral preaching,* or *pulpit preaching.*

I want to zero in on one verse we have read as a take-off point, emphasizing the word Paul employs in our text: "*stewards* of the mysteries of God."

Aboard our flight from San Jose to Houston was a *steward.* Many airlines now employ men again in this role. Our steward had a very clearly defined role. Committed to him were certain responsibilities; certain commodities were given him, to be dispensed to the people in the plane. He performed his role well. He served us drinks. He served us dinner. He made announcements as to what was to be expected of us in various parts of the flight. He was meticulous in his concern that all our needs be met while we were aboard his plane. I commended him when we left on the quality of his *stewardship.*

Now, it is exactly in this sense that the Apostle employs the word "steward" in this verse. In the ancient world, a *steward* was a man entrusted with the care of an owner's whole household. All the treasury was committed to him, along with the distribution of various goods. As Paul thinks here of a preacher, he thinks of a man to whom has been entrusted *a precious deposit.* He is responsible to communicate and to distribute it to other people. Paul uses the term "steward," though it is translated in the King James version a "*dispensation.*" A dispensation has been committed unto the preacher. Now, I don't like to apply that term, as it is often used. I am a graduate of Dallas Theological Seminary, known for its *dispensationalism;* but I am not talking about *that* kind of "dispensation."

If you go back to the original meaning of the word, you find it means "something that is being dispensed." You then get the heart of what that term properly means: we are stewards with the responsibility to *dispense* something to someone else.

I am sure you are aware of how frequently Paul employs this thought throughout the Scripture. In writing to Timothy, he says: "Guard what has been committed to your care." *By that, he means this sacred deposit of truth, called "the gospel" in its widest sense.* Again, to Timothy he says: "Guard the *good deposit* entrusted to you." As you know, in Acts 20 Paul calls this "the whole counsel of God." "I have delivered unto you," he says, "the whole counsel of God." Peter describes this as "the grace which was meant to be yours." He means by that, of course, the dispensing of the Word of God, a stewardship entrusted to a responsible leader that is to be shared with everybody. In Second Peter, he speaks of it as "exceeding great and precious promises."

As I travel around this country I am frankly disturbed by how few pulpits I find employing this kind of preaching today. I thank God that there is an awakening coming again along this line, and that there are fine crops of young expositors coming into being. I rejoice over every one of them as I hear of them. There are some who are equipped to take the Word of God in its uniqueness, and unfold it in such a way that they apply it to the viewpoint of everybody in the congregation.

That is the business of preaching. We are to impart to people what in 1 Corinthians 2 is described in various ways. Listen to these terms: "first I came proclaiming to you *the testimony of God,"* or, as some versions have it, *"the mystery of God."* A little later on he described it as *"a secret and hidden wisdom of God."* Later on, he calls it *"the deep things of God."* Then, in the same passage, he terms it *"the thoughts of God;"* later, *"the gifts bestowed on us by God."* Still later in the passage, he speaks of *"spiritual truths."* Then, at the end of the chapter, perhaps the most remarkable thing he ever wrote appears: "We have," he says, *"the mind of Christ!"*

I think we ought to understand thoroughly what these verses are saying. Paul is not describing certain religious truths which are interesting only to Christians who gather on Sunday morning to hear a preacher. Nor does he speak of a cabalistic body of knowledge which is of no concern to the general outside population. Unfortunately, much of the preaching of our country today *does* deal in such specialized bits of knowledge. We call them *"denominational distinctives."* We major on them; but no one is particularly interested in them.

That is not what Paul is talking about at all. He is talking about vital and essential truths absolutely necessary for the functioning of human beings on this earth. He refers to *truth about God and man,* without which men fumble, falter, go off at loose ends, lose their way in life, and cannot handle life at all. It is what I like to call *"the lost secrets of our humanity."* He is speaking of the missing elements of necessary knowledge about man, his universe, and God himself. Without this knowledge, men make terrible blunders, commit atrocious errors in their thinking, and foul up their lives in endless entanglements. It is the business of a preacher to contradict all of that and correct the thinking of the people in the congregation, so that they begin to return from the fantasies of the world to the reality of life.

I am seeking to convey to you what I feel to be the supreme and paramount value of preaching. In my estimation, there is nothing like it. A preacher has no rivals, either in the scientific laboratory, on the psychiatrist's couch, or in the philosopher's study. They all deal in something quite different from what the preacher is to proclaim.

In fact, the Apostle Paul says the rulers of his age did not understand these truths, and as a consequence, when the Lord of Glory appeared—Truth himself, incarnate in human form—they did not recognize Him, and crucified him. When Paul speaks of "the rulers of this age," he is not speaking of just government leaders, of Pilate and the Chief Priests, and so forth. Rather, he means the shapers of public opinion of that day—the "mind benders," the politicians, the leaders of thought, the writers and authors of influence among men. He says the leaders of human thought are lacking in these truths, therefore, they do not properly understand life. This is why the world in which we live today is a generation where human minds—brilliant minds—are groping in darkness, lost, and do not know answers to human problems.

Some years ago, U Thant, the Burmese leader and statesman who was, at that time, Secretary-General of the United Nations, was speaking to a group of people in New York City. There were some 1,600 leaders from all the nations of the world, gathered to try to find the way to international peace. In his opening address to them, U Thant said these rather remarkable words:

> "What element is lacking so that with all our skill and all our knowledge, we still find ourselves in the dark valley of discord and enmity? What is it that inhibits us from going forward together to enjoy the fruits of human endeavor, and to reap the harvest of human experience? Why is it that for all our professed ideals, our hopes and our skills, peace on earth is still a distant objective, seen only dimly through the storms and turmoils of our present difficulties?"

Those are amazing words to come from a leading spokesman of our day. Here is a brilliant and sincere man, earnestly seeking to find the solutions to problems, who, after years of labor cries out in this pathetic way. What *is* wrong? What *is* missing?

I suggest that the business of preaching is to supply the answer to those questions. Preaching is to help people understand what is wrong with the world, their lives, their homes, their marriages, their businesses, and the economic life of our countries. Preaching is to explain why nations forever engage in terrible, bloody, international conflict; why they cannot solve their problems. Such problems are caused because there are missing elements to their knowledge: there is truth they know nothing about.

This mysterious truth is what Paul says he came to declare. He will not waste his time, he says, in going back over empty philosophies that the world of his day blindly followed even as they follow them today. Instead, he will declare truth that men could never learn anywhere else! I recently read an article in a secular magazine by a secular writer. It listed nine of the great advances of technology of our day. When each of them first appeared in human life, they were widely welcomed as the solution to some of the longstanding problems facing this nation. They included the automobile, the telephone, the television. In the few decades since they have come into being, even secular thinkers have come to admit they are the reason for widespread pollution, for increased urban problems, and for the breakdown and depersonalization of human society. Things we welcomed as saviors are now being regarded as Frankensteinian monsters, threatening our very existence.

That is what Paul refers to as "the wisdom of the world;" and it is the business of preaching to correct it. I preach in a university community. We sit at the very doorstep of one of the major prestige universities of this nation, Stanford University. When I open the Book, I have the privilege of speaking to the physicists, the philosophers, the scientists, the psychologists, the doctors, the lawyers, the bankers, and the engineers—as well as the artisans, craftsmen, and others who comprise our community. I am privileged to set before them *essential knowledge for the operation of human life* that they have never studied in any secular university. *From the Word of God,* I share with them what they can never get elsewhere, and which provides answers to the terrible problems of humanity. I can give them understanding about themselves unavailable from any other source. Now, that encourages me. *That is the content of preaching.*

I believe it is the business of a preacher to change the viewpoint on life of every member of his congregation, so that when they return to their business, or their home, or their marriage, they go with totally different values than the world around them reflects. Therefore, their behavior and everything about will be different.

It is easy to take the phrase from Romans 12: "Be not conformed to this world," and thunder away at people about certain minor applications of that. We all have our own list of the "no-nos" of life. For some of us, not being conformed to this world means you don't smoke, drink, dance, go to movies, or something like that. However, such lists are not what constitutes nonconformity to the world.

Nonconformity to the world is being freed from materialistic value systems. It is being freed from the idea that the business of life is to make as much money as possible; to save for retirement, so you can spend your sunset years enjoying yourself to the utmost. Rather, the *real* purpose of life is to invest your life day by day for the cause that will endure beyond this life. Preaching is to change people's concepts about how to relate to one another, and what is truly important about life.

The instrument the preacher uses to do this is *the exposition of the Word of God.* I agree with John R. W. Stott, who says: "Expos-

itory preaching is the only kind of preaching worthy of the name."
If we are not unfolding the Word of God systematically, regularly, thoroughly, and consistently, then we are not really *preaching*. Preaching is the setting forth of a unique body of truth, the deep things of God—not the opinions and polls and conclusions of men.

Consider some of the "mysteries" Paul saw himself entrusted with as a steward. Entrusted with this sacred deposit, he felt a keen responsibility to impart it to others. He did so by going about, *preaching* these "unsearchable riches of Jesus Christ." Everywhere this great Apostle went, he found whole cities sunk in abject despair, governed by superstitions and magic. He talked to people who were living out their lives in quiet desperation—just as we find them in our cities today. Everywhere he went he planted colonies of people who had been awakened to a new view of life. They were filled with joy and gladness and love. Paul poured out the riches of Christ to them, and saw it transform their homes and their community. There sprang up little colonies of vital life in every city, who then began to infiltrate the whole area. Finally, the whole community, the whole area, the whole nation, began to reflect a drastic change. That is what Paul did with "the unsearchable riches of Christ!"

Certain of these unsearchable riches are called mysteries and seem to be found only in particular passages. They represent themes which run through the whole Scripture, often appearing under other names. Preaching is to proclaim and explain these great, transforming truths. For example, consider one of the best known of these in the New Testament: the *mystery of the Kingdom of God*. What does that term really mean? We may link the phrase also with Paul's reference to the "mystery of the blindness of Israel" (Romans 11). Here are two references to the same mystery. What *is* the "Kingdom of God?" It is God's invisible rule of men and angels. His basic control of history. When we preach about the Kingdom of God, we should not preach just about how that kingdom came to Israel, and that it is going to finally result in a *millennium,* and so on. All that is true, I grant you; but that is not going to change people's lives today, nor does it help them live today.

What the preacher *ought* to be doing is to show how God is still in control of human history, how he is working through the events of *this* day, the very events that fill the pages of the daily newspaper.

History is God's way of getting the work done that he has come to do in this world. Preaching needs to explain, for instance, what the Vietnamese war did to accomplish God's purpose of redemption in the earth. That is the business of preaching! Secular viewpoints only see in Vietnam a struggle, with evil on both sides. They do not understand what is happening, nor why it is happening. Preachers ought to understand it, and explain it. God tells us in his Word how he uses war, what he accomplishes with it, and how he equally judges all the nations who are involved in it. The Bible tells us how God uses a conflict like Vietnam to set up opportunities that would not be possible otherwise, in order for his reign to come to the earth.

Have you ever heard a sermon preached on the reason why America is experiencing such a horrendous upsurge in homosexuality in our day? What is *God* doing through all this? The Scriptures tell us! I often say something about that from my pulpit, because we have, in the City of San Francisco alone, 200,000 homosexuals. On the peninsula where I preach, there probably are another 100,000. We are surrounded by homosexuality. *What is happening? Why?* The preacher ought to be explaining it. He ought to be telling people what God is doing in these human *events.*

Preaching should help men read their newspapers in a different light than they ever did before. Without this knowledge, people everywhere sink into abject despair. That is true not only for Christians, but also for non-Christians. It is the business of the *church* to teach the *world*. The trouble is, today's preaching does not even teach the *church*. If the people of God do not know the answers to these questions, how do we ever expect the people who are locked into the narrow, limited range of secular vision to solve these problems?

T. S. Eliot has beautifully said. "All our knowledge is only bringing us closer to our ignorance; and all our ignorance, closer to death; yet closeness to death, no nearer to God." Then he asks the question that hangs over this whole generation: "Where is the life we have lost in living?" *It is the business of the preacher to answer that question.*

Karl Jung, the great Austrian psychiatrist, said: "We stand perplexed and stupefield before the phenomena of Nazism and Bolshevism, because we know nothing about man. Or, at any rate, we have only a lopsided and distorted picture of him. If we had self-knowledge, that would not be the case. We stand face to face with the terrible question of evil and do not even know what is before us, let alone know what to pit against it. And even if we did know, we still could not understand how it could happen here." It is to that vacuum of knowledge by the psychiatrists that the preacher is called to unfold what God is doing, and how he is doing it. What a remarkable thing happens when people begin to read their newspaper in the light of Biblical information.

Have you ever heard a sermon preached on the mystery of lawlessness? Such a sermon would unfold the incredible secret of invisible, supernatural powers of darkness, who master the psychological techniques for manipulating the minds of men. It would show how these powers hold men in blindness and darkness, no matter how brilliant they may be. It would describe how they have gained access to the inner souls of men, and whisper lies from within that lead to deception and destruction on every side.

Have you ever heard a sermon answer the questions, asked by every human being? "Why do we endlessly struggle with the same problems over and over again? Why do we make no advance in human history? Why is it that we still are wrestling with the same problems the ancient world wrestled with?" Sir Winston Churchill once said:

> "Certain it is that while men are gathering knowledge and power with ever increasing speed, their virtues and their wisdom have not shown any notable improvement as the centuries have rolled. Under sufficient stress: starvation, terror, war-like passion or even cold intellectual frenzy, the modern man we know so well will do the most terrible deeds—and his modern woman will back him up."

Why do not men change for the better? Because of the *"mystery of lawlessness,"* which the preacher is privileged to explain to people. Help should be given to understand that their anxieties, their neuroses, their psychoses, their depressions, and their despair are often coming from a Satanic attack. It has all been cleverly arranged. The attack comes from within, through what Scripture calls "the flesh;" and from without, through what the Scripture calls "the world"—the organized society and culture of our day. "The world, the flesh, and the devil"—that is the only rightful answer to many of the problems of life.

See what amazing truth is committed into the preacher's hands, to help people understand what is going on in the world today. When people begin to see the world system from that point of view, their reverence and understanding and respect for the authority of the Word of God mount like a skyrocket. They see that Scripture is designed for life. The Bible explains man, just like an instruction book explains the latest appliance. It is the business, therefore, of the preacher to declare these great truths.

Take the mystery of the church itself. What a terribly neglected thing is the teaching of this truth in our day. Only in the last decade or so have the churches of this country begun to capture anew and afresh the biblical pattern of God's body, functioning as he intended it to do. Only recently have churches started turning away from the empty, artificial substitutes of an organized religious business. We are now learning again how to love one another, to support one another, to relate to one another. We are rediscovering how to use the gifts with which God has empowered us. We are only beginning to teach the truths about the functioning Body of Christ, so that the world begins to get some clues about what is going on in life.

Recently, I went to Poland to teach a group of sixty Polish pastors. I found a church that was terribly limited, unable to function, scarcely making any impact on the world around it. "Oh," you say, "that is only to be expected in a Communist country. How can a church function in a Communist climate of unbelief and oppression?" No, that is not the reason for their lack of impact! The Polish church has much liberty. For instance, we had meetings without any fear of interruption. We had no supervision from the governing authorities. As long as we let them know what was going on there was no interference in any way. The pastors told me they were free to meet in homes and gather to study the Bible. There were Bibles everywhere. No, the church in Poland is no more deterred by government oppression than the church in America.

But, it was a limited church! Do you know why? Because they did not understand how the Body of Christ was to function. They told me they had never heard a message on spiritual gifts. They did not know they *had* spiritual gifts. They did not know anything about how to meet together and love one another, as the Lord commanded. They were locked into a pattern of gathering in a conventional service, formally conducted. That was their whole idea of what the church exists for—*to conduct meetings!* As I travel around America today I find this is the normal idea of what the church is all about: it is to run a Sunday morning meeting. That is where all the effort, time, and planning is placed. When one Sunday is all over, we start to do it all over again. It reminds me of the story of the man who was taken through an oil refinery. He was shown all the acres of machinery. When he got through, he said: "Well, you have shown me everything but your Shipping Department. Where is it?" "Oh," they said, "we don't have one." He said, "You don't have a Shipping Department? Why not?" They said, "It takes all the oil we produce to run the machinery we have here!" Unfortunately, that is a good description of the church in many places. It is simply operating for its own benefit.

It is the business of preaching to break through that, and to show people what God is doing in the world. Preaching is to declare how he intends to do it, the ways that he works. Preaching declares his mighty power, *the "mystery of resurrection power."* . . . What a theme that is!

God's answer to the "mystery of lawlessness" is the "mystery of godliness." I find that when people understand the mystery of godliness: "Christ in you, the hope of glory," they get so excited that they can hardly sleep. That truth means everything to men. In terms of ordinary, normal performance of ordinary, normal business, it means Christ lives in us to bring about extraordinary results. People who are gripped by this truth spread the word everywhere they go. They cannot even stop themselves from doing so.

I have to tell you that as I have been travelling up and down this country I think the only accurate thing to say about American churches in general is that they are filled with biblical illiterates who know little or nothing about the Bible. True, they honor it in their homes, but they know nothing about what it is saying. They need to be taught the radical, revolutionary truths of the Scriptures. Jesus said, "If you continue in my word, you will be my disciples indeed, and you will know the truth, *and the truth will set you free.*"

Nothing will change a community faster than people who have been set free. People must learn to function as mature human beings, to become grown up men and women. They are to be so taught that they do not run after every doctrine, or every psychological gimmick offered today. Through preaching, men learn how to handle life as it is intended to be handled. *That is the privilege and responsibility of preaching, and I commend it to you!*

9. Christian Education of the Church Today and Tomorrow

Larry Richards

Larry Richards, Ph.D., is a member of the Dynamic Church Ministries team, a not-for-profit mission, committed to encouraging vitalization of the local church. Dr. Richards. a retired seminary professor, has written some forty books.

Christian education of the church, today and tomorrow, has to begin with yesterday. We have to examine some of the theological roots involved in the communication of the Word of God. We must deal with basic theological issues, which shape the way we conduct Christian nurture in the church and the family.

First, then, consider *the theology of communication.* As we think about Christian education, we must think about the communication of the Word of God to people. Our Christian education must be an *effective transmission* of Scripture. As the lives of learners are transformed, God the Holy Spirit takes the written Word and makes it a living expression, coming from the heart of a person who has been touched by Jesus Christ.

Therefore, the basic issue in Christian education to be addressed is: "What is the context which God has designed for an effective communication of his Word to people, so that there is a life-changing impact?"

In order to answer this question, we have to go back to history. Sometimes we take the Word of God for granted. We need to remember that there were many hundreds (perhaps thousands) of years when God communicated with people apart from written revelation. For example, he spoke through prophets; he spoke through dreams; he spoke through tradition. He *did* make himself known!

There then came that time in history when God uniquely determined to begin to communicate the reality of his life to people through a *written* revelation. God then gave a written Word through Moses. It is not surprising, then, to discover in the Book of Deuteronomy, a *written* Word of God given to people, careful instructions about how truth should be communicated. Deuteronomy 6 explains how we are to communicate God's *written* Word. Basically, it is the key to our theology of communication:

> Hear, O Israel: The Lord our God is one Lord; and you shall love the Lord your God with all your heart, and with all your soul, and with all your might. And these words which I command you this day shall be upon your heart; and you shall teach them diligently to your children, and shall talk of them when you sit in your house, and when you walk by the way, and when you lie down, and when you rise. And you shall bind them as a sign upon your hand, and they shall be as frontlets between your eyes. And you shall write them on the doorposts of your house and on your gates (Deut. 6:4-9).

The very first thing we notice is that Moses gives a call. He says, "Listen, Israel! Pay attention, because what I am about to say to you is of utmost significance!" Then he continues with an affirmation about God: "The Lord our God is one Lord. Jehovah, our Jehovah, is one Jehovah."

Sometimes the most insignificant words in the Bible are the most important. Perhaps the least significant word in this sentence—"is"—is the key to understanding what Moses is saying. It is also the key to understanding what our concern must be as we approach the enterprise of Christian education. "Listen, Israel! The Lord our God *is* one Lord!"

Why the emphasis on "is"? We need to remember the historical context. For centuries, Israel had existed as slaves in Egypt. During all that time, they had not had a direct personal experience with God. They had *known* God, but they had known him in a past or future way. We see the same thought emphasized in the term "Jehovah." The word *Jehovah* comes from the Hebrew verb "to be; God is." It is striking that when God called Moses to go to the people of Israel and lead them to deliverance, he suggested that by his name, Jehovah, they had not known Him. It is striking because this name for God had occurred in the Biblical record prior to the time of Moses. God is not saying they had never *heard* the name, but that there now existed a generation who had not *known* him or his character.

How had those people known him? They had known him as the God of Abraham and Isaac and Jacob . . . a God who in the past spoke to their forefathers. They knew him as a God who had revealed himself historically to people in their past. They might also have known God in another way: as the One who had given great covenant promises, as the One who would bring the people of Israel out of servitude into the land which he had promised them. They had known God as One who lived and acted in the *past*, and they had known God as One who lived and would act in the *future* of their race. But as a people bound in servitude, they had *not* known God as One who had acted in their present experience.

Very often the church of Jesus Christ finds itself in that same trap! We know God as the One who acted in Jesus Christ to bring us salvation on Calvary's cross. We know Jesus Christ is someone who will come again and bring the world into submission to God. However, as we look at the task of communicating the Word of God, Moses demands that we face this issue: God wants us to know him as One who *is;* as One who is active and present; and as One who is alive and real in the daily personal experience of His people. So, as we come to this issue of how we are to communicate the Word of God, Moses begins with a call which we, too, must hear: "Listen, Israel—listen, my people—the Lord our God *is* one Lord!" The task of communicating the Word of God is to bring people into a relationship with God in which they experience the reality of his action in their lives *today*.

Moses then goes on, defining that relationship when he says, "And you shall love the Lord your God with all your heart, and with all your soul, and with all your might." God, who exists and who calls us into a present experience of relationship with him, invites us into a relationship which is to be marked not only by love on his side but by a loving responsiveness on our side. As we come to know him and experience him, the totality of our person, our heart, our soul, our strength, and all that we are is to be kept caught up in a love response to him. In this way we grow closer to God in a very personal and intimate relationship.

Now, this initiating call poses us with an interesting problem. Most of us have been brought up in school rooms. To us, a school room *is* "education." This is the way the western world, our culture, our society, goes about the task of teaching and learning. This educational system is tremendously effective within the limitations of its goals. However, it is focused first of all upon teaching *for the future,* not the present. It is focused upon a *cognitive* style of learning, rather than a *"total-person"* kind of learning.

For example, let us say you have a child who is just beginning to learn algebra. Perhaps he has many complaints, and says: "Boy, algebra is dull! I don't like it. It's not any fun. I don't think I'll ever use it." We then try to justify the teaching of algebra. Pretty soon, however, we have to basically say to him: "You will need algebra *some day in the future,* as you go into engineering or certain other career choices."

Now, the same thing is true with almost any other subject within the schooling system. If our children are learning how to speak and write English effectively, we say to them: "This is justified, because some day you are going to need these skills to get along in the world." Very seldom do you have anyone coming home from public school and saying: "Mom, Dad, I want to tell you what I learned in Social Science today. It made such a tremendous difference in my life!" Our school system is designed to communicate information on the assumption that the information will, *some day,* be usable by the learner.

Another aspect of our schooling system is that it is designed to deal almost exclusively with the cognitive processes. We learn and master information. We demonstrate our learning by giving the right answers on tests. If we can pass the tests by demonstrating mastery of knowledge, then whether or not we ever *use* that knowledge, we can get "A's" in our school system. The school system is designed to communicate cognitively and to test for memory of what has been taught. *That is perfectly fine . . . as long as the goal of education is to communicate cognitive information which will be used in the future.*

Our Christian goal, however, is to communicate a living Word of God. In this process, God himself is present *with* the learner, is presented *to* the learner, and calls for a living response of love *from* the learner. Therefore, an educational system designed as our public school system is designed, is totally inadequate for communication of the Word of God. We are dealing with a totally different objective in *Christian* education!

This is one of the great tragedies in the church of Jesus Christ. We have, without thinking, without consideration, without even being *aware* of what we were doing, imported an educational system from our secular culture. We have never gone back to the Word of God to ask whether this is the way God chooses to communicate his Word in reaching his goals. The church of tomorrow cannot afford that kind of worldliness!

Moses has given us a call: "Hear, O Israel: The Lord our God *is* one Lord; and you shall love the Lord your God with all your heart, and with all your soul, and with all your might." This is the context in which the Word of God is to be communicated. We are to bring people into a *personal relationship* with God—a love relationship, in which they experience his presence and his reality.

How are we going to do this? Scripture gives us a careful description of the three elements in a learning situation where the Word of God is communicated with a Christian impact. *First* of all, God said, "And these words which I command you this day shall be upon your heart." He is speaking here not of the *learner,* but of the *teacher!* God is saying that there is a *prerequisite* for communication of the written Word of God. When that prerequisite is met, the communication has a life-changing, God-meeting impact on the learner. *The prerequisite is that the one who communicates the words should have those words alive in his or her own heart.*

This is often perceived as a tremendously threatening kind of requirement. We all realize that, as human beings, we are inadequate. We realize that we live in a world which has been warped and twisted by sin. In spite of our response to Jesus Christ, we ourselves practiciate in that world and are ourselves tainted. We are deeply aware of our own failures, our own weaknesses, our own sins, and our own needs. Therefore, our immediate reaction is to draw back and say: "If this is the prerequisite, who can be a communicator of the Word of God?"

In answer to the question, we have a clue in *this* passage, and clear teaching in the *rest* of Scripture. This passage says: "And these words which I command you this day shall be upon your heart." If Deuteronomy 6 were in the Bible without that one qualifying phrase, we would have tremendous difficulties. If the passage said: "These words which I command you *shall be* upon your heart and *then* you shall teach them," we would all draw back. That would seem to indicate that the total revelation has to be integrated by the teacher into his own life *before* he can begin to communicate it. However, the passage does *not* say this!

The passage says: "And these words which I command you *this day* shall be upon your heart." When I read these words I am reminded of the unique "todayness" of Scripture, as is indicated in the rest of the Word of God. For example, in Hebrews the writer refers to the period of time when the children of Israel came to the Promised Land. God said: "Go into it!" However, the children of Israel drew back, hardened their hearts, and would not go in. The writer says: "*Today,* if you should heart his voice, don't harden your hearts as in the day of provocation in the wilderness." The writer says there remains a "todayness" of the Word of God with the people of God.

God has given us his Word so that he might communicate himself to us. As we open our hearts to what God is saying to us in the Scripture, we hear the Holy Spirit focus and bring into clear perspective his guidance for us. Our responsibility is not to be obedient to those things we do *not* know, but our responsibility is to be obedient to those things which God the Holy Spirit in our *"today"* is saying to us.

In remembering the years I taught at Wheaton, I look back with some chagrin. Some seven or eight years later, I understand many of the things I was teaching so much better. I also have the sneaky suspicion that seven or eight years from now I will look back and say, "Richards, you were so dumb back then! If you had only understood a little bit more."

Such awareness leads us to a striking question: Should I have remained silent as a teacher in graduate school seven years ago, *because I would understand so much more seven years later?* Should I remain silent *today,* because of my conviction that God still has a tremendous amount to teach me, and that I will understand much more seven years from now? The answer is: "No! Of course not!" We have to speak what God has brought into our lives and into our understanding through his Word and by his Spirit *today.*

My greatest comfort is that my students of years ago will not remember the things I taught in error. They *will* remember those things which God had taught me and had made real in my heart and life. "And these words which I command you *this day* shall be upon your heart; and you shall teach them . . ." The only thing which you or I can communicate with life-changing impact to others are those things which God has so taught us that they have passed through our head, entered our heart, and have become a living part of our personality.

That is a very exciting and freeing truth! It means that the newest Christian can go home to his children and share with them what God the Holy Spirit has taught. Out of that sharing, the reality of Jesus Christ can be communicated to those who have never heard of him. It means that as we go on through our lives, there is a continual adventure awaiting us. Each new lesson God teaches us and makes real in our life is something else we can share with others. That is very exciting! The privilege of sharing what God has taught us is a privilege of continual growth, not a demand for perfection in any sense.

That is the first prerequisite of teaching. Notice that we have already begun to move into a unique realm. We have already begun to move away from the cognitive mastery of information into a relationship. We have begun to move into a relationship in which the prerequisite, the key to effective communication, is *the interaction between the teacher and God. The responsiveness of one who is communicating to God and to his Word is the first key to the effectiveness of communicating to others.*

If I had my choice in selecting teachers for any activity of a local church, I would *not* first seek those who had the greatest academic credentials in terms of teaching skills. I would seek a person who is open and responsive, who loves Jesus Christ, and who is growing. That person is listening daily to the voice of God through His Word!

In review: We are not looking at a psychology or sociology of teaching. We are trying to see the context in which the Word of God is most effectively communicated. We are dealing with the communication of the Word of God with a specific goal. The goal is, first, that people might know and come to experience God as a living, present reality in their lives. Secondly, that relationship should be a *love* relationship, controlling more and more of their life and experience. In a learning situation where the Word of God is communicated, there must be a model in the teaching-learning situation. There must be a person who has come to experience the reality of God's Word in himself. We can never get away from the human communicator, the human teacher. The person in the learning setting serves as a model of the reality of the truth which is being taught.

The second element in the learning situation is: "And you shall teach them [or communicate them] diligently to your children." It is rather obvious that the *home* was the original context in which

God designed nurture to take place. If we study the Old Testament and its educational design, it is also obvious that it was not simply the *home,* but *the entire community of Israel,* which was the teaching context for the communication of the Word of God. It is very significant that Moses focused on the family in this passage: "And you shall teach them diligently *to your children.*"

The family is not the only place where the Bible should be taught. Because it is tremendously critical, allow me to reiterate that the family is *not* the *only* place where the Word of God should be taught! If it were, we could chop up the pulpits, get rid of the preachers, destroy the Sunday Schools, and get rid of a few seminaries. We would be very limited in a "mother-dad-children" context. That is not what Scripture recommends.

Scripture clearly teaches that in every situation where the Word of God is taught, *a family kind of relationship* is to be developed. This principle is seen throughout the New Testament. We are "brothers and sisters" within the context of fellowship within the church. Paul says in Ephesians 3:14-15:

"For this reason I bow my knees before the Father, from whom *every family* in heaven and on earth is named." Because God is by his nature the Father, when you and I have come into a relationship with God through Jesus Christ, we take our name and our identity from His character as our Father. That character or identity is shared with all other Christians as our *family.* He is Father; we are "brothers and sisters." Because he is our Father, we have an intimate, personal relationship with every other person who knows him as Father. We must always affirm that family relationship. We must always seek to develop a family relationship with those who are our brothers and sisters in the family of God.

In looking at the communication patterns of the New Testament, we again find this family implication clearly spelled out. For example, in First Thessalonians Paul gives a description of how he ministered as he sought to establish a new church. It is important to notice that this is a ministry of the Word of God. Paul says in 1 Thessalonians 1:5: "Our gospel came to you not simply with words, but also with power, with the Holy Spirit . . ." So here was the Word of God coming to the people with power. Then Paul says they received the Word—"You welcomed the message . . ." This was the second stage. The Word came and the Word was received. Then, in verse 8, Paul says: "The Lord's message rang out from you . . ." Here was the Word of God, which had been received into the hearts of people, finding expression through their lives to others!

That is a beautiful portrait of how God uses his Word in the lives of his people! The Word comes, it is heard and received, it becomes a part of us, and then goes out from us to others. Paul is describing a ministry of the Word. This is not sociological. It is not psychological. It is not educational. It is a *ministry* of the Word of God.

Notice how Paul describes the relationships he had with believers in the church of the Thessalonians. Notice particularly that he went back to the *family* illustration to explain the relationship: "But we were gentle among you, like a [nursing] mother caring for her little children." (1 Thess. 2:7). That is a very beautiful phrase. It is also a fascinating phrase, particularly if you know much about the Apostle Paul.

An early church description of the Apostle Paul describes him as a little man who walked bent over. He had bright blue eyes tucked under some rather bushy eyebrows that met in the center of his forehead, and he had a hooked nose that almost met his chin. Now, picture this little guy walking around all bent over, looking up at you with his piercing blue eyes with his nose almost meeting his chin, saying to these thirty, forty, fifty-year-old people: "I was gentle among you, like a nursing mother taking care of an infant." That always strikes me as being such a peculiar portrait. However, no one saw anything strange about it *because they had experienced Paul's deep love and care for them.* They knew that he was spreaking absolute truth!

Paul continues discussing his relationship with them in 1 Thessalonians 2: "We loved you so much that we were delighted to share with you not only the gospel of God but our lives as well, because you had become so dear to us" (Verse 8). This is also a striking portrait. Here is this busy Apostle making tents to support himself, being harried by his enemies, and yet finding time to spend with his brothers and sisters. Then, as he came to know them better, they became even dearer to him: "I wanted to give you my very self because I loved you so much." In verse 10, Paul says: "You are witnesses . . . of how holy, righteous and blameless we were among you who believed." In other words, he was saying: "You knew our life because we lived an exposed life among you.

There was no question of our motivations." And then he says in verses 11 and 12: "For you know that we dealt with each of you as a father deals with his own children, encouraging, comforting and urging you to live lives worthy of God, who calls you into His kingdom and glory."

That is a fascinating portrait of a father of teenagers: "I dealt with each one of you." How striking it is . . . this busy man in the ministry of the Word of God had time for individuals!

When I had sons myself, I began to realize just how striking it is. I have two sons. Paul, who is the older son, has a rather fascinating personality. He is an artist. That is his profession and his business, and at age 22 he does amazing work. When I tell people he is an artist, they get a certain picture of him in their mind, but Paul is also a body builder. There are times when he constantly works out at recreation centers. Paul is about six feet tall and weights about 235 pounds. It is all muscle. When he was 209 pounds he could press 525 pounds. He is very, very big. He is one of the few artists that no one sneers at if they see him painting a beautiful picture!

When Paul was growing up he was always calm, neat and responsive. If you looked at him cross-eyed, he was so tender hearted that he would just immediately respond.

Then we had Timothy. Timothy is a junior in high school and he gets upset very easily. When he was corrected, he gave a totally different response. Someone would correct Timothy, and his body would immediately go stiff. He would stick out his lower lip, cross his arms, and "boom!" . . . he would withdraw. I tried all sorts of things with Timothy—yelling, spanking, hugging. Nothing worked.

When he would get *very* upset, I would say to him, "Timothy, it is time to go to your room!" He would stay in his room until he had partial control of himself. After that, he knew he had permission to come out. Of course, it was sort of a two-way agreement. No one was to mention the incident for at least five hours. If we mentioned the incident within five hours, it would set him off again. I found that after about five hours, I could sit down and talk with him. However, I first had to *listen* for an hour and a half, as he explained why it was not his fault, how everything else was wrong, what Mom did that she should not have done, and all the other factors of the matter. Then he would be at a point where I could explain to him what actually happened and what should be done.

Here are two young men—same family, same heredity, same environment, and yet totally different people. When I study this passage in Thessalonians, I realize how striking Paul's words are. He says: "For you know that we dealt with each of you as a father deals with his own children, encouraging, comforting and urging you to live lives worthy of God." People were also "different" then! Some of them needed encouraging. Some of them needed comforting. Some of them needed urging, or a good kick in the pants. Paul not only dealt with people individually, but he came to know them so well that he could motivate them toward a goal of life "worthy of God, who calls you into His kingdom and glory."

As a father, I have come to realize how important this principle is. If I had treated my two sons in exactly the same way, I would have destroyed one of them. We need to build relationships with each other, to develop a family context into which the Word of God can come with its fullest impact. Within that relationship, we also need to know one another intimately, so each person's needs can be met. The only analogy for the kind of relationship which is to exist for the teaching of the Word of God is that of a family . . . the church!

So we find two qualities from Deuteronomy for the educational context in which the Word of God is taught to people, with a life-changing God-experiencing impact: "Hear, O Israel: The Lord our God is one Lord; and you shall love the Lord your God with all your heart, and with all your soul, and with all your might. And these words which I command you this day shall be upon your heart; and you shall teach them diligently to your children." First, there must be a human model in the teaching-learning situation. This model must personally know the reality of the truth being taught. Second, the model must teach in the context of a loving, family relationship between the people of God, the church.

Finally, Moses says: "And [you] shall talk of them when you sit in your house, and when you walk by the way, and when you lie down, and when you rise." This is the *third* element in a learning situation. The context in which the Word of God is to be taught is the context of life itself—in lying down, in getting up, in sitting down, in walking along the way. All too often, in our churches and in our educational approaches, we have created an artificial context. We have taken people away from the reality of their lives, put them in classrooms which are isolated from that reality, and talked to them about Biblical ideas. God calls us to invest ourselves and our lives with people, to walk with them through the reality of their lives, and to bring His Word to bear on the reality of their daily experiences.

Somehow, the church of Jesus Christ must design and develop an educational approach that treats the Word of God according to the design God himself has given us. *Is it possible for the church of Jesus Christ to teach the Word of God as he designed it to be taught?* Is it possible for the church of Jesus Christ to discontinue its dependence upon a secular educational system which is not rooted in theology, but in something entirely different? The answer is, "Hallelujah! Of course!"

10. The Body of Christ:
God's Setting for Learning the Bible

Larry Richards

In the previous chapter, we began by taking a look at the theology of communication. We looked at Biblical principles for teaching of the Word of God, which is the objective of Christian education. In doing so, we must recognize that God intends us to use His Word uniquely, and has planned a unique way for the Word to be communicated.

We saw in Deuteronomy 6:4-9 that we are called by God to experience Him as a present reality in our lives. Through our personal experience with God, we are to grow into a deepening love relationship with him. He is to capture upon every dimension of our human personality, drawing us into an ever closer relationship with him.

In Deuteronomy 6, we also took a look at the communication setting in which God defined how we are to communicate his Word with impact. First of all, we see the words which God has spoken to us are to be *in our heart*. Then, we are to communicate those words. The communicator is someone who has taken into his own *heart* and *life* the words of God. Secondly, we saw that there is to be a unique kind of relationship between those who gather together to hear the words of God. It is to be a *family* relationship. We saw in the New Testament that this concept of a family relationship—a context of intimate love—is the community into which the Word of God is to come. Finally, we briefly described the context into which the Word of God is to be applied, and into which it is to be heard. It is not to be conveyed in a classroom isolated from life, but rather in *the context of life itself*. It is there we hear the words of God—as we stand together in the morning, as we rise up, as we walk, as we sit down.

I would now like to show you an illustration of all the qualities I have described, present in one teaching/learning situation. Afterward, we will address the critical question: *How, in traditional settings, can we bring people from their present essentially cognitive, impersonal, non-relational dealing with Scripture to a pattern which is closer to the Biblical ideal?*

Let us begin by looking at a very simple prayer fround in Ephesians 3:14-15. Here is Paul, saying, "For this reason I bow my knees before the Father, from whom every family in heaven and on earth is named." As I commented in my last chapter, because of God's character and essential nature as *Father,* we who know him take our essential nature as *family.* We are brothers and together we have a relationship with one who is Father. In the context of a family, Paul goes on to pray that out of God's glorious riches, we would be "strengthened with might through His Spirit in the inner man, and that Christ may dwell in your hearts through faith." (verses 16 and 17.) Here, of course, he is describing the *nurture,* the *growth,* and the *maturing* of members of the family.

Paul then adds: "(and I pray) that you, being rooted and grounded in love, may have power to comprehend with all the saints what is the breadth and length and height and depth, and to know the love of Christ which surpasses knowledge, that you may be filled with all the fulness of God." (verses 18 and 19.) One of the things that strikes me as I study the passage is the phrase *"that you, being rooted and grounded in love, may have power to comprehend."*

The first question I ask myself is: What kind of love is the writer talking about? Is he talking about *God's* love for *us?* Or, is he talking about *our* love for *God* that is the rooting ground for growth? As I studied the passage, I became convinced that what he is talking about here is *the necessity for members of the Body of Jesus Christ to be rooted and grounded in their love for one another as family!*

As we trace through the concept of love in the New Testament, we find that God speaks more often of love between the brothers and sisters in the family than He does of God's love for us, or of our love for God. This is buttressed by the fact that God says, "When you have been grounded and established together in love within the family, *then* you will have the ability, together with all the saints, to comprehend." The relationship of togetherness with other saints is tremendously important if we are to come to know a love of God which surpasses our knowledge or ability to comprehend. We experience the reality of that love as God Himself reaches out to love us *through the brothers and sisters* with whom we have established an intimate relationship of fellowship.

The passage in Ephesians 3 is the reflection of the Deuteronomy 6 phrase: "You shall teach them diligently to your children." We are to teach the words of God in a context where a family relationship has been established. It is very striking to note that, in this context, a unique kind of teaching and learning takes place. This kind of teaching and learning is reflected in many other Biblical passages.

In Romans 15:14, Paul writes to the people of Rome: ". . . my brethren, I myself also am convinced that you yourselves are full of goodness, filled with all knowledge, and able also to admonish one another." Here is the great Apostle, yearning to come to Rome, desiring to share something with the Christians there, desiring for them to share something with him. Yet, as he is held back from coming, he writes to them with this word of reassurance: "I . . . am convinced that you yourselves are full of goodness, filled with all knowledge, and able also to admonish one another." Here we see just the beginning of an idea—the idea that when the brotherhood has grown together *as a family,* teaching and ministry is no longer the providence of a single individual in that fellowship. When the brotherhood has grown together *as a family,* teaching and ministry becomes an expression of God's working through each member to the others.

The same concept is present in 1 Corinthians 12. There Paul talks about each believer as having been gifted by God. He says in verses 4 to 7: "Now there are varieties of gifts, but the same Spirit. And there are varieties of ministries, and the same Lord. And there are varieties of effects, but the same God who works all things in all persons. But to each one is given the manifestation of the Spirit for the common good." Each believer gains a relationship with Jesus Christ, and is indwelled by the Spirit of God. Each believer is also given a unique capacity to contribute to the common good. When we are together in the loving relationship of the family, God the Holy Spirit ministers through each one to the other and makes the common good, the common growth, the common strengthening of the Body, the outcome of His Work.

We see the same concept in Ephesians 4, where Paul talks about the fact that believers are part of a whole body which is joined and held together by *every supporting ligament*. The Bible says the whole body grows and builds itself up in love *as each part does its work*. Again, we see the theme that there is to be a contribution of each part to the other if growth and love toward maturity is to take place.

One other passage, Hebrews 10, gives us an addition to this portrait. When I was first converted, I joined a little Baptist church in Brooklyn, New York. The phrase "Do not forsake the assembling of yourselves together" was often quoted by the pastor. Unfortunately, what he meant was: "Be sure to be here every time I speak!" He took that phrase out of its context. If we read this phrase *in its context,* we get a striking picture of the gathered church. "Let us consider how to stimulate one another to love and good deeds, not forsaking our own assembling together, as is the habit of some, but encouraging one another; and all the more, as you see the day drawing near." (Hebrews 10:24-25).

What is striking is *the call to gather together*. We also see what is to happen when we gather: We are to minister to each other, to encourage one another toward love and good deeds, and to stimulate each other all the more as the day approaches. Here is a portrait of God at work in and through the "together" setting, in and through the family relationship setting, where each person has a teaching contribution to make to the nurture of all the others.

With these verses giving the setting for learning, here is a model of these concepts. I share with you now a model of a small group Bible study. At least, it certainly *started* small! It started with just four of us meeting in a house. We met together, just the four of us, for about eight or twelve weeks. All that time we were asking God to make us willing to grow if he wanted to bring others into the group. We particularly wanted to be willing to see if anyone who did not yet know Christ might come into our little fellowship and come to know him. We invited a few people, but no one came. Yet we stayed together, and we kept sharing among ourselves, studying together, praying together.

After about eight or twelve weeks, when we had developed a core fellowship among ourselves, God brought in a couple named Charlie and Barbara. Barbara had heard me speak at a church one day. She then heard about our Bible study, and came, dragging Charlie along. To understand Barbara and Charlie, you need to realize that they were social Christians. They were very rigorous in attending their church, but essentially viewed church as a social club, a place for excellent business contacts for Charlie. (Charlie was a builder and was always very aggressive and very alert for a good business contact.) However, they did come to our little Bible study and, amazingly, they kept coming back. And, as they came, others began to be added.

Now, I say "amazingly" because Charlie was very embarrassed when he came to our Bible studies. As we talked about it later, Charlie told me that he was not embarrassed for himself. He was embarrassed for the other people in the Bible study. There were people there who were talking openly about their problems. There were people who talked about their inadequacies. Charlie sat in our midst and said to himself, "Oh, my! These poor, inadequate, horrible people. If I were in as much trouble as they are, I would really be embarrassed." So he sat there and suffered the embarrassment. He kept coming because *Barbara* was coming, and because he wanted to make sure that Barbara did not get any crazy ideas about the Bible. Now, of course, Charlie had never read any part of the Bible for himself. Nevertheless, he was quite *sure* that he would be able to instruct his wife if she got any screwball ideas! So, he kept coming.

Now, Barbara had a peculiar reason for coming. In fact, Barbara and Charlie had both developed the same reason to *keep* coming after they had been with us for a month or so. That reason was a very simple one. As we talked about it later, they said, "Well, you people were different. Never in our lives had we seen people love each other like you did. Somehow, that love was something we felt we had a desperate need to receive. *We kept coming back because of the reality of the love we saw.*"

A lot of other strange things began to happen as Charlie and Barbara kept coming. One of them was that the guy who was embarrassed by *other* people's problems began to realize that he had some of his own! He began to have some doubts about the morality of some of the practices that were going on in his business. Amazingly, he began to talk about them with the group, to talk about his uncertainty, his snatches of guilt. The group began to pray for him. Barbara, too, began to talk and to share and to participate. She studied the Bible, and came back each week with her answers to questions about Scripture.

About six months after they began to come, both Barbara and

Charlie accepted the Lord Jesus Christ as their personal Savior.
Bill, one of the original team who started the group, came over for
supper one night. Barbara asked him: "How does a person really
become a Christian?" Bill told her. The next morning as she was
cleaning up the table, she leaned her head against a doorpost and
accepted Christ as her personal Savior. Her face literally changed.
Suddenly, for the first time in her life, she knew that she was totally
loved and accepted by God. She knew that somehow she was
secure in a relationship with him that she had never dreamed
possible.

During the next months, it was fascinating to see both Charlie
and Barbara grow and change. The thing that struck me was the
tremendous commitment of these people who were new Christians. They moved on into a discipled life that I had not seen in the
lives of many people who had known the Lord for twenty or thirty
years!

Another example: we had one young woman who began to come
to the group. Unfortunately, she had had some rather difficult
experiences in her past, and was having a very difficult experience
in her present. She was an organist at a church and had developed
an illicit relationship with the Chairman of the Deacons. We dealt
with her. She kept coming, and we continued to deal with her very
directly and very honestly. She became, of course, more and more
uncomfortable. She began to call Barbara many times during the
day, and explain to Barbara why her actions were all right. She
would quote Greek (which she did not know) to buttress her
opinion.

Barbara began to feel tremendously pressured. One day Barbara
said, "I don't want to stop caring for her, but I think she is using
me. What do I do?" We went into Scripture and took a look at the
concept of discipline. We saw that discipline is not something that
God calls the church to do to *punish* people, but to help them
experience the reality of the separation which sin caused between
them and the Father. Discipline is a loving way to communicate the
reality of someone's spiritual condition to them, with the hope for
change. The striking thing was that as soon as Barbara saw the
principle, her response was, "Oh! I can't wait to go over to her
house tomorrow and explain to her why I can't talk with her
anymore!"

I had just returned from a retreat in California, with Ministers of

Education and Pastors. I had talked to about twenty-five of them individually, and every one of them had had the same problem. The problem was: "I am having difficulty with my relationship with the head Pastor;" or, "I am having difficulty with my relationship with the deacons;" or, "I am having difficulty with my relationship with someone here or someone there." As we talked about it, they asked: "What can we do?" I replied, "Well, there is a simple and beautiful answer. Christ says that if you have anything against your brother, you are to go to him and have it out with him and work toward a reconciliation. If your brother has anything against you, leave your gift on the altar and dash off and be reconciled to your brother." The answer was very simple. We are told, "Go share with this person your concern and your feelings and seek to have him share with you his feelings. Then work toward a reconciliation." Every one of the men that I had talked with had had the same reasponse: "Oh, that is hard!"

But here was Barbara, a new Christian, who said, "I can't wait until tomorrow to go over and do what the Word of God tells me to do!" I became tremendously impressed as I watched that group disciple each other into obedience to God.

We saw some other fascinating things, too. Barbara's background was very, very socialite; she came from an upper social set in St. Louis. After Barbara's conversion, she began to try to convert her mother. She talked to her mother on the phone about Jesus, and sent her Christian books. Now, her mother resented all of this! Her daughter was telling her that there was something *wrong* with her spiritual life! Her mother began to send Barbara one book for every book that Barbara sent her. The relationship, which had previously been very beautiful between the two women, began to deteriorate.

As we talked about the situation one evening, Barbara shared something very interesting. She said, "You know, when we started coming to the group we were actually kind of ashamed because we were deceiving you. You thought we were real Christians just like you are." I laughed, and said: "Why, Barbara, we didn't think that you were real Christians at all; *we knew!*" She said, "Oh, you *did!*" I said: "Yes. You see, Barbara, it didn't make any difference to us, because we loved you just as much then, and God loved you just as much then, as we do now."

I then asked her: "Barbara, what would have happened if a

month or so after you had come to the group we made it very clear that in order to be acceptable to us you would *have* to make a profession and believe what we believe?'' Barbara thought for a minute and said: ''Well, I would have never come back.'' I said, ''Exactly! Don't you see, Barbara? By communicating to your mother that she is not acceptable to you because she doesn't believe the way you do, you are creating a tremendous barrier to her hearing the gospel? What you need to do, Barbara, is a very simple thing. Act as though you assume your mother is *already* a Christian. Talk to her in the same natural, loving way about Jesus that you talk to us. Just assume that she is going to listen with the same kind of enthusiasm and interest that we listened to you.''

Barbara began to do this. While Barbara's mother is not yet a Christian, the relationship is *totally* changed. Barbara is now able to witness in a very natural and spontaneous way, without the communication of condemnation which often comes in witnessing. Only in a setting of group life could Barbara have worked through this problem.

There are many other people I could tell you about who came into this group: For example, there are Gary and Eileen. Gary and Eileen were a Catholic couple, brought up in New York. They had been brought up in a Catholic grade school, a Catholic high school, a Catholic college, and had never owned or even read a Bible. (There are many, many, Catholic schools where this is no longer true, which is very exciting, but for them it *was* true.)

Gary had been a very successful man in the construction business. He quit that business, because his best friend and partner left his wife and five children and began to live with his secretary. Somehow that event seemed to destroy everything, in terms of the integrity Gary and Eileen had been trying to build into their business. There had to be *more* to life, but they did not know what it was! They bought a trailer, and started from New York to explore the world. They finally ended up in Phoenix.

Along their journey, they kept running into Christians. They ran into Christians in a trailer next door, when Gary went over to help install part of the sewer system. The man invited him in, and gave Gary his first Bible. They stopped at a Christian camp in Michigan and stayed for three or four days. They noticed the fantastic difference in the lives of Christians, but did not know exactly what caused it.

When Gary and Eileen arrived in Phoenix, one of Gary's resumés ended up on Charlie's desk. Charlie was to interview Gary for a job. Now, Charlie still happened to have quite a few prejudices. First of all, he did not like people from New York. Secondly, he did not like Catholics, Thirdly, he did not like the fact that Gary was overqualified for the job. But, in spite of all these "not likes," he hired Gary. Then, something amazing happened. They began to like each other tremendously, and began to talk about their shared adventure as they moved toward God.

Gary and Eileen began to come to our Bible study group. It was very tough for Eileen, who was a very traditional Catholic. She felt a terrible sense of guilt because she went to a Protestant Bible study. Before too long, both Gary and Eileen accepted the Lord Jesus Christ as their personal Savior.

Then Gary wanted to start a Bible study himself, and asked me to teach him how to do it. I said, "Gary, you don't need me to attend your Bible Study." He said, "I really wish you would come." I went over to Gary's house, and I never said a word the whole evening in the Bible study. Gary opened his Bible as soon as the group had arrived. He said: "I was reading something very exciting in Galatians this morning." He then started talking about Galatians, relating it to his own background. All the people there were Catholics, except for one Jewish lady. They all immediately identified with what he said. They had all been through similar experiences. Paul's comments in Galatians 2 about the Law spoke to their own hearts and their own previous experiences with religion. It was a joy to me to watch Gary, as he suddenly discovered that God the Holy Spirit in his life had made him an able communicator of the Word of God. Somehow, a "professional teacher" was not necessary in his life any more.

The purpose of this illustration has been to show a context where the Christian family together ministered to each other. I have shown a context where a Christian family actually *functioned*. In fact, it functioned in such a way that people came to know Jesus Christ, that believers were discipled to a unique and totally committed obedience to God, and that God spoke to them through the Word.

The format was so ridiculously simple! All we did was get together for about two and a half hours a week. For the first forty-five minutes, we talked about what had been happening in our lives; we renewed our friendships. If someone had been sick, we asked about them. We were just *friends.*

Next, I would have previously prepared a simple "do-it-yourself" Bible study, which everyone would have completed. When everyone arrived, they were ready to share with each other what God had been teaching them that week through his Word. They simply talked about those questions, and about what they had discovered as they studied Scripture to answer them. They talked about what God had been saying to their lives, and how he had been ministering to them.

Finally, we would pray. We all kept a prayer list. By the way, one of the reasons Gary came to know the Lord was because he was absolutely stunned to hear people pray about "daily life" kinds of things. What stunned him most of all was how, week after week, people came to share how God had *answered* their prayers! Gary realized that he did not know the tremendous reality of a personal relationship with a God who lives and answers prayer.

It was extremely simple—sharing Scripture, praying for each other, sharing from each other's lives, taking time to let each person know love. *We reproduced the context for dealing with the Word of God which is reflected in Deuteronomy 6!*

There were models of Christians to be observed . . . not just *one* model, but *many,* who had all taken the Word of God into their hearts and were teaching it. Every member of that group was a teacher, a valid model for the others. Every one *taught* because every one *studied.*

The striking thing was that our daily lives became the focus of the study of the Word of God. Charlie talked about his business problems. People talked about their jobs. Pat talked about her divorce, and the two children she was struggling to raise—as well as her inadequacy as she tried to learn how to make decisions. In the past, her husband had made every decision for her.

As we studied the Word, prayed, and related the Word of God to these experiences in our daily-life patterns, God began to infuse and work in our daily-life patterns, bringing them into harmony with his Word. We did not get into doctrinal disputes, because the focus of our study of the Word of God was to see what God would say to *us,* that we might learn to *live* his Word, to experience his *reality,* in our own day-to-day experiences.

That group has been disbanded now for about three or four

years. I am much more heavily involved in travelling, and they are all involved now in their own churches. Recently, I had the privilege of marrying my son, and they all came. It was such a delight to see them all again. The exciting thing was, as we met each other and hugged and were overjoyed at the chance to meet again, our old relationship was immediately reestablished. *There had been no loss of love.* Why? Because we were family. We had been part of a love relationship

Now, even though this is an exciting model I have presented, it is a rather *discouraging* model for some people. The difficulty is that every time I tell about this model, it becomes almost a condemning story.

So many times I share with other people my experiences, and how we have discovered the Body at work. Then, they share that they are in a congregation where there is a great suspicion of this model. There is a great fear of intimacy and of deep relationships. There is a real antagonism to any kind of change.

Many of us know the kind of church where the whole approach to dealing with the Word of God is something which has been structured by our *society* rather than by *Scripture*. Many churches have come to feel that the only appropriate way to study the Bible is to line up chairs set in rows, listen to one person talk, agree with the information he gives. If any questions are asked, if any thoughts are shared, they must be safely kept on an intellectual plane. The hurts, pains, and realities of our daily experiences are never to be revealed. We fear how others in the group might perceive us. Whenever I talk about the intimate small group fellowship, the anguish in many hearts is: "I live and work in a congregation where this would be so threatening that, if I dared to try to introduce anything like it, I would be cast out!"

As a result, one of the questions we have to ask is this: as we take a look at Christian education today and tomorrow, *are there ways that we can begin where the church is at the present time?* Are there things we can introduce into the lives of our congregations that will, through experience, modify their patterns of learning and thinking? Are there things we can introduce into the lives of our congregations which have traditional classes, where the teacher drones, "What is in the text book?" Can we turn that class into the kind of a shared-life experience, where each person takes responsibility to listen to God, to hear God, and to share what God has

been saying to him with others? I believe there is. I do not believe it
is easy, but I believe there is!

Let me now share with you another model—a *"change model."*
I will tell you about how a change model works, and how it
originated. Then we will look at how even things like *technology*
can be used to build an interpersonal learning center that dupli-
cates the conditions for hearing and learning his Word that God
outlined for us in Deuteronomy.

Several years ago, I was invited with others to the Billy Graham
Center at Wheaton College to consider a very basic question. The
people there felt it was very important to ask *why,* in view of the
Bible teaching and preaching over the years, tests constantly show
that people in the United States are Biblically illiterate. They
wanted to know *what* we can do to teach the Bible in a systematic,
meaningful way. It was a very fascinating time, and there were
many suggestions. None of them, however, had any value at all!

I think the closest thing to a model anyone proposed was to put
on a series of seminars on Bible teaching all around the country.
(That is a horrible suggestion, because that model is *again* not in
harmony with the Deuteronomy passage!) It would have been
another one-way communication of informational truth, without
opportunity for the other dimensions needed to hear the Word of
God to be effectively in place.

After that conference—where absolutely no answers were
derived—I had an experience which started me thinking in a rather
wild vein. I was in Grand Rapids, Michigan, and someone asked
me if he could spend some time with me to show me something he
had produced for use on television. I have a principle that if people
want to talk to me, whether I am busy or not, I will usually try to
find the time. So I took the time to listen to him and to watch what
he produced.

What he had done was very simple. It was a television Bible
study, which was essentially a human head on a screen, talking
about content. The head on the screen started with the history of
James, and moved on to the outline of James, and the details of the
book. Very seldom did it ever mention anything about human
beings, life, reality, or experience. He had shown it to a number of
people, and they had all been quite enthusiastic.

From my perspective of the Deuteronomy approach, I had to
say, "To be honest with you, what you are doing is absolutely

horrible, and is perpetuating the very thing that got us into this mess!" And then, because I also try to be as helpful as honest, I suggested that perhaps there *would* be a way to use media to do something significant—but that certain conditions would have to be met.

The conditions would be, number one, that the system would have to contain something that motivated people to study *before* they came to a viewing. We who are committed to a ministry of the Word of God have as a goal to get God's people into the Scripture for themselves, so they can hear *his* voice, not ours. People need to become responsive to God the Holy Spirit, so he can speak to them through the Word he has inspired. This is the first condition: *there must be some way to get people motivated to get into the Bible.*

The second thing I suggested was that *media must be used in a way which is suitable for its character, nature, and strengths.* As utilized as a media in our culture today, television taps *below* the cognitive level and engages the emotions, the attitudes, and the valuing processes of people. To do this, it uses drama and a variety of other means. Uniquely, it can relate concepts to multiple levels of human experiences.

I suggested that whatever television should contribute to a teaching/learning system, it certainly should not be viewed as the primary communicator of information. The *content* ought to come through personal Bible study, and through personal involvement with Scripture. Of course, the use of television can summarize, crystallize, and bring into focus key teachings. Then it must go beyond this, and somehow engage the heart and attitude and "daily lifeness" of human experience. It should apply truths that have been studied to human experience, making it bridge the kind of sharing that is described in the Deuteronomy model . . . the "sitting-up, standing-up, walking-by-the-way" kind of experiences.

The third dimension was this: *any system which moves to a Biblical approach would have to have a time of sharing and ministering by those who are with each other in the study group.* It is not enough to simply have them study something, watch a television program, and react to it. People need to be in a context where they minister to each other, support each other, pray for each other, share with each other. When this happens, the *family character* of that group is developed.

Before we left the motel room that night, my new friend and I had decided, God willing, to try to put together some such system. It took us two years before we could begin.

I had been writing a series of Bible study books called *Bible Alive*. These are a series of twelve books, published by David C. Cook Publishing Co., which survey the Old and New Testament. This series had come out of my teaching of Bible survey for seven years at Wheaton Graduate School. I found students became excited when they dug into Scripture, not to learn *facts*, but to *hear God speak to them*, and to understand the great movements of God in Biblical history. They were excited to discover that when they read a passage they could actually *hear* and *see* what God was saying. I tried to apply the principles I had learned about teaching as I wrote that series of books. Then, based on that series, we decided to try to develop a television-based Bible study approach.

It took a number of years, but we finally did do it! The television component alone cost over a quarter of a million dollars. It took my house, my boat, my two cars, and my washing machine. God performed many miracles to bring the funds in to make the project possible. We finally ended up with a system which has been tested on broadcast television and in many other modes. We have found it has a surprising impact.

Let me share with you the elements, and then go back and relate this to theory. I am doing this to show that there *are* ways to take people from traditional settings, and to introduce them to the elements of the teaching learning situation which Scripture demands.

The kind of format we finally ended up with is very simple: each student has a kit. At first, we just gave them a text book which I had written; they not only did not read the *text book*, but they did not read *the Bible*. After this failure, we developed a full-color Bible study magazine in which each person writes down what they discover in the Scripture. When they were given this kind of a support system, people would do the preliminary Bible study. They wrote down their answers, and even took notes on the television program. They were prepared with content from Scripture they themselves studied.

Next, we developed the television format. For the first book of the series, *The Servant King* (the study of the Gospel of Matthew), we developed thirteen twenty-eight-and-one-half minute television programs. It is important to consider the features of these television programs, because they illustrate some of the elements of a teaching/learning situation.

To begin with, people need to see what the Bible is talking about. So, where it made a difference, we went to Israel and shot over 20,000 feet of film. In this way, we actually took people to the location where Scripture was taking place. People saw the space, time, and historical reality of the Scripture.

We received permission to go into the Garden Tomb, and photographed it in great detail. The last program in the series begins in an Easter-like setting. It takes people into the garden, shows them the track on which the great stone rolled away, and shows them every detail of the Matthew account, etched in the stone of that location. It is a fascinating and moving experience for people who watch it.

As well as giving some teaching that summarizes the basic concepts people have been studying, we have tried to apply these key truths to personal experience, causing sharing and discussion. To do this, we utilize a family as a dramatic tool. The television family has a dad, mom, and two teenagers. Throughout the series, this family dramatizes experiences which bring them into applications which have been indicated in Matthew's gospel. We have found this to be very effective. It has been a great way to launch discussion and sharing; it taps the *emotional* part of life. It makes it possible for people in the church to talk about personal experiences that are similar to the ones they have seen acted out on the television screen. It has been a great help to get people sharing on a personal, daily-life kind of level.

To make sure that sharing and interaction take place, we provide a special Leader's Guide, which has about eighty pages explaining how to lead a group. We also provide a ninety-minute cassette for every session, with suggestions for the leader to involve the group in sharing, in discussion, and in building fellowship relationships.

One thing is very important to the whole concept; *avoid having the leader of the group be a teacher!* The television is effective here, because the teacher is on the screen. The leader of the group is *not* the teacher of the course. In this particular series, I happen to be the teacher on television. When I am turned off, the teacher is gone! Instead of being a detriment, this is actually an aid. The people in the group have to go to Scripture for answers; they have to go to each other! They have to go to the resources God has given to every believer—*the Word of God,* and *the Spirit of God,* to discover *his* answers.

Of course, if there are problems or questions, there is always a pastor to go to for help. Essentially, we have used this format to force members of a congregation to take responsibility for seeking God's answer to their questions, and to force them into a pattern where they minister to each other rather than rely on one person to minister to them.

We have tested this whole concept in a variety of ways. We put it on broadcast television in Los Angeles, California, Miami, Florida, Phoenix, and in Indiana. We made an interesting discovery: when it was on broadcast television, people utilized it for *entertainment.* People liked it, but they did not study the Bible for themselves. There was also another problem—whatever was happening on the television media was not utilized through the local church. Therefore, it was not building the ministry of local fellowships of believers.

After a number of tests, we decided to use videotape instead. What we are now doing is making this kind of a study system available to local churches so that they can utilize it in a variety of ways. It has been used in such ways as prayer meeting Bible studies, adult classes, and young people's classes.

Once people have been through this series in their own church classes, they feel comfortable in inviting people into their own homes to do a Bible study of an evangelistic and outreach nature. What we found has been very exciting to me, because I am not an evangelist by my gifts. There have been many people who have come to Christ through these Bible studies. For example, one group with twenty teenagers met in the home of a youth pastor on Wednesday nights to study the Bible. Five of those young people came to know the Lord during that thirteen-week study!

Another young man was interested in the Bible, but was not interested in coming to church, reading a Christian book, going to a class, attending lectures, or even coming over to someone's house to study the Bible. When this twenty-six-year-old man heard of the television Bible study, he said, "Yeah, I'll come over." He not only came; he accepted the Lord. Somehow, people who have been brought up in a media culture are responsive to the media approach.

The main point is this: it *is* possible, in spite of what tradition has done to churches and people, to use carefully designed educational systems and modern technology, which will help people interact with Scripture and each other in a Biblical way. *It is possible even in the most traditional settings.* People *can* accept transition, to experience that which they do not now understand. After they have experienced it, they can then be taught to implement the simple Biblical principles of Deuteronomy. It *can* happen!

11. Technology and Future Church

Eugene Kerr

Eugene Kerr has received his doctorate in the field of education. In addition, he has a wide range of academic and practical experience relating educational processes to modern technology. He is currently the Northwest District Manager of Control Data Education Company.

I would like to help you accept the fact that *God* provides the technological knowledge we now possess! It is through his grace that all of the electronic devices we now possess have been invented, and they are to be used for his glory.

It was also through his grace that a Christian school teacher with whom I worked made me realize that I had a need for Jesus Christ in my life. As a new Christian, I joined our evangelical, Bible believing church. They looked at me and said, "Here is a man who has great talent and skills in teaching, recreation, and education [my fields at the time]. Let's use him immediately!" So, I became a Sunday school teacher and a youth leader with literally no background in the Scriptures. I was very successful as a youth leader. I had a lot of skills that I had developed in the secular world, but unfortunately my work was not biblically based. No one in that church ever sought to discover whether I was doing things from the *Lord's* point of view, or whether I was just operating as I would have in any other social group. The trouble was, of course, that I was totally "secular" in what I was doing in the church. That led to no personal growth, and that led in turn to disappointment in my ministry. I didn't really enjoy serving the Lord; it became a duty, an obligation. I very quickly came into a period of doubting and questioning.

The Lord was gracious, however. He brought some problems into my life that caused me to stop and look at my experience as a Christian. As I fellowshipped with a pastor who discipled me, I discovered there is a lot more to Christianity than just "playing the game." That eventually led me to search out what God might do with my life. With many others, I did not clearly see his plan for a long period of time. I was ambitious. I came from a material-istically-oriented generation. I wanted to be successful. I got into industry and was very successful. I became the president of my own company. It was then acquired by a large corporation. All through this, I still did not see what God had for me. Though I was working and ministering in the church, I did not see any clear direction from the Lord for my life.

In 1970, I was involved with computers and education in the secular world. I was speaking to a large group of educators in the state of Utah. I had been invited there by the State Board of Education and some of the university staff, and I was sharing with them the use of computers in education. They were raising a lot of questions and problems, very similar to the ones pastors raise with me today: "Isn't this impersonal? Isn't this technology expensive?" I said, "Yes, that's all true." But, I was saying to *myself:* "You know, these problems are real—but what is the *result* of what is happening *here?* Why use my life to give people a *general* education? If I am going to contribue to the educating of people, how much more valuable it would be to do it in the light of the Lord's purposes for man! From that point forward, God has led me to make my goal in life not to become a corporate executive or a millionaire, but to seek out the ways that technology might help Christians. Technology can do much in the area of instructing others in the use of the Bible, and showing them how to grow as a Christian.

Unfortunately, even though I was on the cutting edge of my field at the time, my forecast was that it probably would be 1990 before we could even hope to consider the use of technology in an educa-tional setting within the Christian church. But, through his grace again, the Lord has allowed open minds among church leaders to develop much more rapidly than I anticipated. Major corporations, including the one I currently work for, have started to pour millions and millions of dollars into this whole field of technology. What Control Data Corporation *alone* has done has moved technology in education ahead at least ten to fifteen years. Secularization of our Christian environment, as Os Guinness points out, has not only *overcome* us, but has *permeated* our lives. We, in Christianity, unfortunately have gone to the secular world for our models. How we apply technology and new systems or techniques has not yet been done from a biblical base. Let me illustrate.

I was invited to speak to a group of pastors. They were related to a large denomination in a major city. The whole objective of this particular Friday and Saturday retreat was to develop a set of goals. Sounds like *business;* of course, that is exactly what it was! The group was to set goals for their particular organization. We gathered together on Friday evening and started the process. I just sat back as an observer, not participating. They met in small groups, using industrial goal-planning techniques. That is what I do in my business life. I consult with industry, showing them the applications of "systems technology." I do a lot of this with very large corporations. About 3 o'clock on Saturday afternoon, we had been focusing down very rapidly (as is supposed to happen in these kinds of exercises), and were to come out with ten goals before 5 o'clock. The moderator said, "Go back to your small groups. Each group is responsible for a goal based on the area that has been assigned." My pastor got up and said, "Wait a minute . . . We have been going almost two days now, and not once have we prayed for God's guidance. We have used new techniques, we have played simulation games, and things of that sort. Yet not once have we sought God's guidance and spiritual help, or sought the help of his Holy Spirit in our decision process. I really think before we close we ought to pray about what *God* wants us to do." All of the other pastors agreed—but they had been afraid to do so. The church leaders didn't know how to deal with the new technology. They used it as a substitute for seeking *God's* plans for his church. That is the *wrong* use of technology! We live in that kind of environment. We can easily fall into being seduced by technology.

Technology, in itself, is not evil. Technology is a tool which is available to us by the grace of God. Technology which can be useful in Christian service does not come along very often. Technology has mainly touched our lives in the area of the business world, and it is now invading our homes. We forget that this *printed* Bible shattered the world—the result of technology which came from Gutenberg. The initial thought of the inventors and developers of the printing press was to print God's Word. That was their *immediate* thought! The new technology would be used to print God's Word. I am sure the Lord oversaw the whole procedure. Historians tell us that the printing press was a major factor in the Reformation, the modernization of Europe, and of America's development. The printing press made a significant change in everyone's life-style.

Today, industry has used the new electronic technology to cause new revolutions. Their motive is, "How much money can one make?" . . . not the question of, "How can this be used for the glory of God?" That has been a real burden on my heart. That burden has led me into the ministry that I am in today. Even though I am still working in industry, I have set myself to educating Christians in this area, and bringing unused technology to bear on Christian problems. Technology is almost impossible to keep up with; it's changing so rapidly that even those of us who are in the field cannot keep up with it. It took about 200 years for Bibles and books to be distributed among the western cultures after the printing press was invented. It was not common for people to have a book in America—except for a Bible in their homes—until after 1900. The massive use of books has not been with us for very long!

Because of the rapid implementation of communication and computer technology, it will invade the home in a period of no more than six to ten years at the most, and probably within three to five years. Computers now interactively communicate and teach. I can send a message today to any place in Europe or in the United States or Canada in seconds. There are over 150 sites today where people can sit at a terminal and be taught by the same computer. That is just the tip of the iceberg as far as technology is concerned! Projections are that by 1985 there will be 10 million such computers and terminals, located in peoples' homes within middle-class America. They will be accessing all kinds of education, learning activities, and entertainment.

Industry knows this is taking place. There are four major companies in industry that are gearing up right now to get into this business in the 80's. Those four major companies have more dollar resources and financial resources than 90 percent of the nations of the world, with the exception of the 30 or 40 major countries! These economically powerful corporations will create a rapid dispersion of this technology not only in the United States, but across the whole world! There will not be a continent or a major city in the earth where interactive education will not be available by 1985.

Cost factors are going down. This technology is the only thing in the world that is dropping in cost. In banking, when I got into the computer industry in 1961, we were spending about $100,000 a month for a computer to do bank processing work. A year ago last Christmas I bought my son a small micro-computer for his own personal use. That computer was *more powerful* than the computer that we rented in 1960 for $100,000 a month! It cost me $600. That cost will *again* be cut in half *this year*. By 1990, scientists tell us that the Library of Congress will be storable in a unit about the size of a church pulpit.

If we think that *television* is a powerful detriment to our society, wait until the unscrupulous people who are now trying to make money from media—along with totalitarian regimes who use behavioral techniques—control the children of the world. It's a scary kind of thing—but at the same time, *we* are here by God's grace. We need to free ourselves from cultural entrapments. We do not have the possibility of saying, "This is 2,000 to 3,000 years in the future!"

About four to five years ago, I used to visit with churches and pastors and discuss these things. People would say, "Oh, that sounds Buck Rogerish. That may come about in the year 2250. Maybe 100 years from now we can look forward to that—or, at the soonest, twenty to thirty years." Of course, that is *not* the case at all. The new technology is going to be upon us *shortly*.

How is it going to be used in the church? A number of projects are already under way. A major area is the use of computers for making Bible research material available in the home. Many of us now use libraries and Christian books, but most of us don't have ready access to in-depth research, archeology, and so forth. I am now working with a seminary trying to establish a nationwide network and eventually a worldwide network that will make such knowledge available, first of all, to churches. Then, as the technology becomes available in the next three to four years, it can be furnished to homes. Anyone who has the desire could do in-depth research in fields of Christian education, any aspect of the Bible, or biblical knowledge. We now have the ability to do these kinds of things. As with the printing press, we must make the Bible the basis for truth. The Bible is the key to making use of technology. The

Christian who studies and searches the Bible will find himself the most profited person when it comes to using these new technologies God has provided.

The church, however, does not seem to be searching the Scriptures to see what *it* should do. I say that in love. I'll give one example: A local church was looking at learning materials. Videotaped Sunday School materials—the finest yet produced—were introduced. Like a lot of things that are new, it takes a lot of education to train people to make use of such things. I returned to the church after a brief period of time, and discovered they were just in the process of throwing out these materials. You see, they were not like the "traditional" *written* materials that had been used in the past. I had been aware of these new materials, and considered them to be among the most scripturally sound in the country!

The majority of Christian education materials that use a lot of Bible do not follow the *pattern* that God would have us use in the *education* of people. I then taught a class to the leaders of that church. It took about six months. We went through the Bible, discovering what it says about Christian education. Finally, a couple of the members of the Christian education committee members said, "Wow! That's why those new materials were the way they were! They had a theologically sound base."

The materials were *theologically* sound from a scriptural point of view. However, the leaders and policy makers for the Christian education program of that local church had never searched the Bible to find out *what* "Christian education" should be. *Have you?* We accept materials without questioning their ability to get the task accomplished. The materials had been thrown out originally because they did not follow the pattern of these older materials. That church group is now doing a biblical examination of other materials, and finding a tremendous amount of holes, biblically speaking, in the methods they use to transmit truth. My point is that sometimes we just do not operate from a Bible base of education. Technology can, and hopefully will, help us to search the Scriptures. It can assist the local church first, and then move into the homes of believers.

In the same study, we examined the area of how much Christian education *really* takes place in the church. Statistically speaking, an elementary school child will watch more *television* in a *month or two* than he will receive Christian education in the church *in his whole elementary school career,* from grades one through six! Yet, we expect that such Christian education will give him a Christian life-style. It's impossible.

It is no wonder my generation is biblically ignorant. My generation is now taking over the leadership of churches from elderly people who were *not* biblical illiterates. Unfortunately, we do not have the biblical knowledge to make *Christian decisions.* Where does technology fit here? Consider an individualized program for learning how to be a Christian parent that will be video as well as computer based. It will use a lot of the techniques Larry Richards has pioneered in Christian curriculum. It will *also* provide *interaction* with a computer, providing the ability for people to see for themselves the mistakes they are making. It will ask them *hard* questions. Their answer will be "private," with no loss of face if they are wrong. Consider the constructive criticism that faulty parenting can receive using technology.

We are also working with some people in an area we call "individualized revival." This is a combination of technology, plus small-group sessions, to inventory the spiritual lives of Christians. Imagine a man driving up to your church in a small truck. He converts a room into a learning center. Members take inventories of their Christian life, using conversation with a computer. They then come together and share their felt needs. One of the problems we now face is that people are a lot more willing to communicate with a computer about their *real selves* than to communicate with each other in small-group settings. It may take six to nine weeks to get to know other persons well enough to be willing to share with them inner problems. For some reason, when a person "talks" to a computer console, and nobody has access to the information, it is different. The computer quizzes him about what he is *really* like. He is more likely to explore that subject with a computer, and find out what it means biblically to live the Christian life. Computers have a lot of potential in these areas. Other areas, such as pastoral continuing education, can also be strengthened. It is a very threatening thing to some pastors to be evaluated by their peers. Computers can help a pastor, in a totally *impersonal* way. However, many people are also threatened by a *computer* evaluation. Does that sound strange?

Why is being evaluated by a computer threatening? My experience in the secular world tells us why. Teachers are definitely

afraid of computers, because *it threatens their jobs*. That runs all
the way from public school teachers through university professors.
They are definitely afraid of computers. It is very hard for a man
who has a Ph.D. to say, "I'm really afraid of that machine; it could
take my job away from me." He doesn't say that. He says things
like: "Well, I think that will apply to *engineering*, but it doesn't
apply to *literature*. I think that computers will really apply to
solving math problems, but it just can't help in philosophy and
things of that sort." You go to the engineering school, and the
professor says: "I can see where that might work in teaching people
basic music, but I can't understand how it could ever work in
engineering." I think we will see the same kind of threat at the
pastoral level, because what we're really doing is threatening
peoples' very livelihood, the place where they get their ego support. We might wish that in a Christian setting that would not exist,
but unfortunately it does exist. A pastor feels very good about what
he is doing, because he is the fellow standing up there talking to
everybody. The Sunday School teacher likes his job because he
gets to be the expert for an hour, and he needs ego support. That's
not scriptural, of course, but it *is* the real world.

What happened when the Bible was first printed? Was it welcomed with open arms by the church? Was the translation printed
in English accepted? We might think churchmen would just run out
and welcome the translator with open arms! No . . . they burned
him at the stake. The preacher said, "How *dare* you allow my
people to learn about the Bible and God? They need to come
through *me* as priest and preacher to learn about God. They are
uneducated. They cannot understand God's Word without my
interpretation." Have we changed much? I do not think so.

How soon will the new computer technology be available? What
is it going to cost. The cost of computers is going down. They will
be cheaper than the price of a TV set within two years. They could
be in *any* home, in *every* home, and within two to three years.

The biggest use I see for this system in the near future will be to
ask people hard questions about their Christian faith, because most
Christians are really afraid to face that issue with other people.
Most of us are really afraid to be challenged by our brothers with
the hard questions about whether we are *really* living a Christian
life. If we apply technology as it should properly be applied, it will
enhance the fellowship and brotherhood of the church, reinforcing

it. The Bible is the major resource for day-to-day living and the performing of Christian ministries. This means that foundation programs will concentrate on the improvement of *biblical* instruction, and also emphasize the practical use of the Bible in the everyday life of all believers. That is where technology can be a tool to help us. I pray, as it says in First Corinthians, that *all* we do might be to the glory of God. I am convinced we *can* apply new technology for that purpose!

12. Oikos Evangelism:
Key to the Future

Thomas A. Wolf

Rev. Tom Wolf has been pator of the Church on Brady in Los Angeles for ten years. During that time the church has gone from stagnation to exciting growth and vision in a changing, pluralistic community. He and the church are featured in the film: They Said It Couldn't Be Done. *Rev. Wolf is married and has three sons. He obtained his education from Moody Bible Institute, Baylor University, and the School of World Missions, Fuller Seminary.*

In the Los Angeles Southern Baptist Association he is chairman of the Committee on Discipleship and Church Growth. He is also a part of the American Institute of Church Growth lecture team. His lectures on Church Growth, Comparative Religions and Apologetics in universities and seminaries across the country are calling for new levels of commitment and skill to meet the cry of the future.

Today many churches are almost overwhelmed by the task of evangelizing their own communities. Exhortations to evangelize the world only further darken the cloud of guilt and frustration. To this picture we add the future with its ominous speed, mass, pressure, and confusion; we wonder: What is the key to evangelism?

But, by cleaning the lenses of our socio-historical spectacles, we can gain perspective regarding the future, wrestle with the impact of our calling, and discover the kind of evangelism that will reach the masses of the future. Oikos Evangelism is normative, New Testament evangelism. It is the God-given and God-ordained means for naturally sharing the supernatural message. It tran-

scends cultures and is relevant to the struggles of any generation.
In considering the Church of the Future, three sharp focal points
come into view:

1. Shape of the future
2. Strategy for the future
3. Stasis of the present

THE SHAPE OF THE FUTURE

From the front door of the present, I can see the outlines of the
future silhouetted against the horizon of the 21st century. As best
as I can discern it, the shape of the future is *urban*, and the shape of
the future is *open*.

The Future Is Urban

It should not be too surprising that the future will be urban. After
all, the past has been urban. World history is urban history.

> Anyone who scrutinizes the history of cities will not only redis-
> cover world history; he will see it more compact and in sharper
> focus, more colorful and more cruel. Whenever there were wars,
> cities were starved, plundered, burned down, completely leveled
> by furious hatred. Whenever revolutions took place, they origi-
> nated in cities or were aimed at cities. Whenever a culture came
> to full bloom, it was connected with the name of a city: Babylon,
> Athens, Rome, Florence, Paris, Vienna, Weimar. At times, the
> power that ruled half the earth was concentrated in a single city:
> Rome, Byzantium, Baghdad, Peking, Madrid, London, Mos-
> cow."[1]

But to say the future is urban *does* cause surprise, even more,
alarm. For the urban past was far different from the urban future
speeding our way. In 1900, 13 percent of the world's population
lived in cities and 87 percent in rural areas. Within one century,
that will reverse. By 2000, 87 percent of the world will be urban, 13
percent rural. These figures hint at the four fundamental facts of
modern urbanization.

One fundamental fact is, the *incidence* of urbanization. Never
before has the majority of all the earth lived in or near urban
centers. But such will be the fact by A.D. 2000.

> Metropolitan Tokyo is greater than half the population of
> Canada, and the first 10 cities of India equal half the population of
> Britain. Our century began with only 11 cities with a population

of over 1 million, but today there are more cities than that in Asia alone, which claim populations of more than a million.[2]

Another fundamental fact is, the *influence* of urbanization.

All people everywhere are increasingly coming under the dominance of the urban centers and the influence of the urban way of life. This is virtually true now, but the process will be complete in the foreseeable future through the combined technology of communication, transportation, and politics, if not immediately, through direct industrial and economic development. Already such people as the great nomad tribe of the Masai of Eastern-Central-Africa, who once roamed freely with their cattle over thousands of miles, are now restricted to certain areas and are forced to pay taxes to their city-controlled governments.[3]

Significantly related to the influence of future urbanization is the primate city pattern across the world. A primate city is the dominant urban center of a nation. Characteristics of the primate city include: population concentration several times that of the nearest rivals; dominance in political, economic, educational, and cultural arenas, and greater growth than other urban areas. Take, for example, the urbanization pattern of Southeast Asia. Southeast Asia is one of the least urbanized areas in the Third World: in 1975, only about 10 percent of its population was in urban centers over 100,000. Only Africa and perhaps China have a lower level of urbanization when considering the regional blocks of the Third World.

T. G. McGee, geographer at Victoria University, New Zealand, points out that:

Of the urban population resident in centers of over 20,000 the percentage who are concentrated in the large cities exceeding 100,000 is 70 percent in Malaya and Singapore. It is thus not surprising that it is the 'great cities' which dominate the urban structure of Southeast Asia. In Burma, Thailand, Cambodia, South Vietnam, and the Philippines, the largest urban concentration is at least five times as large as its nearest rival. In Malaysia and Indonesia the dominance of the 'primate city' is unquestionably the most important feature of urban structure. So much so that the characteristics of the 'great cities' of Djakarta, Singapore, Rangoon, Bangkok, Manila, and Saigon-Cholon are justifiably held to be representative of the characteristics of the pattern of Southeast Asian urbanization[4]

But what is true of Southeast Asia is especially true in Latin America. Latin American urbanization is primate city urbanization. The largest city is normally the political capital, center of commerce and industry, and seat of culture, education and the arts.

In sixteen Latin American countries, the population of the primate city is almost 4 times that of the second largest city. Mexico City illustrates the primate pattern graphically. In the mid-70s, 8 million of Mexico's 48 million lived in metropolitan Mexico City. Yet, Guadalajara, Mexico's second ranking city, had not yet reached the million mark. The most extreme example of primate cities is Montevideo, Uruguay. Of Uruguay's 3.1 million, 85 percent are urban; and 38 percent of the nation lives in Montevideo. The influence of the Third World primate cities establish their strategic importance. The real, enduring victories will be won in the hearts of the masses in these urban jungles.

Another fundamental fact of modern urbanization is the *increase* of pace. The sheer speed of urbanization is different from what has ever gone before. In the past, the capacity for urban development was limited because of food production, trade-transportation, and communication. But in the 20-year-period, 1940-1960, Brazil's urban population rose 148 percent. Mexico City absorbs people at almost 1,500 each day—over one half million per year.

Harvard Professor, Harvey Cox, sinks the shaft of insight deep when he says:

> Future historians will record the 20th Century as that century in which the world became one immense city. We know already that America is an urban civilization. In one lifetime America has changed from an agricultural to a metropolitan nation.
> ....
> But America is not the pacesetter in urbanization. Overseas the transformation is even more jarring and accelerated. In fact, the most pertentous phenomenon of our time is the urbanization of the nonwestern world. The cities of India, for example, are growing at the rate of 50 percent per decade. They will have to absorb 140 million new immigrants from the villages before the end of this century. Already carts circulate through the teeming alleys of Calcutta every morning to shovel the dead from the sidewalk. Already the city is glutted to the point of paralysis by a daily increment of babies from heaven and immigrants from villages. But Calcutta's real problems still lie in the future. Un-

less its growth rate is greatly retarded, its present population of 2.5 million will have swollen to the staggering figure of 66 million by the turn of the century.[5]

And the press of the pace increases. Nothing stops the surge, as French anthropologist Claude Levi-Strauss describes:

> Filth, promiscuity, disorder, physical contact; ruins, shacks, exrement, mud; body moistures, animal droppings, urine, purulence, secretions, suppuration . . . everything that urban life is organized to defend us against, everything we loathe, everything we protect ourselves against at great cost . . . all these by-products of cohabitation never here impose a limit on its spread.[6]

Cox carries us further:

> The cauldrons of misery in Asia and Latin America need no cunning Communists to stir them up. They are already seething. Mobility and urbanization have supplied the revolutionary kindling; hunger and sickness add the kerosene. No spark need blow from Moscow or Peking, for such conditions in society can produce just as much spontaneous combustion as gasoline soaked rags in a suffocating attic.

> Hope and despair stride hand in hand in the new world city. In India 61 percent of the urban residents questioned told interviewers they would prefer to go back to their villages if they could. But they know that what awaits them there is only stagnation, sickness and death. With retreat cut off, the only alternatives remaining are resignation or insurrection. At the crossroads of the throbbing new cities of our new world, aspiration and bitterness collide. Out of the cities come life-giving medicines, thrilling new forms of art, the vision of life on a richer and vaster scale. Out of the same cities come the angry shriek of the beaten and oppressed and the sobs of hungry children.[7]

Sheer speed is the scream of the future. No wonder Alvin Toffler defines future shock as: "The shattering stress and disorientation that we induce in individuals by subjecting them to too much change in too short a time."[8]

Finally, the fact that makes today's urbanization unique from what has gone before is its *inversion*. Two items account for this inversion of the past's urban development: The *way* and *where* of current urbanization.

The Way Urbanization Has Happened

In the past, industrialization, economic development and urbanization have gone together. The urbanization of western, industrialized nations during the 19th and early 20th centuries experienced all three factors. Not so today. Third world urbanization is different, inverted. Kingsley Davis, Columbia University, explains:

> It is in this respect that the non-industrial nations, which still make up the great majority of nations, are far from repeating past history. In the nineteenth and early twentieth centuries the growth of cities arose from one half and contributed to economic advancement. Cities took surplus manpower from the countryside and put it to work producing goods and services that in turn helped to modernize agriculture. But today in underdeveloped countries, as in present-day advanced nations, city growth has become increasingly unhinged from economic development.[9]

Economic development, that broadly diffused rise in per capita income throughout the population, is not keeping pace. That is why J.D.N. Versluys, Social Sciences UNESCO, Paris, can write: "The most typical feature in city life, particularly in Asian countries, is the glaring difference between the rich and the poor. Where in western countries the ratio of income for a professional and an industrial worker may be 3 or 4 to 1, it is 15 or 20 to 1 in Asia or even higher."[10]

This striking difference between the rich and the poor even in their dwellings also shocks the observer. The filth and squalor of the bustees of Calcutta are indescribable. The descent from manicured lawns to miserable lean-tos is steep. Seventy-nine percent of Calcutta's families live in rooms 5 x 10, (that's smaller than the average American bathroom). In these small quarters a whole family will sip, sweat, spit, sleep, and have sex.

Where Urbanization Is Occurring

Where urbanization is occurring is also part of the contemporary and future difference. Until 1975, United Nations' studies showed that the majority of the world's urban masses lived in more developed countries (MDCs). Since 1975, however, the balance has shifted. Now for the first time in recorded history, the majority of the world's urban population is in the less-developed countries (LDCs).

According to UNESCO projections, between 1950-2000, LDCs urban population will increase almost eight times. MDCs increase will only be 2.4 times. Therefore, while only one third of the world's urban population lived in LDCs in 1950, two thirds of the world's 3.1 billion urban inhabitants will live in LDCs by A.D. 2000. This also means that from 1950-1975, LDC cities absorbed about one third (35.3 percent) of global population increase. But between 1975-2000, these same LDC cities will absorb more than half (53.4 percent) of the increase of 1.2 billion new persons.[11]

Never before has urbanization happened in this way. All is inverted. Never before has city growth been unhinged from economic development. And never before has the explosive growth of cities occurred in the nations least able to respond. The kerosene fumes spread.

First then, the shape of the future is urban. This is not only the first fact of the future, it is the great fact of the future. It is the umbrella fact, the overshadowing fact. In the *incidence* of future urbanization we see a unique fact of human history: never before has the majority of the earth lived in or near urban centers. In the *influence* of future urbanization we are confronted with new forces: the dominance of a single primate city on multitudes. Also giving significant shape to future urbanization is the *increase* of tempo, the sheer rapidity of population increase. But the urban future will also be different from all that has gone before by the inversion of all patterns to this point:the disassociation of urbanization from economic development and the concentration of the world urban masses in less-developed countries.

The Future Is Open

The same forces shaping an urban future converge to shape an openness in the urban masses of the future. The bold new fact of urbanization is fracturing the mold of the past . . . the rural past. From birth in the city, men are severed from contact with nature, the regular order of the seasons. Urban man is without roots, without traditions. The migrant to the city has no ready-made, accepted community. The world urban dwellers of the future have several distinguishing characteristics.

First, the urban man is *lonely*. Surrounded by millions, he knows very few. Faces flood his consciousness, but tears fill his eyes. The urban dweller is usually from somewhere. And that somewhere was smaller, more manageable, more intimate than the new urban complex. The more rural setting was close-knit with face-to-face primary relationships. The city is diverse, impersonal, institutional. The laughter of loneliness mocks him under the night's neon lights. He would prefer to return to his village like 61 percent of those urban residents interviewed in India, but retreat is cut off. Little is here, but nothing is there. The somebody of the small town is another nobody in the urban center. From his homogeneous security he is catapulted into heterogeneous anonymity.

Second, the urban man is *lean*. Millions in Africa, Latin America, and Asia have left their peasant, small-town past. Forging into the urban future, they arrive at the terminal only to find themselves alone and near the bottom of the socioeconomic scale.

Between 1948-1960, Cairo doubled in population, but available living quarters rose by only 15 percent. Thousands more migrate into misery. In 1960, some 275,000 Italian peasants abandoned their fields and rural poverty. By moving to Rome, they now live in "horrible barracks, in caves, and in sheet-metal shacks, in even more wretched and squalid conditions than they endured in their villages."[12] Nightmares cannot match the mire, the filth and the flies of the unemployed poor of Calcutta. And since the reasonably successful individual has less incentive to move, it is usually the ambitious unsuccessful who migrate. But, in spite of starvation wages, wretched working conditions, and appalling accommodations, the urban unskilled usually fare better than the toiling farmworker. With higher wages for ligher work during fewer, more regular hours the urban man may be lean, but tonight he will sleep in the city. Tomorrow he will choose another day among the crowds.

A third distinguishing characteristic marks the urban dweller. He is *longing*. Man cannot live by bread alone. The ruthless money economy of the city, the merciless materialism of the populace may strip down his value system. Life may mean little more than trying to get coins for mere existence, a place for the family. But the heart longs for more. Inflation intensifies the insistence for the infinite. Urban man is a searching man. He is lost, wandering in a far country. The gods of the past seem so inadequate here, yet the forces of the supernatural, especially the evil supernatural, are so evident. Many shed the amulets of village gods for the clothes of secular scorn. But darkness knows many forms. Demons of darkness crowd the streets of Bangkok, Bombay, and Brazilia; superstition and the supernatural is alive in Mexico City; and deep longings claw the mind in Long Island as well as Los Angeles.

Fourth, the urban man is *listening*. Many in the city have ears that can hear. Radio reaches everywhere. Television touches millions. Satellites shower down imput. Mark it well: in all six continents, the rootless are responsive. Jarred from old associations, standard social and religious patterns, migrating city dwellers are searching. "People away from home are off balance . . . impressed by what they would have considered unthinkable or strange back home. . . . As Ed Dayton points out, the migrant is forced to be a 'learner in the city. New ways are accepted out of necessity.'"[13] So out of the hardship, suffering, sacrifice and survival, he learns to listen . . . to new voices . . . to many voices, and listen he does. It is from this lonely-lean-longing-listening urban man that the openness of the future is forged.

"The strategic people are the responsive people." Edward Murphy, Professor of Missions, Biola College, speaks of a theology of harvesting the responsive. God has sent us to reap a spiritual harvest, not just sow seeds. Thus, genuine evangelism will bring people to Christ and incorporate them into local churches. Anything less is sub-Christian, for New Testament evangelism *intends* church growth.

Therefore, the theological truth of responsiveness must be grasped. God intends that those who want to be liberated have a higher priority than those who resist liberation. That is why Jesus told the disciples to let responsiveness determine the "where" of church planting. Wherever people firmly rejected the message, the disciples were to disassociate from that group and pass on to more responsive people (Matt. 10:14; Mark 6:11; Luke 9:5). Paul's actions in Acts 13:43-52 and 18:1-6 evidence the use of that criterion in the early church.[14]

Urbanization encourages openness, and openness will be part of the future. Those moving to the cities are open, looking for new jobs, new opportunities. The urban man is free: free to experiment, free from restraints, free to think in new channels, free to accept Christ.

The cities of the future will be filled with migrants. Studies show that for the first ten to fifteen years after arrival, the urban new-comer is especially open to new ideas, including the gospel. That is why urban strategist, Ralph Neighbour, Jr., reminds us: "Reaching migrants is one of the oldest successful strategies for evangelism. Migrants took the gospel to the Roman empire. The seed of the Word of God was not scattered everywhere in equal measure. It was sown specifically among the *diaspora*, the migrants. Such groups are often more responsive in the city than in the village."[15]

For example, only 1 percent of Japan's population is Christian. But 43 percent of the 700,000 Japanese in Brazil are Christians. And though less than 1 percent of mainland Chinese were Christians after 10,000 missionaries worked among them, 7 percent of the 40 million Chinese world migrants are Christians today. Or again, 57 percent of Brazil's total population lived in urban centers in 1970. The cities of Sao Paulo, Rio de Janeiro, and Belo Horizonte constitute Brazil's triangle of urbanization. The highest growth rates of evangelicals is in the terminal points of immigration into the urban triangle. And so the future forms firm outlines. The future is urban. And the masses of our future are, and will be, open.

THE STRATEGY FOR THE FUTURE

But to many, the future forebodes dismal disarray for the church. What can be done in the face of such horrendous numbers, such crushing speed, such staggering rootlessness? Can the gnashing numbers realistically hold anything other than the numbing of hope and initiative? Is not the impending future also the impenetrable future? Not really. For hysteria hurries too quickly to our side. That place, however, is reserved for another: the Comforter called to the side of the early church.

We have already noted that world history is urban history. But too often we have forgotten that early Christianity was urban Christianity. Question: How did that early urban Christianity spread? How did the primitive faith become the pervasive faith? The critical dimension can be found in R. Kenneth Strachan's dictum: "The expansion of any movement is in direct proportion to its success in mobilizing its total membership in continuous propagation of its beliefs."[16]

Applied to the church, that means: *Early urban Christianity experienced what appeared to be spontaneous, explosive expansion in direct proportion to its success in mobilizing its total mem-*

bership in the continuous propagation of the Good News of Jesus. And this fact has not gone unnoticed by historians of the Roman period. K. S. Latourette, Sterling Professor of Missions and Oriental History, Yale University, explains that the primary change agents in the spread of the faith in those urban situations were not professional missionaries, but the mobilized "men and women who earned their livelihood in some purely secular manner and spoke of their faith to those whom they met in this natural fashion."[17]

Almost a century ago, Adolf Harnack stressed the fact that the church did not grow just because of spectacular confessors and martyrs. Instead, Harnack was quite clear, "All who seriously professed Christ participated in propagating the faith. In the middle of a suffocating swamp of moral decay and social disintegration, informal missionaries, women as well as man, made a profound impression on pagan neighbors by their moral life."[18]

C. G. Kromminga, writing for the Vrije University in Amsterdam, The Netherlands, says:

> With respect to the early period especially . . . we are able to document the fact that ordinary believers spontaneously propagated the faith which had come to them as astounding good news. The spontaneous communication of the gospel by the members of the church appears to have increased rather than diminished in the early post-apostolic age. In fact, up to the issuance of the Edict of Milan in A.D. 312, the spontaneous transmission of the gospel by the life and witness of ordinary church members appears to have been one of the chief reasons for the rapid spread of Christianity throughout the Roman Empire.[19]

Rapid expansion, then, denotes high mobilization of membership in continuous transmission of the message of the early church. Total membership mobilization was the arrow. But what was the target? Whatever it was, they hit the bull's eye. They certainly hit center mark in their outreach . . . they were *on target* in their ability to bring large numbers to Christ.

The target struck by the arrow of the highly mobilized early urban church was the *oikos*, the household. An oikos was one's sphere of influence, his social system composed of those related to each other through common bonds of kinship ties, tasks, and territory.

The household of the Graeco-Roman culture was a basic unit of that society. It was broader than the nuclear family, for the oikos household included one's entire estate, people and property forming one interlocking sphere of influence.

The strategic importance of the oikos in the capture of the cities is startling. They were right on target. Their accuracy was uncanny. Their penetration power was undeniable. Equally amazing is the illumination shed on the significance of the oikos in the light of recent anthropological studies. In fact, one of the purest rays of hope penetrating into the cities of the coming generation is from this research.

Several fundamental insights from contemporary anthropology can help us understand more clearly the biblical pattern of evangelism which flowed so freely, fearlessly, and forcefully through that first urban church. For cultural anthropology has documented three cultural universals relevant to our investigation. According to anthropological research, three universal units of societies are the social systems of:

1. Kinship
2. Community
3. Association

David G. Mandelbaum, Professor of Anthropology, University of California, Berkeley, explains:

> Whatever diversity there may be among social groupings the world over, there are at least two types which are found in every human society. The *family* is one of them . . . . In every land, among every people, the child is ordinarily raised and nurtured within a family.
> . . . .
> The other type of group universal to humanity . . . is the *local community*. Just as no person normally lives all his life alone, devoid of any family, so does no family normally live entirely alone, apart from any local group . . . of neighbors.

Mandelbaum goes on to point out a third group (the clan) which is also a cultural universal, if one allows for its evolution in the contemporary Western setting. The clan has developed into ". . . the social units which are extensions of the local group . . . *voluntary associations* based on common interests."[20]

Paul G. Hiebert, Professor of Anthropology, University of

Washington, gives pertinent clarification when he writes about the three cultural universals of kinship, community, and association:

> One of the few cultural universals is that of groups based on the principles of *kinship*. This does not mean that all societies have the same kind of families or even see kinship ties in the same ways; in fact, humans have developed a surprising variety of simple kinship groups. But in some form or other, kinship groups are found in all societies.
>
> Many Americans grow up with few important kinship ties other than those of their immediate family and are surprised to learn of the elaborate and varied kinship systems found in many parts of the world. Relationships to kinsmen take precedence over other social bonds in much of the world. Kinship groups serve important functions in all societies, particularly in less complex ones.
>
> *Associations* play an important part in all societies. By organizing roles, setting norms, allocating authority, and mobilizing resources, they provide the organization necessary to achieve certain tasks. They also help to integrate a society and to provide the people within it with a sense of identity and belonging.
>
> Associations are organized on a great many bases: friendship, sex, age, power, prestige, and common interest are a few. Moreover, in urban societies, kinship groups often play a decreasing part in organization above the level of the family. The result is rapid growth in the numbers and types of associations.
>
> *Geography* ranks with kinship and association as one of the important principles by which human groups are organized. As we have already noted, kinship and associational groups are influenced in large measure by the geographic distribution of their members. For instance, family members and relatives who live in the same town generally have more to do with with one another than with kinsmen who live in a distant city.
>
> The basic stable geographic group is the "community," a territorially localized group of people, in which the members satisfy most of their daily needs and deal with most of their common problems. Communities are found in all societies, from the simplist bands to the most complex cities."[21]

Now let us go one step further. Since this triunity of social systems is a part of present-day human life, would we be so surprised to discover the same central characteristics in the human matrix of social life in the times of the New Testament? That is in fact exactly what we find. For this phenomenon is not only transcultural, it is also transhistorical, reaching across centuries.

The apostolic church used the interlocking social systems of common kinship/community/interests . . . the oikos . . . as the backbone for communicating the gospel. The basic thrust of New Testament evangelism was not individual evangelism, not mass evangelism, and was definitely not child evangelism. The normative pattern of evangelism in the early church was *oikos evangelism.*[22]

Oikos Evangelism is the God-given and God-ordained means for naturally sharing his supernatural message. It is sharing the astoundingly good news about Jesus in one's own sphere of influence, the interlocking social systems composed of family, friends, and associates. So then, oikos corresponds to what contemporary anthropologists define as the three universal social systems of common kinship, common community, and common interest.

Michael Green, in *Evangelism in the Early Church,* confirms that "the [oikos] family understood in this broad way, as consisting of blood relations, slaves, clients, and friends, was one of the bastions of Graeco-Roman society. Christian missionaries made a deliberate point of gaining whatever households they could as lighthouses, so to speak, from which the gospel could illuminate the surrounding darkness . . . . [We are, then,] quite right in stressing the centrality of the [oikos] household to Christian advance."[23]

Cornelius of the Italian cohort is a case in point. Acts 10 has a casually given, though faithful, definition of oikos. It says that "Cornelius feared God with all his oikos/household" (10:2). An angel of God instructed Cornelius to send for Peter, saying "He will declare to you a message by which you will be saved, you and all your [oikos] household" (Acts 11:14, RSV). When Peter arrived, Cornelius was expecting them and had "called together his kinsmen and close friends . . . many persons" (Acts 10:24,27).

But now, other questions arise. If the oikos, that sphere of influence composed of kin, friends and associates, was the channel of conversion in the early church, and if those three social systems are intrinsic to all human cultures, and if these are not only transcultural but also transhistorical, then why are the channels so often not working today? It worked for the first urban church. Why does the contemporary church languish in so many places if the same three systems function today. And what is the word for the future?

The early church spread vibrantly through oikos evangelism, captivating those who saw before their own eyes, the old sinner of the family become the new saint; neighbors who saw such a difference as peace and joy invaded their old friend; associates in the local trade union or the athletic events who asked about the transformation.

It is here that we stand before the stark, straight and searching key to oikos evangelism: *life transformation*. For if *oikos evangelism* is God's key to the natural and rapid spread of the Good News, then *life transformation* is the Holy Spirit's key to oikos penetration and persuasion.

"Believe in the Lord Jesus, and you shall be saved, you and your [oikos] household" (Acts 16:31, RSV). That is the promise God gave to the manic depressive, suicidal prison guard in the Philippi Municipal Prison during earthquake aftershocks of 7.5 on the Richter scale. It was an Asian talking, not an American. In one gulp of air, under intense pressure, Paul pointedly proclaimed: "You and your oikos!" Now an existentially conditioned, atomistic American with an individualistically isolated concept of personal salvation would probably have stopped with: "Believe in the Lord Jesus and you will be saved." But not so with the apostle: "You will be saved, you and your oikos." For the spread of the gospel is inherent in the sharing of the gospel.

It is the lack of life transformation that especially hinders the church from growing. Bill Gothard, lecturer for Basic Youth Conflicts Seminars, makes a telling point when he says the non-Christian has basically only two problems: First, he does not know a Christian. That is a problem of information. If a believer can make contact with the person, he will be able to hear, believe, and receive Christ. But the other problem of the non-Christian is: he *does* know a Christian. That is a problem of reputation. Because he knows a Christian and that believer's life does not adorn the doctrines of Christ, the unbeliever has no taste for the things of God, he has no attraction towards Christ. You may go to his home and talk about sin, salvation, and the Savior, but his ears are closed because of what he has seen in the life of the Christian: things he has found objectional, odious, offensive.

If, however, the believer's life has undergone genuine (though maybe not even rapid or dramatic) change, then the non-Christian will manifest amazing openness and responsiveness to the gospel message and life transformation is the key to that openness.

In Cali, Colombia, a group of eleven believers sought help to begin a church in Barrio Villa, Colombia. With just a few nights of evangelistic emphasis there were over 100 professions of faith. The decisions were followed immediately with studies in the Christian life. Public testimony of their new faith was the outcome. Investigation confirmed that 95 percent were either relatives or friends of the original eleven believers. Within a few months most of the new converts were baptized and formed into a vigorous church.[24]

Why such rapid spontaneous growth? Because of oikos evangelism. Believers shared Christ and invited to services those within their own spheres of influence . . . their family, friends, and associates. And because of the life transformation Christ had effected in their own lives, their oikoses had living proof, living verification of the message. Thus, life transformation is God's key to the penetration of any oikos. It is this pattern of natural, rapid growth along the natural social networks that accounts for the joyful proliferation of cells of Christians throughout Latin America. Without gun, gimmicks, or goading, the church can and will grow when believers' lives become living demonstrations of the Holy Spirit indwelling his people.

John Stuart Mill, in *On Liberty,* knew the kernel truth when he wrote, "And what is a still greater novelty, the mass do not now take their opinions from dignitaries in Church or State, from ostensible leaders, or from books. Their thinking is done for them by men much like themselves. Addressing them or speaking in their name, on the spur of the moment."

Sociologists have documented the same truth in other areas. In a report of the Bureau of Applied Social Research, Columbia University, Katz and Lazarfeld investigated the process of decision-making in daily household marketing, fashion, movie-going, and public affairs. Conclusion: The influence of prestige persons is fairly well restricted within narrow limits. The real influences are persons very much like the people they influence. Women influence other women in marketing, fashion, and entertainment trends. In public affairs, men (especially husbands) influence other men. What Katz and Lazarfeld have researched in this century has been recognized through the centuries in the business proverb:

word of mouth is the best advertising. Businessmen around the world agree that the most powerful and desirable form of recommendation for a product, a performance, or a precept is word of mouth recommendation by an enthusiastic owner or user.[25]

And so it is with the gospel. In Asia, Africa, or the Americas: oikos evangelism is normative evangelism. The word-of-mouth sharing about Jesus by persons very much like those they are sharing the Good News with. The conviction of the new convert is verified by life-style behavior changes. So that vibrant, personal verbalization with the lips and verification of the life is a potent persuasion for others. And with those conditions, you cannot keep the church from growing.

So it was for the first several hundred years of the early church. And so it must become in the next several decades in the urban church of the future. The past was won through the oikoses and the future; if it is won, it will be no different. But we are not in the future. We are in the present. Let us turn our attention for a moment to the present precipice overlooking the future.

THE STASIS OF THE PRESENT

Stasis is a medical term. Stasis is the slowing, stagnation, or stoppage of the normal flow of fluid in a vessel or semifluid material in an organ of the body. In the blood stream, stasis is the abnormal slowing of circulation in arteries or veins.[26] Applied to the church, stasis is any agent causing a slowing, stagnation, or stoppage of healthy church growth. There are two major stases in the present church which interact to impair the growth of the church:

1. The lack of pastoral incarnation
2. The lack of the people's mobilization

The first major stasis to the church growing is: *the pastor.* Bear in mind that I am a pastor. I know emergency calls in the middle of the night; problems of properties; little ones crying in the middle of my best sermon point; tears of weeping with broken hearts; hands weary under the load, shoulders strained by the hours; days off that aren't, and hugs from my boys (Chris, Shane, and Matt) after football in the street.

Study in the social sciences, observation of the business world, exposure to management concepts, exegesis of the Scriptures, experience garnered at Brady, and personal interviews with scores of pastors across this nation and on several continents have led me to a conviction. I have attempted to be unrestricted to imput and impartial about the direction the data would lead. But now, almost 20 years have passed. I am no longer undecided. I do hope my parochialism on this point is because I feel a compulsion to be partial to truth.

And the truth I see from where I stand is this: This major stasis-slowing, stagnation, stoppage of church growth in the present is the pastor. Not the people. Not the programs. Not the place. Not the province. The pastor. We cannot blame the people of God for not obeying our harangues when the real problem is that we won't pay the personal price of leadership so that they can respect, trust, and follow our direction. The pastor is the point of retardation to the local church being what God wants it to be entering the 21st century.

Throughout history when God blesses the multitudes, he calls a man. Churches today look for more money: a full church for finance. God searches for a man: a pure church for power. If his people are oppressed, he calls forth a Moses. If his people are affronted, he finds a David. If his people are scattered, he sends a Paul. And the work of God through the centuries has demanded of his men that they give their whole life. God's call is their consuming. What is disclosed in a moment is unfolded in a lifetime (Acts 9:15-16).

This is what is needed today: men with a vision for the cities, the urban centers clamoring over the walls of the future. Men with a willingness to lay down their lives in the streets so that the cities may know Jesus. A generation past went to the tribes. The next will be called to the tenements. Our fathers died of disease in the jungles. But we will fall ill in the intersections. And it will take a lifetime. No short sprints from church to church. But a lifelong work of hacking life from the dead, cold concrete quarries; rooted in one church for integrity and reaching across a city for impact. The emperor Decius declared that he would sooner have a rival emperor in Rome than a Christian bishop.

In the American present the average evangelical pastor will stay eighteen months in a church. Of course, some stay longer . . . three or four, maybe even six to eight years. But then they move on. And thus 50 percent of the churches have seventy-five or less on a Sunday morning; 80 percent have 200 or less, and 95 percent have

350 or less. Not only that, but the average conversions per church worldwide was two per church per year. Need we say more? That will never win our generation. Something must change. In the early church a pastor shepherded the same flock until he died. Even the emperor trembled under the shadow of a steady standard of righteousness. Pastors came and stayed. Emperors came and went. Today, politicans come and stay while preachers come and go.

We could learn some lessons from the Levites. Numbers 4:3,35,39,43,47 and 8:23-26 tell us about the service of the ministers of God. When we combine 1 Chronicles 23:24, 2 Chronicles 31:17 and Ezra 3:8 we find the full picture.

The two recurring points about the ministry of the Levites are: 1) Active service was twenty years (thirty to fifty years of age) and 2) apprenticeship ranged from five to ten years, beginning when twenty or twenty-five years old. No matter when a man began, he retired at fifty. Active duty (Numbers 4:3: saba, warfare) of 20 to 30 years was considered a legitimate and reasonable norm. That is still the accepted formula for retirement in the military, civil service, and other areas of business. After 50, the Levites could assist the service and frequent the sanctuary but they ceased to be on regular staff. They themselves no longer did the heavy work. In the prime of life they carried the burdens of the work; in retirement they knew the honor of the work.

Will Durant, in *The Story of Philosophy,* garners wisdom from Plato on the kind of man who is fit to rule the state.

> After five years of training in this recondite doctrine of ideas, . . . and after this long preparation from childhood through youth and into the maturity of thirty-five; surely now these perfect products are ready to assume the royal purple and the highest functions of public life?—surely they are at last the philosopher-kings who are to rule and to free the human race?

> Alas! not yet. Their education is still unfinished. For after all it has been, in the main, a theoretical education: something else is needed. Let these Ph.D.s pass down now from the heights of philosophy into the 'cave' of the world of men and things; generalizations and abstractions are worthless except they be tested by this concrete world; let our students enter that world with no favor shown them; they shall compete with men of business, with hard-headed grasping individualists, with men of brawn and men of cunning; in this mart of strife they shall learn from the book of

life itself; they shall hurt their fingers and scratch their philo-
sophic shins on the crude realities of the world; they shall earn
their bread and butter by the sweat of their high brows. And this
last and sharpest test shall go on ruthlessly for fifteen long years.
Some of our perfect products will break under the pressure, and
be submerged by this last great wave of elimination. Those that
survive, scarred and fifty, sobered and self-reliant, shorn of
scholastic vanity by the merciless friction of life, and armed now
with all the wisdom that tradition and experience, culture and
conflict, can cooperate to give—these men at last shall automatically become the rulers of the state.[27]

How much better we would be if no man was allowed to teach in
any ministerial training school until he had *done the work successfully for 20 years.* In the future, learning must be linked with life;
out of the local churches of the cities, young men must be appren-
ticed to do the work of the ministry. There they learn, observe, and
are tested. Then they are promoted according to character and gift,
authenticity and accomplishment.

In Latin America, the Pentecostal churches are doing just that.
Their explosive growth has little to do with their doctrine, for other
non-Pentecostal groups have grown just as fast by adopting their
simple system. Through an apprenticeship rather than an academic
training system they are capturing the cities. Congregations of
25,000 are common. Seoul, Korea alone has one church of 85,000
members.

It is time now to change two things for the future. The kind of
pastor: from a short-stay to a long-stay. And the kind of ministerial
training: from an academic model to an apprenticeship model.

In discussing the future, Earl Joseph, Editor of Minnesota
Futurists' *Future Trends,* makes two crucial points: 1. The world
that we will experience in five to twenty years is being shaped by
decisions made now. 2. Almost anything can be done in twenty
years.[28] If God has called you to pastor, go and lay down your life.
Go to stay twenty to thirty years.

According to the Ephesians exhortation (4:11 ff.) the function of
the pastor-teacher is to mobilize the believers for their ministries.
And their ministry is "to grow up in all aspects into him" (4:15; see
2:19-22). Therefore, believers are to live lives distinct from the
surrounding pagan patterns (4:17ff.). The result is evangelistic light
splattered everywhere (5:7ff.). This light is especially brilliant in the

quiet and clean new ways of living at home (5:21 to 6:4) and on the job (6:5-9). In this simple, basic process is the core of the spiritual battle: life transformation penetrating the connecting oikoses (6:10-17). The most intense prayer in all this is for boldness to speak as we ought (6:20). Such a "love incorruptible" (6:24) creates a church growth unstoppable.[29]

The clear concept men must have for the future is the concept of longevity for life-transforming equipping. Go to stay. Go to root among the rootless. Go to incarnate with the flesh of the city. Go and do not go back home. Go and make that city your home. Give it your life. Unfold your calling.

THE FUTURE IS OPTIONAL

Harvard theologian Harvey Cox delineates three strikingly different views of the future as seen by Christians. The three views are: apocalyptic, teleological and prophetic.

Apocalyptic motifs describe the future as dark and disastrous, encouraging fatalism, world negation, and a retreat from earthly chores. The world will come to a cataclysmic end. Cox concludes that their modern counterparts see only the disastrous end itself, a deeply antipolitical nihilism.

The teleological approach sees the future as the unfolding of an inherent universal purpose. Today's secularized teleology is embedded in Darwinian biology and points to a great intelligence moving toward still un-thought-out life forms.

The prophetic view is characteristically Hebrew. From deep biblical roots the prophetic stance says the future is an open field of human hope and responsibility. Cox makes the point that prophecy is not soothsaying. The pagan seer foretold the future because the gods had already determined all future events. To attempt to evade the future was futile.

But not so with the Hebrew prophets. To talk about the future in Hebrew prophecy was to get people to change their present behavior. The future, according to the Bible, is what Jehovah will do unless his people change their ways. The Lord of the past-present-future is free. He can change his mind. The future is a response. The future is our responsibility.

Cox says of prophecy:

> Prophecy insists that the future will be shaped not by invisible malevolent forces or by irresistible inherent tendencies but by

what men decide to do . . . This unconditional openness to the
future also allows prophecy to escape from the paralysis of past
decisions and policies. The prophetic call always requires repentance, the candid recognition that one has made mistakes, but
will now do something different. Policies need not be papered
over with spurious claims that they are simply extensions of
decisions made in the past. The prophetic perspective requires
incessant innovation and the continuous reappraisal of past
policies because tomorrow will not be just an unfolding of yesterday's tendencies but will include aspects of unprecedented
novelty.[30]

Standing within the doorway of a biblical perspective, I see the
future as optional: open to our input for good or evil. We know
the future will be urban. Intensely, immensely so. And we know
the future will be open. Undeniably, unquenchably so.

So our real root question is: what will we do with such a future?
The option is ours. We are not limited to the stagnating stasis of the
present. For God has given us his answer. It is locked into the
example of the early urban church: believe on the Lord Jesus and
you will be saved, you and your oikos. The spread of the gospel is
embedded within the sharing of the gospel. Anthropologists confirm what God has created: men live in the universal web-
relationships of family, community, and association. And when
lives are transformed in obedience to the indwelling Spirit of God,
oikoses are penetrated and open to Christ. Any movement will
expand in direct proportion to its success in mobilizing its total
membership in the continuous propagation of its beliefs.

The need of the future is a new generation of men who will give of
themselves in the urban centers of the world, the primate cities of
the LDCs to equip and mobilize the believers for their ministries in
their God-given and God-ordained oikoses. Oikos evangelism won
the urban centers of the first church. And oikos evangelism will
win the cities of the future church. Oikos evangelism: God's key to
the future.

NOTES

[1]Wolf Schneider, *Babylon is Everywhere* (New York: McGraw-Hill, 1963): 18.

[2]Roger Greenway, *An Urban Strategy for Latin America* (Grand Rapids: Baker, 1973): 217.

[3]Francis M. DuBose, *How Urban Churches Grow* (Nashville: Broadman, 1978): 28-29.

[4]T. G. McGee, *The Southeast Asian City* (New York: Prager, 1967): 23-24.

[5]Harvey Cox, "Mission in a World of Cities," *International Review of Missions* (July, 1966): 273.

[6]McGee, *Southeast Asian City:* 20.

[7]Cox, *International Review of Missions:* 275-276.

[8]Alvin Toffler, *Future Shock* (New York: Bantam Books, 1970): 2.

[9]Kingsley Davis, "The Urbanization of the Human Population," as quoted in Greenway, *An Urban Strategy:* 25.

[10]Nels Anderson, *Urbanism and Urbanization* (Leiden: E. J. Brill, 1964): 42.

[11]Roger Greenway (ed.), *Discipling the City* (Grand Rapids: Baker, 1979): 87.

[12]Schneider, *Babylon:* 315.

[13]Ralph W. Neighbour, Jr., *Strategic Planning for Urban Evangelism* (Nairobi: Brackenhurst Baptist Assembly, 1978): 5.

[14]Edward F. Murphy, "Guidelines for Urban Church-Planting," in Arthur F. Glasser, et. al., *Crucial Dimensions in World Evangelization* (Pasadena: William Carey, 1976): 248.

[15]Neighbour, *Strategic Planning:* 5. See also, W. R. Read, V. M. Monterroso and H. A. Johnson, *Latin American Church Growth* (Grand Rapids: Eerdmans, 1969): 236-243, 269-280.

[16]Kenneth Strachan, *Evangelism—In—Depth* (Chicago: Moody Press, 1961): 25.

[17]Kenneth Scott Latourette, *A History of the Expansion of Christianity, Volume I: The First Five Centuries* (New York: Harper, 1937): 116.

[18]Adolf Harnack, *The Mission and Expansion of Christianity in the First Three Centuries* (New York: Harper, 1961): 367. See also, pages 147-218.

[19]Carl G. Kromminga, *Bringing God's News to Neighbors* (Nutley, N.J.: Presbyterian and Reformed, 1976): 44.

[20]David G. Mandelbaum, "Social Groupings," in Peter B. Hammond, *Cultural and Social Anthropology* (New York: MacMillan, 1964): 146-163.

[21]Paul G. Hiebert, *Cultural Anthropology* (Philadelphia: Lippincott, 1976): 221, 243, 257, 261, 263.

[22]Thomas A. Wolf, "Oikos Evangelism: The Biblical Pattern," in Win Arn (ed.), *The Pastor's Church Growth Handbook* (Pasadena: Church Growth Press, 1979): 110-117. See also, Joseph A. Grassi, *The Secret of Paul the Apostle* (Maryknoll, N.Y.: Orbis, 1978): 130-136.

[23]Michael Green, *Evangelism in the Early Church* (Grand Rapids: Eerdmans, 1970): 210, and the discussion, 207-223.

[24]Murphy, *Crucial Dimensions:* 248.

[25]Elihu Katz and Paul F. Lazarfeld, *Personal Influence: The Part Played by People in the Flow of Mass Communications* (New York: The Free Press, 1955). Cf. H. G. Barnett, *Innovation: The Basis of Cultural Change* (New York: McGraw-Hill, 1953).

[26]See David A. Womack, *The Pyramid Principle of Church Growth* (Minneapolis: Bethany Fellowship, 1977): 57f.

[27]Will Durant, *The Story of Philosophy* (New York: Time Incorporated, 1962): 32.

[28]Edward Cornish, et. al., *The Study of the Future* (Washington, DC: World Future Society, 1977): 98-99.

[29]Frank Stagg, *The Book of Acts* (Nashville, Broadman, 1955), shows the theme of Acts to be the struggle for an unhindered Gospel in the early church, the primary barriers being not geographical, but religious, racial and national, as demonstrated by the unusual usage of the Greek adverb *akolutos*. Stagg's work should be consulted by every student of the future church.

[30]Harvey Cox, "Christianity's Conflicting Views of the Future," *The Futurist* (August, 1969): 95-96.

13. The Fault Does Not Lie With Your Set

Cal Thomas

Cal Thomas is a veteran of 20 years in broadcast journalism. He spent 7½ years with NBC News in Washington, D.C. and cofounded International Media Service, a daily broadcast news service that reports on news of moral, ethical, and spiritual natures. He is the author of two books, A Freedom Dream *and* Public Persons and Private Lives, *and coauthor of* Target Group Evangelism *with Ralph Neighbour, Jr.*

It has been said that history is a *process,* a *slope.* The Swedish Parliament didn't decide "out of the blue" to pass a law banning parental spanking of children, or treating them in a humiliating way. It took time! America didn't arrive *suddenly* at the point of being a "litigous" society, where we rush to court to settle disagreements of any kind—from singing Christmas carols at school, to children suing parents for mal-parenting.

Even as the erosion of a shore line cannot take place without the constant battering of the sea against the earth, neither can a society or nation erode from only a single wave.

Therefore, I would caution those who single out the wave of television in particular—or the media as a whole—as the source of the erosion of American moral and ethical standards, and the breakdown of communication and the family. Television *is* part of the problem; it is also *part of the process.* It only reveals the "slope." The erosion itself, the result of all the individual waves, is the erosion of authority and absolutes.

Jesus was frequently asked by what authority he did or said certain things. As his followers, we must be aware of where our authority and absolutes come from. At the same time, we must be

177

careful not to lord it over others. We must understand that the natural man does not understand spiritual things. Tossing Bible verses to support decency, family, or any other cause to a non-believer, a person who doesn't accept the Bible, is like trying to break through a wall of concrete with a feather.

Nevertheless, we have a clear responsibility to try to make a difference in the world we live in. Jesus told us to be the salt of the earth, a lamp shining out for all to see. Though he talked of continuing wars and rumors of wars until he returns, he also called the peacemakers "blessed."

At the National Prayer Breakfast in Washington this February, Bishop Fulton Sheen noted that there is no freedom without an accompanying responsibility. He pointed out that the signers of the Declaration of Independence suffered much for their courage. Some lost their lives, all lost their fortunes, but none lost his sacred honor!

This is our calling . . . regardless of the outcome, regardless of the consequences, we are to be followers of Christ in the world. We are to have an impact *on* the world, while refusing to be *of* the world.

In less than twenty years, television has become the dominant force in American life. Short of the plagues that swept Europe in the Middle Ages (and there are some who see a parallel here), no force in human history has had such an impact, such an influence in so short a period of time. Television is the major source of news for the overwhelming majority of Americans. Because we are pro-grammed to fast food, we also have become programmed to fast news and fast living. Therefore, we have little time to digest the newspaper or read news magazines, periodicals, and books that treat subjects in-depth. The attention span of today's adult is rapidly approaching that of an infant. No sooner is an election over than we start thinking about the next one. A star is born and we are busy looking for who will be next.

We are living so superficially, so near the surface of events, that we have approched an era of decadence. In its final issue this past January, *New Times Magazine* put it beautifully in a caustic editorial called "Decadence: America Shrugged." I share it with you now because it is a perfect illustration of where the slippery slope has brought us. You may be offended at portions of this . . . but it *is* what's happening:

Welcome to America. Our Miss Shields will show you to your table. Such a pretty baby. What'll it be? Have a drink, have a puff, have a snort, have some smack. Legalized gambling in the front room, skinflicks in the back, mirrors, mirrors everywhere in glorious profusion.

C'mon in. Something for every palate. Reproductions by Rockefeller. Senators by David Garth, exploding Pintos by Ford. Hey, and that's not all. Carcinogens in 31 flavors. Opium from Saint Laurent, Seconals from Graceland . . . funky, punky, junky . . . you want it, we got it.

See the Mayor of San Francisco shot dead in his office, see the homosexual supervisor dying down the hall, see 900 bodies bloating in the jungle sun. Parental guidance suggested. Get your top hat and your spike heels, grab a whip, grab a chain and get it on for the Rocky Horror Picture Show. Sorry, Norman Rockwell doesn't live here anymore.

Join the looters in New York, a police strike in Memphis, an orgy in L.A. Say hello to Harry Reems, get a rattlesnake by mail. (Who invited Solzhenitsyn?) Catch some herpes, get a face-lift, rent a boy . . . .

There's something in the air—a sense of slippage, the perfume of decay. Life is slick and bright and noisy, but there's a softness here, a crumbling behind the gloss. Chuck Barris is the man of the hour. Tacky? Sure he's tacky, but he's having a swell time. Chuck Barris is perfect.

Disco, with its red-raw beat . . . , is the anthem of the seventies. High voltage, quick hits, that's what we want, nuance and texture can wait. It doesn't have to be good—we're talking bottom line here. We have raised image over substance and reduced sensuality to its crudest, most efficient forms . . . .

Come July it will be ten years since Neil Armstrong stepped on the moon—and ten years since Teddy Kennedy and Mary Jo Kopechne rode off Dike Bridge. Of the two events, Chappaquiddick far better presaged the decade ahead. It was so callous, so sloppy.

We shrug off almost everything now, moving on—with a lot of help from the omnivorous media—to the next fleeting titillation . . . . Bianca Jagger, Billy Carter, Gary Gilmore—all hipe, show, diversion. There's a new rock group called The Dead Kennedys. Shrug.

It's as if we are beyond making distinctions, beyond caring. Do
Teddy's celebrated indiscretions continue? No problem—his
Gallup ratings have never been higher. Third graders are selling
dope. White House aides are buying it. Our appetite for violence
is insatiable. Sid Vicious is just a mixed-up kid.

Exhausted from our exertions of the sixties, all we ask for now is
relief. Six hours of TV helps to get us through the day—life once
removed is close enough, thanks. The impetus to rethink-
reform-transform has long since slid into the ennui. After two
centuries, we have reached a consensus of indifference.

"We do it all for you"—that's the spirit of '79. Proposition 13,
with its shimmering promise of something for nothing, is a
metaphor for the times. The beauty of Werner Erhard's PR
project to end world hunger is that you don't have to do a thing.
Small wonder Jerry Brown is our quintessential politician. Liberal, Conservative, Jesuit, Buddhist—Jerry will give us what we
want. No sweat.

Don't think about it. Don't think about anything. Turn up the
volume, have another toke, ... Say, heeeeere's Johnny -
Dolly - Reggie - Woody - Angie - Amy - Betty - Donny -Chevy -
Henry - Goldie - Liz and O. J. Immerse yourself in their glossy,
empty lives, all the better to forget your own. Jackie oh Jackie oh
Jackie ohhhhh . . . There are almost no famous people anymore,
only celebrities—'personalities'—Fame is passe. It is much too
solid, too suggestive of steady achievement. There still are rip-
ples of grace and distinction, commitment and courage, but all
seem in shorter supply now. It's not time for heroes. Bob Dylan
at Caesar's Place, coming soon.

And when . . . the fevers of a thousand Saturday nights and all
the massage parlors in Wichita still aren't enough, there remains
surrender, body and soul, to an Emperor Jones. Like the man
said, 'Choose your poison!'

Aw . . . forget it, we'll just ease on down the road. And, hey,
welcome to America, drinks are on the house. Bottoms up.*

Television can roughly be divided into two categories: (1) Escapist fare, which brings us everything from occasionally good

---

entertainment to the more prolific banality of soap operas, game shows, and situation comedy complete with canned laughter. (2) Information, in the form of news which seems to consist mostly of gloom and doom. (3) There is a third category, found mostly on public television. For the purpose of this discussion, we won't deal with the high quality programming you'll generally find there.

In his book *Christ and the Media*, Malcolm Muggeridge takes the position that the New Testament kingdom of God is our true habitat, and the devil's kingdoms are as deceiving as travel brochures are as they describe countries they seek to persuade us to visit. In view of this, the media seems reversed—its facts are fancy, its documentation is myth—and has provided the devil with a great opportunity. All he needs to do is to get into religious broadcasting! Screwtape was taught that there is far more mileage in corrupting good, humane people than in corrupting wicked, cruel ones. Muggeridge says, "King Herod has always had a bad press for slaughtering the innocents, but let Screwtape keep it in mind that nowadays a good campaign on the media for legalized abortion will facilitate the slaughter of millions on the highest humanitarian principles before they are ever born."

In another part of the book, Muggeridge goes on to say: "As far as I am concerned, there are no studies that could be mounted capable of convincing me that [the] eight years of a normal life span that an average Western man spends looking at the television screen have no appreciable influence on his mores or way of evaluating his existence."[1]

This is really the point. We can become programmed by the network programmers and lose our reference point. Then the difference between reality and illusion is hard to find. If we see enough shows with illicit sex and violence, emaciated men under the influence of domineering women, and dirty jokes we begin to accept that as the norm. I am convinced that anti-Christ will speak to us live via satellite, and that by the time he comes, the majority (the elect excepted) will not be able to determine the difference between right and wrong. They will have lost their reference point. We can see it upon us at some points already.

If you don't think media is important in controlling the people, why is it that the first thing the revolutionaries take over in a coup is not the presidential palace? That comes later. The first thing they grab is the radio station. Control the flow of information and you control the people who listen.

This past January, I attended a hearing on the cults chaired by Kansas Senator Robert Dole. There was a lot of testimony about the evils of programming . . . of taking young people and putting them in a closed environment, controlling what goes into their minds and stomachs until the desired mental state is reached and then using those programmed people to do the bidding of a Sun Myung Moon, Mahareshi Mahesh Yogi, Guru Maharaj-Ji, L. Ron Hubbard, or even Jim Jones.

In a more subtle and sometimes more insidious way, that is precisely what television is doing to us and to our children. It often presents a truncated and false view of life so that what is not true begins with repetition and the absence of perspective to take on the resemblance of truth. Some believe this is a plot, a conspiracy. They are convinced that men get together in New York and Washington and decide each day how to slant the news, for example, to their viewpoint. That doesn't happen. It's more subtle than that. It's a mindset that says, "We know what is best for America, and we know what sells, and what the people want."

But can we *expect* anything else from television? Doesn't the natural man behave naturally? I used to get upset when I heard someone swear, particularly when they took God's name in vain. I don't get upset anymore, because that is the natural man behaving naturally. If he knew God, he would be revering, not slandering, his name.

The media, as active or passive tools of Satan, will go to any length to keep us from confronting the reality of sin and the need for a Redeemer. For example, we have never had so many "experts" delivering so much advice for so many problems. Experts fill up the guest lists on talk shows. Experts proliferate in magazines. Doctors, lovelorn column writers, psychiatrists tell us it's old fahioned to be married . . . you can have sex before or even after marriage with someone else and if you feel guilty about it there's another expert to help you get rid of your guilt.

Horoscopes take care of our future. Dear Abby takes care of our present . . . but only Christ can take care of our *past,* after which he *deals* with our present and *guarantees* our future.

Having said all this, having demonstrated that the media, like fire, can be a friend when properly controlled, what should be the response of the church and of individual Christians to the power of television and the rest of the media in the world today?

First, we must realize that now, perhaps more than ever before, mankind is spiritually hungry. Men are looking for a messiah. We have come out of the *God is Dead* philosophy of the 60's, to *"Born Again"* headlined on the covers of *Time* and *Newsweek*. We look for a deliverer to extricate us from the bad economy, from the energy crisis, from global conflict, from the Republicans or Democrats, from personal failure and a feeling of unimportance. The media is all too quick to deliver that messiah, whether it be in the form of a government program, a campaign promise, a Presidential candidate, a get-rich-quick scheme, or a new religion that fails to deal with sin and its consequences. Star Wars and Superman are perfect examples of messianic figures that offer everything, requiring only the price of admission, delivering illusion which fades soon after the theatre lights come on. Jim Jones offered nothing, required everything, and delivered death.

"What shall we say then to these things?" the apostle Paul might ask.

Dr. John Stott has reminded us that we Christians are the salt of the earth. He recalls that before refrigeration we used to preserve our meat with salt. When the meat goes bad, he asks, is it the fault of the meat? Or, does the fault rest with the *salt,* which was supposed to preserve it? "If salt goes bad it is good for nothing except to be ground underfoot."

We are the salt. The world is the meat. If the world goes bad, whose fault is it?

We have in the Christian West what I call a "rapture syndrome." We want to wait for Jesus to return and make everything right. But, we are to be laboring in the fields even at the moment of his return.

In responding to things we do not like in the media (and we should also respond to the *good* as we find it), we must never predicate that response on the chances for success. This is not the basis for Christian involvement. We are to get involved because Jesus commanded us to do so. That involvement flows from a relationship with the Holy Spirit. We can respond in a number of ways. The most effective is to send individual letters to the offending network, if it is a network program, with copies to the local station and the sponsor. Don't bother writing the FCC. The FCC does not control the content of the programming. The First Amendment prohibits that.

If you want your power to really be felt, affiliate with organizations such as the National Federation for Decency operating out of Tupelo, Mississippi, or the PTA, which is zeroing in on bad programming in a very effective way.These organizations multiply your letter and have a lot of clout with the networks and local stations.

A second way to have an effect is to be selective in what we watch. We are selective in what we eat, but digest anything television offers us without assessing whether it nourishes or whether it is "junk" food. What goes into your mind can sometimes have a greater effect than what goes into your stomach! If you take poison, your body dies. But you can take in poison through your mind and live a demented life.

A third and, I believe, very important alternative that Christian leaders should consider is the offering of alternatives to television. In an interview in the April, 1979, *Eternity Magazine,* Dr. Frank Gaebelein says, "We need a restricted watching of television. I am convinced that undisciplined use of television has been sapping the mind and imagination of youth." Parents need to say no when it comes to children's viewing of some television programs. There must also be an *alternative* to television which offers escapism, something we all need once in awhile. Thought must be given: As a Christian, I escape *from* what, *into* what? How do we then find the way back to our Christian reference point in the real world?

Enter the church! We are sadly in need for the church to become what Francis Schaeffer has called an "orthodoxy of community." We often have an orthodoxy of doctrine, without having a very good orthodoxy of community.

I believe the greatest need of people in today's world is to feel that someone loves them unconditionally, that someone cares, that they are important to someone. Certainly, Christ offers ultimate meaning and purpose and direction in life. But his love must also be seen revealed in the lives of others, reflected through the prisms of others' hearts into our own.

If I come home and say to my wife, "Instead of watching television tonight, let's go to the airport and get on a plane for Paris, France, and spend a week there having a good time," which do you think she'll choose . . . TV or Paris! She'll choose Paris! I've offered her something far greater than the cheap thrill of television. Through true fellowship, through caring, through involvement in each other's lives, we need to present a "Paris, France" kind of alternative to television. Then, television will become the exception for an evening's entertainment rather than the rule.

I think the church should organize itself into caring units. One unit would look out after the physical needs of the body of Christ. If someone is a severe victim of inflation; and he doesn't have enough food in the house—his needs would be met. If someone is unemployed—a unit of people would specifically pray for and act on that problem, using their influence and experience to help the person find a job, pooling resources of the church to make sure the needs of the unemployed are met. If there is strife in a family—a caring unit could be sensitive to that need, and move accordingly. If a child needs some guidance or there is a need for discipleship—a caring unit could move in at that point.

What I am saying is that I personally do not have much interest in television, even though I have been involved with it for most of my life. There are so many other things I would rather do . . . so many people I'd rather be with . . . a friend dying of Lou Gehrig's disease, a man I worked with at NBC News who is not a Christian and whose son was killed in a traffic accident last month . . . a brother in Christ doing life for murder . . . a youth choir . . . a concert or play . . . friends with whom I can have dinner or coffee . . . a pastor to call up and tell him I love him and how much his messages mean to me, and how they have contributed to my knowledge of God and spiritual growth . . . a child who loves to have his back scratched and have bedtime stories read to him.

Our problem with television is that we have exchanged the greater excitement of the real world for the phony superficiality and temporal excitement of the unreal. The best example of this was during the Gemini space program when it appeared for awhile that two of our astronauts might not come back to earth. There was a news bulletin on ABC reporting the trouble. The bulletin interrupted a popular television program. Viewers called to complain that their favorite program was interrupted by a news bulletin about astronauts in trouble. The fictitious program they were watching was called "Lost in Space." They were more interested in watching a dramatization of an emergency that was not real than they were in watching the real thing!

At the National Gallery of Art in Washington, there are many priceless and beautiful paintings. They are one of a kind, never to be repeated masterpieces. Also at the National Gallery there is a gift shop where you can buy inexpensive reproductions in various sizes of the original paintings. The question is, which has the greater value . . . the original or the cheap imitation? Television is a cheap imitation of life, of reality, and we so often are willing to make the trade because we don't realize the value of what we are giving up in exchange for an illusion.

NOTE

[1]Malcolm Muggeridge, (Grand Rapids, Michigan: William B. Eerdmans Publishing Company, 1977).

14. The Future Church Faces Radical New Religions

John Newport

John Newport holds numerous degrees and has written several books, including Demons, Demons, Demons *and* Christ and the New Consciousness. *A former faculty member at Rice University and Southwestern Seminary, he now serves as the vice-president and academic dean of Southwestern Seminary.*

All of us who are believers in the sovereignty of God believe that God is working in history. Although there is a personal evil force tempting and working in our universe, that force is limited. Satan is on a leash—perhaps a long leash—but there are limits beyond which he cannnot go. God is still on the throne, and He *is* working! Even out of the radical new religions which seem far away from God's redemptive purpose, God could well be preparing us for a great new era in Christian evangelization.

Some evangelical Christians, such as Richard Loveless of Gordon-Conwell Seminary in Boston, see these New Consciousness groups as providing an exciting evangelical opportunity. These groups are revealing the limitations of scientism and secularism as ultimate world views. They are forcing people to think of life's spiritual concerns. "In the fullness of time," Christ came into the first century. From this perspective, "the New Consciousness groups are helping to constitute," says Loveless, "a new fullness of time for one of the fresh and exciting moments of all evangelical history."

No one can deny the fact that these New Consciousness groups exist. *Psychology Today* calls them "God in the gut." Someone else has said that there are 8,000 ways available in America today to "turn on." Robert Ellwood, of the University of Southern California, says there is a new alternative view of reality that has become powerful in our time.

New Consciousness Groups refers to groups that are primarily based on the presupposition that we are divine, essentially divine; and that there are techniques which can awaken that inherent divinity within all of us. Many years ago, William James said we used only three to six percent of our abilities. The New Consciousness movement builds on this kind of principle. I recently heard Jean Houston, a dynamic professor from New York City, speak on the emergence of New Consciousness groups. She told about attending a conference at the Menninger Clinic in Kansas, where they talked about awakening this inherent or latent potential we have within us. A year or so ago at a Rice football game, an airplane flew over the large crowd with a banner which read, "Scientology: how to make the able more able." Scientology was paying for it! They are capitalizing on the quest all of us have to find the meaning of life. They are building on one of the great basic drives of life.

One way to approach the subject of the new religions is to look at it in terms of a great world movement in history, such as abberations out of Hinduism or Voodooism or Islam. However, it is also a Western secular movement. I was recently in Phoenix and was reminded that Phoenix was where L. Ron Hubbard had his vision of Scientology, at least in its more developed form. The manager of John Denver recently told me that John Denver is caught up in Erhard Seminar Training and pyramid power. He says there are no gods. He said, "I see my music as a vehicle to spread the gospel of a new secular religion where 'Godhead' is in one's *own* head. I want to wean people away from the vain hope of a supernatural intervention in the world by God. Man is alone." He went on to say that "one of these days I will be so complete personally that I won't be human; I will be a god." On a talk show recently, I heard a woman saying, "My hero is the 'religious' man John Denver. I think he is the hero for our young people today." John Travolta is also caught up in Scientology, and is spending a great deal of time in it. These people, of course, have a tremendous impact on the youth of our country.

Then, there are groups which may not be called New Consciousness groups, but are very dangerous. They use Christian terminology somewhat like Christian Science did in earlier years.

They are similar to the Unity movement that came out of Missouri; or the Jehovah's Witnesses, who call themselves Bible students under Pastor Russell; or the Mormon church, who use the Bible many times to make an initial impact. Today, there is a group like the Unification Church, which claims to be a Christian school or a Christian movement. They have a seminary in New York, where they are using many Protestant theologians to teach.

Then, of course, there has been a tremendous revival of a new form of magic and witchcraft. The University of Texas has seven departments requiring the work of Castaneda, which is a sophisticated presentation of shamanism, magic and witchcraft.

So there are many movements in our country. There are also tremendous lessons to be learned from these movements. The movements create occasions for teaching authentic theology to many of our young people, who otherwise would never listen to abstract courses on theology.

First of all, what are some of the reasons why these New Consciousness groups have arisen? There are many explanations. The psychologists, sociologists, and theologians have all tried to explain why, at this particular time in the history of our culture, these groups have arisen. One reason, of course, is that America has always been something of an experimental group. As far back as the 19th century there was a heretical type of philosopher in this country called Ralph Waldo Emerson. Emerson became enamored with Hinduism, and developed a movement called Transcendentalism. (Incidentally, Mrs. Mary Baker Glover Patterson Eddy was influenced by Transcendentalism.) We have always been an experimental society, with religious freedom and liberty.

Another reason is explained by Charles Glock of the University of California. He contends that a new mode of consciousness has been developing in our country for many years. One sign was the drug culture in the 1960's in California. This new mode of consciousness is now sweeping out to the masses of young people in our country. Young people are saying that this is "Better Living Through Chemistry!"

I was at Harvard University on Sabbatical leave when Leary and Alpert were experimenting, trying to give people a religious experience without having to go through moral and spiritual rubrics of repentance and faith and meditation and prayer. Incidentally, Leary has now given up all of this and has gone into the UFO business. He recently spoke at the University of Houston about UFO's. Alpert went to India, found a guru, changed his name to Ram Das, and is working out of a place in Llama, New Mexico.

According to Theodore Roszak, who teaches at the University of California in Haywood, many young people have gone to these groups because they want to be religious. They have found that so many of our church people and churches are identified with the status quo and rationalism, identified with what Roszak calls "the urban industrial ecological chaos of our country." Young people want to be religious, and they see Christianity identified with the *status quo,* legalistic, rationalistic, negative approach to reality. They look somewhere else for their religion.

There may be just enough truth in their statement to hurt! Roszak, in his books, *Where the Wasteland Begins* and *The Unfinished Animal,* goes so far as to say that the most dangerous person in the community is a businessman going to a middle class church on Sunday morning with his black Bible. This is the most dangerous person in America, because he is the one who is trying to put a divine halo around his own private financial situation, around his own private little empire.

Sociologists have studied why so many young people are interested in the New Consciousness groups. Robert Whatnow of Princeton University suggests that these groups are a short-cut for middle-class young people to meet the overwhelming chaos of the world and the university situation. Many of our young people are confused; the universities are so overwhelming now! People come to the campuses from everywhere, from different schools and curriculum. It is an overwhelming experience. So many of these religions which require an escapist sort of mentality, like Hare Krishna, emerge. All a student has to do is turn himself over to these groups. The groups will then take care of his needs, and simplify his life.

Those of us who are evangelical Christians have also given suggestions about why we think these groups have arisen. Os Guinness, in his book, *The Dust of Death,* suggests among other reasons that Biblical ignorance and a doctrine of the decay of Christianity in the 20th century has permitted us to be infected by such groups. We do not know *what* we believe! We do not know the Bible. We do not know doctrine. Others see these groups as a reemergence of paganism. Like the homosexuals, they have been there all the time, but have just come out of the closet. Hal Lindsey, of course, sees many of these groups as the direct fulfillment of Biblical prophecies related to the last days of history. He sees this along with earthquakes, the return of the Jews to Israel, the reemergence of pagan groups, and the so-called "falling away of the churches" as definite signs that we are in the last days.

The Spiritual Counterfeits Project, a very helpful group in Berkeley, suggests that these groups are the fulfillment of a vision of the Apostle John, of an anti-Christ kingdom at the end of history. They suggest that mankind is being brought together in the last days of history in a common expression of humanistic spirituality called "yoga," "illumination," or "the divine principle." There are some truth to these indications.

Other evangelical Christians, as I mentioned before, see these New Consciousness groups as providing an exciting new evangelical opportunity.

Now, one of the very crucial problems that all of us who are Christians have to face is the problem of how to approach other world religions. This is a problem for all who have tried to work in the secular universities. In my classes at Rice University, I had Jews, Buddhists, devout members of the Baha'i faith, Islams, and all shades of Christians. Empirically, I think that the Buddhists are gentle people; they are a kind people. Some of the Islam people are very devout. Many of them fall on their faces five times a day to pray to their god; some of our people do not even fall on their faces once a week! The Hindu group is perhaps the most religiously oriented group of all of the peoples of the world. How do we approach these people? What should our attitude be toward them?

There have been the *liberal approaches,* like Toynbee, who said we ought to purge ourselves of all exclusiveness, join with them, and take the best out of their groups. Then there are people like Trueblood, who comes out of the Quaker tradition. Even though he has become more evangelical, he still has the lingering of the Quaker principle, the idea that Christ actually lives in one sense or another in all of us. He uses what is sometimes called "the highest rung on the ladder" approach. That is, people are climbing up steps, and Christianity is the last step.

But I think most of us are coming out of a deep biblical tradition. We cannot use our own human wisdom, or even judge individual personalities with whom we have some rapport. We have to look into our own hearts, as well as their hearts, with biblical perspectives, such as Romans 1. We have to go with Henry Kramer's famous dialectical approach, where he says that these people are seeking after God, but at the very same moment are rebelling from God. These people are searching for God, yet they are turning from him. In one sense of the word, they know God.

In another sense, in a *saving* way they do not know him. None of us know him, apart from someone penetrating this egocentric and sinful veil that surrounds all of our lives. That is why we have to go to these New Consciousness groups. But if we go to them, we have to have a profound understanding of the gospel of grace, which denies that any person can know God apart from grace. It has nothing to do with whether we are Eastern or Western, or whether we are smart or ignorant, poor or rich. The gospel of grace has nothing to do with this. It has to do with the grace of our Lord Jesus Christ, who comes to all of us despite the veneer we might have from our background. We are all sinful, alienated, egocentric, prideful creatures who desperately need the gospel of grace!

Let me point out what I consider to be some key principles that we have to face with these groups. Often these principles are very subtle.

The Hindu tradition is one of the oldest religious traditions in all of mankind's history. The Hindu religion had almost died, until evangelical Christian missionaries—such as William Carey in the early nineteenth century—confronted these people with the gospel. Their reaction to the gospel actually sparked Hinduism back to life.

However, Hinduism did not gain any ascendancy in the United States until the latter part of the nineteenth century, when Swami Vivekenanda came to this country. The United States had just gone through the Great Revival, and some of the people had been "burned over" by Christianity. (Finney used to call the country of New England the "burned over" country.) So, it would seem, they were right for this new, more tolerant type of religion. Still, it appealed only to the masses.

Then in 1959, Maharishi Mahesh Yogi came to the United States. Maharishi Mahesh Yogi had been a disciple of Guru Dev, who was the leader of one of the oldest traditions in Hinduism. Guru Dev believed that there is some ultimate spiritual reality we were once a part of. We have fallen away, and our soul is stuck in this evil body. Therefore, the goal of all humanity is to somehow reattach ourselves, to get out of this body and sink back again into the great universal and personal Brahman. Just before Guru Dev died, he said to Maharishi, who had been a physics student at Allahabad University: "The American people are so non-philosophical; they are so ignorant philosophically. (After teaching at a seminary for 25 years, I can attest that this is true.) You need to digest this, capsulize it, get it down on their level, and then take it to America."

When Maharishi Mahesh Yogi first came to America, he tried to sell his movement as a religion, but it was not accepted. Americans were seemingly not ready for this Hindu religion. So Maharishi Mahesh Yogi went back to the drawing board, those caves up in the Himalayas, and meditated.

Then in 1972, Maharishi Mahesh Yogi came back to America. He chose Houston, Texas, as the spring board to announce his new plan to win the world for Transcendental Meditation. I will never forget that day. Maharishi was brought in, and he sat on a throne. The people stood in adoration. He smiled and grinned at everyone. Then he told about his plan. This time he decided not to call it a religion; he called it a psychological technique.

Maharishi soon realized that the Federal Government had the most money. He quickly began to get Federal and State monies to teach this technique as a means of overcoming alcoholism and drug addiction. Transcendental Meditation began to be taught in public schools in states such as Illinois. The Federal Government and some of their agencies were using this method in teaching. Maharishi even started his own university, Maharishi International University (the old flunk-out Parsons college).

A key issue is that they have a right to speak in our country. However, they must be fair! A lawyer by the name of Woodruff led the fight in the New Jersey courts to have Transcendental Meditation decreed as a religion. Transcendental Meditation says that the world is created by sound, and holds together by sound. If you can get your sacred Sanskrit word—their sacred word in their language—you can repeat your own particular word 20 minutes, twice a day. It is never said out loud—only silently. You will then sink back into Brahman. It will reduce metabolism, blood pressure, and bring peace and tranquility. In their ceremony, they have an adoration of their great line of Hindu gods, which they call the

Puja. The average American does not understand what is happening, but it is a very devout religious ceremony. The New Jersey courts have now decreed that Transcendental Meditation is a religion, like any other religion, and cannot be taught with public money.

Here, then, is a religion in a very simplified form. It is very subtle. Many people who profess to be members of a Christian church have been taken in by Transcendental Meditation. However, Hinduism and Transcendental Meditation and most New Consciousness groups believe that man is basically divine. They believe in pre-existence and reincarnation. They believe a person just has to "turn on" the divinity within himself, and they have no sense of sin. This particular type of religion does not call for a radical break with moral or spiritual evil. Unfortunately, this seems to appeal to many people in our country today.

Another New Consciousness group is the Hare Krishna movement, or the International Society for Krishna Consciousness. It is a completely different sort of religion, which comes from a different tradition of Hinduism—a fundamentalist type of Hinduism. It goes back to a man named Chaitanya Mahaprabha. Chaitanya Mahaprabha appeared on the streets of the Hindu cities with his cymbals. His ideas were very similar in some ways to Transcendental Meditation.

Hare Krishna is the most fundamental of the Hindu groups, and in some sense is more closely akin to Christianity. Hare Krishnas believe that Lord Krishna created the world, and is a personal being. However, people have fallen away from him and have lost fellowship with him. Many Hare Krishnas chant the *mantra* five or six hours a day. Their famous call is: "Hare Krishna, Hare Krishna, Krishna, Krishna, Hare, Hare, Hare Rama, Hare Rama, Rama, Rama, Hare, Hare." By chanting this call, a person can revive the "original pure consciousness." This group believes that there is no need for any emphasis on ethics, because one will automatically do right after chanting the *manta*.

When Swami came to America to introduce this religion in 1965, he started out in the lower part of New York City, in Greenwich Village. I went down with some other people to hear him. No one knew what he was doing. However, it was not long before multi-colored posters were hanging in California saying: "Get away from drugs and alcohol! Stay high forever . . . follow Swami Prabhupada."

Shortly after Swami died in 1977, I was in their headquarters in Berkeley. At that time I met the man who is now heading the Counsel of Seven (I believe it is called) who said that the movement will go on even though their original founder has died.

There are several problems when we get into this form of Hinduism. First of all, there is the problem that they can swallow you up by saying Christ was one of the great saviors. They claim you can be illuminated by him, you can come back into fellowship with Brahman by him, or you can have your divinity reinstated by him, along with many of the other great religious leaders of mankind. This is a very subtle danger. This form of Hinduism also lacks the doctrine of sin.

Another subtle problem is the problem of pre-existence or reincarnation. I gave some lectures at Stetson University, in which I tried to give a dramatic presentation of natural, or pagan, immortality. I then tried to contrast it with the great Biblical doctrine of creation, and that we must depend upon God and upon the Resurrection. Paul tells us if Christ had not been raised from the dead, there would be no hope for us or our loved ones. The whole context of the entire speech was that I was trying to use the Biblical doctrines of creation and resurrection to fight the pagan doctrine of natural immortality. Many people do not understand what the authentic Biblical doctrine is concerning the hope of the life beyond. We Christians do not believe in *pre*-existence. We do not believe, like Plato and the Hindus, that you are naturally immortal. You do not need a savior if you are *naturally* immortal; you automatically live on!

There is another group that is rather interesting in our time. It is a Buddhist-related group coming to this country, an offspring of the world's fastest growing religion. The fastest growing religion in the world is not Southern Baptist, Assemblies of God, or any similar group. It is the religion called *Soka Gakkai*. Soka Gakkai is a religion which developed in Japan after 1946, when they had to separate the Shinto religion from the State. To a large extent it is a lay movement, and is tremendously effective. A man named Nicheren Shoshu, who lived in the thirteenth century, developed the idea that the Buddhist religion, with all of its gods, was so complex that the average lay person could not understand it. He says that Gautama, who lived in the sixth century before Christ, who was called The Buddha, The Enlightened One, gave us many writings. There was one writing, he explained, which was especially important: the *Lotus Sutra*. It summarized everything that the great Buddhist said.

Nicheren said that it was not necessary to understand the *Lotus Sutra*. (It is very much like our Book of Revelations which many people find very complex.) All a person has to do is put the title in a little box and chant the title of the *Lotus Sutra*. (Incidentally, when a person comes into the religion, they rent him a little box with a picture of the scroll for as long as he is in the religion.) Members of Soka Gakkai point out that the body and mind and spirit are so closely integrated that if one will chant the *Lotus Sutra* over the title in the little box, a person can get anything he wants. He can get money, power, and job security. You can get anything you want. There is a close tie, they teach, between the mind and the body, the body and the mind.

Soka Gakkai became so aggressive in Japan, because they used forced conversion, that it obtained a bad reputation. Therefore, they changed the name for the "export version." They called it *Nicheren Shoshu*.

Now, Nicheren Shoshu from the Christian standpoint falls short. Christianity never equates the will of God for a human life with immediate material satisfaction. In Nicheren Shoshu, you do not find a holy God who calls for repentance and change, who calls us to conform to a prophetic way of life such as found in the life of Jesus. Nicheren Shoshu is very close to magic. Whatever you want, whether morally constructive or not, is granted if you chant. This sort of emphasis reveals that Nicheren Shoshu is a manipulative type of religion. Evangelical Christianity would also question their discounting of study and evaluation, in favor of chanting. Jesus said we are to love God with our mind, soul, and heart.

We can learn some lessons from this group. In Nicheren Shoshu, their techniques of recruitment are very questionable, but they are tremendously aggressive. They are concrete in their method, their techniques, the power of the arts, and their enthusiasm. They have a strong sense of fellowship, and recognize the need for positive thinking.

Nicheren Shoshu shows us what we already ought to know from what has happened in Christian circles: religion can be prostituted to gain less than authentic ends. Sometimes I think we are very close to it. Have you ever heard the old phrases: "How I can get where I want to go through religion?" or, "How I can get rich through prayer?" One church I belonged to had a "test me, try me, prove me" tithing program. I do not know whether or not the pastor actually meant it, but he implied that if you did not get a better job in three months, you could quit tithing. I disagree. We should tithe as a sense of proportionate fellowship with Almighty God. If we tithe in this way, we will have a sense of being a part of the great worldwide redemptive program. We will also get many spiritual blessings, and in some cases, we will get physical blessings. *However, physical blessings are not guaranteed.* They are not the primary end.

Islamic-related New Consciousness Groups fascinate me. Whether we like it or not, we are going to have to face the whole matter of the Islamic religion. It is now the most aggressive religion in the world outside of Marxism, if Marxism can be considered a religion.

There are many divisions of Islam. One is the *Sunnites,* who are dominant in Egypt, Syria, Saudi Arabia, and similar countries.

Another division of Islam has been in the news recently in relation to Iran, and the recent takeover by orthodoxy there. This division of Islam is the famous *Shi'ite* tradition. The *Shi'ite* is a smaller division, but very prominent in Iran, Pakistan, Yemen, and Lebanon. The Shi'ites believe that those rulers who took over after Muhammed died in 632 A.D. were usurpers. (Islam is based upon a man named Muhammed who had a mystical side of his life.) Muhammad's cousin and son-in-law, Ali, who married Muhammad's only daughter, Fatima, was supposed to have carried on the true tradition of Islam. After Ali there came twelve other *Imams,* who were all killed except for the twelfth *Imam.* The Shi'ites believe that the twelfth Imam escaped and went into a spiritual realm, very similar to the fact that Jesus has gone to the spiritual center of the universe. The twelfth *Imam* is now living in an invisible state. He is waiting for the fullness of time, when he will come back to this earth and establish justice on the earth. At this time, he will elevate Islam as the outstanding religion.

Incidentally, the Baha'i religion flows out of this same tradition. The Baha'is believe that their leader, Baha'u'llah, is the twelfth *Imam,* who came back to the Middle East in the middle of the nineteenth century to rescue mankind. Their headquarters are now in Israel, and they are very active and popular in the United States.

Another division of Islam is what I called the *Subud* division.

Indonesia and Pakistan are the two great large Islamic nations. When Islam flowed down to Indonesia, some mystical traditions developed. This we call *Subud*. It started with a man named Subud, or Bapak, who had a light glowing out of his head. People claimed they could see the light glowing from his head for several miles. Bapak felt God had called him to share this light that had been revealed to him around the world. Therefore, he went to England, where he was considered a kind of messianic figure. Then Bapak came to America.

Subud teaches that intellect is a *secondary* part of us, and that emotion is the *chief* part of us. In order to arouse the great emotion part of our lives, they have the "*latihan* experience." To prepare for *latihan*, a person must study the writings of Bapak for three months. Then, he must listen to the people inside the latihan room for three months before he is allowed to go in. After having read about the "higher energy," an emotional energy comes to the person, bypassing intellect—which is a "coarser quality" of energy. A helper takes the beginner into a darkened room. The beginner takes off his watch and glasses. He is not to try to control his mind. He will begin to shout, croon, leap, weep, speak in tongues, utter wordless chants. If the beginner gets completely out of control, helpers come in to try to rescue him. It is different, they say, from a trance. The *latihan* experience is supposed to open a person to God. This enables them to bring out their subliminal.

Another technique is to go into the *latihan* room with a question about a job, marriage, sex, friendship, or any decision they have to make. The *Subud* member then speaks in tongues and goes into ecstasy. When he comes out, he will have the answer to whatever question he had.

I mention *Subud* because it is an example of a movement that is almost sweeping the world—an emotional, sometimes almost primitive emotional expression in religion. We are finding that many new Jesus groups, such as the Witness Lee groups, do the same thing with their endless chanting, only they do it in the name of Jesus.

This is an example of a new, sweeping, non-rational approach in our world. It teaches that with the right key or technique, you can bypass your intellect. They claim it will make your life meaningful. It is very close to Primal Therapy, which is now operating on the West Coast. However, *Subud* does not have techniques. *Subud* members do not know how to describe the things that are happening. This is another example of a New Consciousness group that is part of the worldwide charismatic sweep.

We need to consider how we are to deal with this sweep. We all know that one of the great Christian movements of our world today is the "charismatic movement." Henry Van Dusen used to call it "the third force." It is especially appealing to the South American people, and to people of a more primitive mentality, like the people of Africa. It is appealing to people in our country who are befuddled, and to many of the intellectuals in the Episcopal churches. Kelsey was caught up in this movement when it began in the 1950's in California. He is now at Notre Dame, writing books in which he is trying to develop a more intellectual approach, basing it on Jungian sub-rational arch-type approach to theology, philosophy, and psychology.

How do we deal with this constructively? How do we handle this great worldwide sweep? John McKay used to say that if he had a choice between the rather uncouth life of many of the Pentecostals and the deadness of many of the churches, he would choose the uncouth life . . . but he also said that we do not *have* that choice! We do not have to *make* that choice, because there is a delicate balance in Pauline theology. One of our problems is that we label one another. We are struggling *not* to be labeled, and yet we must ask, what *is* the "gift of the Spirit?" What *is* the place of the so-called "speaking in tongues?" Where *is* the place of the Spirit? This is one of the great struggles today. *Subud* is a religion which is symbolic of this great worldwide movement.

Scientology is one of the most subtle groups in our country, and is perhaps one of the most dangerous groups. Many of our movie stars, such as John Travolta, are into Scientology. I mention this New Consciousness group because it is very similar to the other pagan groups, except that it is done in the name of Western man.

L. Ronald Hubbard is the founder and central figure of Scientology. Hubbard started out as a science fiction writer, and wrote part of his first book for a science fiction magazine. It is a "science fiction religion." He has the idea in his finalized scientology that all of us at one time were divine. We were all *Thetans,* and once lived "up there" and had fun as gods. Then, because we were bored, we created this world. As we started playing around in this world, we became so interested in it that we forgot we were gods. We then became so integrated with this world that we fell away and lost our potential divinity. Then we had to start evolving up out of the slime through a long evolutionary process. Many of these religions, as in Hinduism, were struggling to help us recognize our divinity; but it took a man in Phoenix, Arizona, named Ron Hubbard, to discover what he called the "E-meter."

The "E-meter" consists of two tin cans with an electric power switch. Hubbard teaches that people have problems because, as Thetans, they had shocks. These shocks have caused people to fall away from their divinity. If a person will hold the two tin cans of the "E-meter," an electric shock will go through him. The shock will cause the needle to fluctuate when there has been a deep shock. This deep shock not only might be in *this* life, but also in an *earlier* life. A person might have fallen off a horse when he was trying to fight in the Trojan war, or he might have had some sand in his craw when he was some type of a shellfish. That may be why he now has problems with crying all the time!

Scientology members have many techniques to get these shocks out in the open. Once the shocks have been brought out into the open, they will disappear. Gradually, if you pay up to $15,000, a person can recover his "Thetanhood." A person then can almost have supernatural power.

Again, the inherent doctrine that man is divine is appealing to people. This time, however, it is in a sophisticated Western version.

I add a brief note about Erhard Seminar Training. I took this unbelievable course, and have never been called such nasty names in all of my life. Werner Erhard has been attracted to Scientology, to Voodooism, and to selling the Silva Mind Control. Erhard says a person's problem is that his parents, his religion, his church, his country, and his school have "determined" him. He wants to shock people out of their "determined" mold, and teach them that they are on their own. Your mother not loving you is not the cause of your problem. You are the result of your own problems. Once a person has this realization, he can realize his own individuality. This group, of course, does not have any conception of the Christian doctrine of man, of the doctrine of grace. It puts a great deal of emphasis on experience.

The Unification Church is one of the most subtle of the New Consciousness groups in the United States, because it claims to be a Christian group. Many people think this group will make a big push and become a denomination—a move from being a *cult* to becoming a *sect*. The Unification Church has built a seminary in Perrytown, New York, and is employing prestigious Harvard, Yale, and Princeton graduates to teach in it.

When I taught at Rice University, Unification Church members were quite often in my office. One day, Dr. Bergman, a Jewish psychiatrist and graduate of Columbia University and UCLA, came to speak at Rice. He is the head of their mission group for the United States, and is one of the most powerful men I have ever heard. Incidentally, a young architectural student heard him that day. The student went off for a weekend, and never came back. His father discovered that the Unification Church had paid his son's rent and taken his things. His son had joined the Unification Church. The Unification Church has had a tremendous, universal influence on young people around the world.

The Unification Church's basic idea is that God created Adam and Eve and wanted them to live without sexual relationships, without being husband and wife, until they could develop maturity. At that time they were to have fellowship with God, have children, and begin to create a perfect family. Unfortunately, Satan, seeing how pretty Eve was, seduced her. She succumbed to Satan and they had sexual relations. Then she had sexual relations with Adam. Because she tainted Adam, all the human race is tainted.

God's great plan to restore the family was Jesus. Jesus was not a divine person, but was a sinless man. God wanted Jesus to mature, marry, and live without sexual relations. At a certain time, they were to have children. Therefore, Jesus was the one who was supposed to create the perfect family. Unfortunately, John the Baptist did not teach the Jews well, and they crucified Jesus. Jesus' crucifixion was not a part of God's plan. Therefore, Jesus was only able to save us *spiritually*. If mankind is to be saved, someone has to save us *physically*.

Sun Myung Moon then goes into Biblical prophecy, and uses the Book of Revelation. He teaches that 2,000 years after Abraham lived, Jesus lived. Then, 2,000 years after Jesus lived, the "Lord of the Second Advent" will come. The "Lord of the Second Advent" will be born in the Far East (according to a text in the Book of Revelation about the coming out of "the land of the sun and the moon.") The country could not be Japan, because of its evil

background. The country could not be China, because it is a
Communist state. Therefore, the country is Korea. Many different
signs are coming. By the 1980's, the "Lord of the Second Advent," who will save us physically, will be revealed.

I asked the National Director if Mr. Moon were the "Lord of the
Second Advent." He told me I would have to come into the
movement in order to know. However, if things develop as they
are supposed to develop, it will be revealed that Mr. Moon is the
"Lord of the Second Advent." Korea is to be the world center, the
Holy Land, and there will be peace. All of this will be revealed in
the 1980s!

The whole matter of mind control, deep programming, and the
relationship between evangelism and the improper kind of mind
control, is a problem of interest to evangelical groups. We, of
course, as evangelistic Christians are trying to win people to Jesus.
How far do we do? I remember so well preaching at youth revivals,
where we would sing twenty stanzas of "Just As I Am." How close
was I getting to this sort of practice? This raises some very great
problems. We believe in religious liberty. We believe in zeal. But
surely we believe in enough humility that we are still finite; we are
not God. We believe we have the revealed truth in the Holy Bible.
We are not going to force anybody psychologically, sociologically,
or politically, to accept Jesus as Savior. We are going to *witness!*
This is the importance of the lay witness, the non-professional's
witnessing out of the context of his life.

Evangelicals also do not believe in removing people from the
world to keep them in our movement. In fact, one of the purposes
of worship is to give people vision, perspective, and power to go
back into the dirty stuff of the world and relate to it in Christ's
name. One of the advantages of religious liberty in a pluralistic
society is that we have many more contacts with people who do not
know Jesus than we would have in a theocratic society.

Several new Jesus movements use these same techniques. An
example is *The Way*. When I was interim pastor at College Station,
one of the prominent men at A&M came and said, "A most
exciting thing has happened to me. I have just been appointed as a
faculty advisor for a new Christian group called *The Way*. Will you
tell me all about it?" Well, I tried to find out about the group, but
there was not much information on it. I did discover that a former
United Church of Christ minister had thrown away all of his books

and had gone back to study the Bible. He then worked out the idea that there is no Holy Spirit; only a human spirit. The Way denies the doctrine of the Trinity in any orthodox sense. They talk about speaking in tongues with what we call the human spirit.

Let us look at man's continuing passion for magic. Magic is as old as mankind. I think it is very important for those of us who are working with unbelievers to realize the fascination that magic has for them.

Carlos Castaneda was a Peruvian who came to America. He attended the University of California at Los Angeles. In order to prepare for his graduate work in anthropology, he was told to study the place of psychotropic plants in the religious experiences of the Mexican Indians. While he was in Mexico, he heard about a magician named Don Juan. Carlos became fascinated with Don Juan, and spent several years with him. Don Juan taught him how to break down his western, rationalistic thinking by using various kinds of psychotropic plants or drugs. Don Juan then led Castaneda into the world of magic and into the world of "helpers," who are very much like demonic helpers. He taught him all the techniques of power and magical rituals.

Castaneda then began to write books on the teachings of Don Juan. UCLA became fascinated with him. They gave him a Master's Degree for one of his books, and a Ph.D. for another. Many scholars now think some of it was a hoax; that Don Juan never existed. If, in fact, there was reality to his findings, they are probably the result of a composite study of many Mexican magicians or shamanists.

The point for Evangelical Christians to consider is that Castaneda's writings have literally fascinated American young people! At the University of Texas, there are seven Departments that use his writings. Students are fascinated because Castaneda spells out in an intellectual way the whole ancient world of magic, witchcraft, shamanism, manipulation, and taboo. He also explains how to get a "divine helper."

Magic has a continuing fascination for Americans. The heart of magic is *power,* the *ability to manipulate.* Some people think power is just holding strongly to your will, until you will other people to do what you want them to do. Other people think you can develop an "ESP" power," thus manipulating people. Still other people, like Corley and the Great Beast, claim that a person can get in touch with Satan—even sell your soul to Satan. Satan, they teach, will then give unique power, foreknowledge, and other powers which a normal human cannot have otherwise.

One of the most intriguing things in magic is sex magic. A magician—like Sybil Leek will say, "We can teach you how you can get a sex mate." There are certain rituals a person can go through; afterwards, a man can seduce any woman—or, a woman can seduce any man.

The Bible speaks against magic in a very dramatic way. God's people, after living for so many years in a sheep culture, were brought into the pagan land of Canaan. Canaan had a highly developed magic culture. Magic infiltrated the very community of Israel. As part of the diplomacies of his time, Solomon became intrigued with magic. Later, Jezebel brought 800 "Magic" preachers from Tyre and Sidon to Samaria, where she set up her own "seminary." The greatest problem, however was Baal worship. Manesseh even offered up his own children to the iron god, Molech. This was done in an attempt to get better crops and better rain for his people. All of his was based on magic.

Magic runs close to true Christianity at all times: There is a very close parallel, for example, between White Magic and Christianity. Yet, the contrasts are great! Christianity is not used for *bending* the will of God, *manipulating* the will of God, or using God. Rather, it is a matter of *surrendering to the will of God!* The Bible is true: when we surrender to the will of God, we will have all things added to us *in the way God wants us to have them*. Consequently, we will find joy, happiness, and fulfillment.

We have not done a good job of getting these Christian concepts over to our American young people. Magic appeals to the rootless, single people of our culture; to young people who are frustrated, who do not know how to get a "handle" on life. They are lost and lonely. Possibly the whole dramatic story of magic in our time is going to be another example of how we ought to go about teaching what *authentic* religion is all about!

I close with three ways to approach New Consciousness groups. We obviously have to use *the practical approach*. We have to answer the critics of Christianity. Secondly, we should use *the basic conflicts approach*. Everyone has a religion. Our great approach is to take the basic concepts of Christianity and throw them over against these pagan concepts. Although not many people are converted by argumentation, there is a place for *the testing approach*. Which of these approaches has coherence, comprehensiveness, creativity, and hangs together?

Christians can learn lessons from the New Consciousness groups. For example, we can learn *devotional practices*. Practically every one of these groups demand disciplined devotional techniques, such as twenty minutes twice a day by Transcendental Meditation, and five to six hours a day by the Hare Krishna Movement. At the same time, we have dropped our great devotional techniques in our churches. These groups put tremendous emphasis upon worship; again, we have neglected this. I personally believe that in today's secular world we need worship more desperately than ever before. We need to recover and restate the depth and breadth of our views. We need to point out the weaknesses in the New Consciousness groups. We need to emphasize *being* as well as *thinking*. Jesus said, "If I am lifted up, I will draw all men to myself."

In a context of religious freedom and openness of commitment, we should be unafraid. Because Christianity is the authentic religion, we should not be afraid of other religions in our world. We cannot, of course, go back to any kind of "closed system" or theocracy in our country or in our world. Andrew Greeley, the world-known Roman Catholic sociologist, said: "It is in a society of pluralism and religious freedom that Christian orthodoxy is best maintained with intellectual virility and social vitality." It is also in this kind of society that we are going to have more contact with people who are not Christians.

Our greatest tool to combat these groups is not through official pressure. Rather, it is for us to become so radiant, disciplined, and evangelistic, that people will see deep commitment to Christ in our lives. Persuasion, witness, incarnation is our approach. An authentic religion based on reality should prosper in this context. I pray that God will help us to take advantage of this opportunity in our time!

15. The Impact of Rejection

Charles Solomon

Charles R. Solomon, Ed.D., is founder and president of Grace Fellowship International (GFI), 1455 Ammons Street, Denver, Colorado 80215. He is the author of The Ins and Outs of Rejection, Handbook to Happiness, *and* Counseling with the Mind of Christ. *GFI is a counseling and counselor training ministry.*

I want to write about rejection—what it is, how it takes place, and what it does to people.*

In a way, it seems simplistic to boil down the problems related to rejection to a single syndrome. Nevertheless, we have seen over the past ten years that people have experienced rejection in many, many ways. It is usually very easy in the counseling interview to pick up how rejection took place in the life. Most people, when they hear the word "rejection," think of actions that were very harsh, unloving, and unkind. Many times, that is exactly the case; but there is also rejection that takes place in somewhat "loving" or more subtle ways.

Two types of rejection, therefore, are seen to exist. There is an *overt rejection*—an open, obvious rejection that everyone understands, such as a child being told by his parents, "I wish you had never been born." Many people in a counseling session verbalize feelings that they should never have been born. Often, all they are

---

*As a Christ-centered counselor who is a pioneer and reformer, I find myself in tension between Christian therapists on the one hand and some noted Christian or theological counselors on the other. The reader should not infer that the editor has taken up the cudgel by the inclusion of this chapter.

doing is agreeing with what their parents have told them. They heard their parents make such statements, or, perhaps they observed other children in the family thrown out of the house. If a child were thrown out at five or six years of age, the door slammed behind him and locked, and he is put in an orphanage, he would obviously get the idea he is unwanted! This is *overt rejection*. He may not know that big word, but at least he would know that his parents did not want him.

Rejection makes a great difference in the life of an individual. Overt rejection can also take place when a person is twenty-two, instead of age five. However, the earlier in life that it occurs the greater the impact it makes on the individual. For instance, parents sometimes tragically die when a child is two years old. The child is then left all by himself! *This is a form of rejection*. You may say, "But they didn't commit suicide, they did not *intend* to die!" Try to explain that to a two-year-old child. It doesn't really make a lot of difference to *him* whether they left the country, had heart attacks, abandoned him, or committed suicide. The net result is that the parents are not there to show him the love and acceptance he needs. This is a subtle kind of rejection. In the case of premature death of parents, the rejection is not *intended* by the parents, but is *perceived* as rejection on the part of the child. As this child grows older, further rejections will be handled in distinct ways.

I recall one lady I counseled who had a stepdaughter whose mother died when she was thirteen years of age. At age seventeen, she still had not forgiven her mother for dying. We might think she was old enough to know better than to take that attitude, but the daughter had still not forgiven her mother.

I remember a woman who "adopted" into a family at the age of thirty. Her father had died when she was two years of age. She has kept men at arm's length ever since. She could compete with the best of men, and competed with them strongly enough that no man would ever have married her! Her very strong personality goes back to the time when her father died and she developed compensatory behaviors. Her stepfather probably *tried* to show her love, when he married her widowed mother. She was then five or six years of age. In all likelihood, he found it was like trying to embrace a *porcupine* when he tried to hug her! Whether she knew it or not, she probably reacted from a feeling that no one would ever take the place of her father. To this day, she says that her stepfather rejected her. He might have, but it is debatable that he *started* the rejection. We see, then, that a premature death is a subtle form of rejection.

In any large group of people, there are some who have been adopted, or have children who are adopted. An adopted child, by definition, has experienced rejection. The parents may both have been killed in a car wreck, or the child may have been the product of an illegitimate relationship. Nevertheless, when he looks at his adopting parents they are not his *real* parents, his natural parents.

An adopted child is always faced with an identity crisis. From the beginning, he really does not know *who* he is. The vast majority of all children who are adopted, at one time or another, attempt to find out about their natural parents. They just want to *look* at them, one time, so that they will know who they are. The adopted parents can do all of the right things. They may say, "We picked you out! You were not just *born* to us, we picked you out. From the start, we loved you." They may show all the right kinds of love, but the identity crisis will still be there, *until the child finds his identity in Jesus Christ*. He can have a secure identity as a part of his adopted family, of course. Yet, until he gets his *eternal* identity nailed down—understanding his identity in Jesus Christ—he can't really let go of his search for his true parents.

Another type of rejection is *overprotection*. It is so subtle that many people have been thoroughly rejected through this device, and do not even know it! Since they *don't* know it, they do not know what to *do* about it. They have feelings inside they don't understand. Generally speaking, the adult who has been over-protected has ambivalent feelings toward his or her parents. They love the parents for the many good things they did *for* them as children, and also resent them for what the parents did *to* them. When loving overprotection has taken place, the person generally doesn't understand the dynamics of what has happened, because all the parents have done is to show love. When overprotecting love is shown and the child or adult feels resentment or hatred toward the parents for which he knows no basis, he hates himself more for hating such wonderful parents without a cause. Consequently, he hates himself. As he feels more and more guilty, you can see that he gradually digs a hole until he winds up in the pits by not understanding why he feels the way he does.

For many people, it is difficult to see how loving a child *too much* can become a form of rejection. Let me tell you a little story; see if you can fit children into this. Let's assume you have found a little fox pup. You have no pet at home, so you decide the fox would make a good pet. You pick him up, take him home, and you build a nice tall fence around the lawn. He can't get out; you have protected him from getting killed. You then install a watering device, the type used for cattle, so all he has to do is nudge it with his nose to get water. You give him the best animal food—possibly fresh horse meat. You have it chopped up. Perhaps you are a "food nut;" you even put food supplements in the horse meat. He has everything a fox's heart could desire, and some things that it couldn't!

He also needs exercise; you install a treadmill machine, so he can get plenty of exercise. You love him so much you even let him sleep in the bed with you. Everything is great! Naturally, with all the exercise, good food, and tender loving care, he has a beautiful frame. He grows up to be an adult and has all of the standard equipment. He could take the first prize in the local fox show!

When he is about eighteen months old and well-developed, because you are a Christian you start praying about your fox. It just isn't quite fair that he should have to be penned up all of his life and not be able to go out and mate or do the things that other foxes do. You are a little slow in your praying, so it takes you about three months to finally "pray through" on the issue. When he is twenty-one months old, you say to him: "Happy Birthday, Foxie! Today you become an adult—although it is tearing my heart out, I have to let you go into the world of adult foxes."

Now, he probably doesn't understand a word you are saying! You then pick him up and take him back to the exact spot where you originally found him. You water him with tears, because you really love him. You were not hypocritical; you have loved him like he was your own child . . . *but you didn't love him like a fox!* After you have cried your heart out, you let him go.

We may wonder what will happen to such a fox. He has been used to sleeping on your nice warm mattress. Now, it might rain during the night; he is sleeping on the cold, cold ground. He could wind up with laryngitis the next morning. He looks for the watering device, and does not find it. Instead, he finds *puddles!* He waits for someone to bring him his chopped up horse meat, and finds no food. As he gets weaker and hungrier, he may see a little four-legged rabbit going by, but he doesn't even know that rabbit is to be his food; he has always seen food chopped up in a bowl. As he gets weaker, a much larger four-legged animal comes by. The fox does not know that *he* is food for that large animal. Instead of *getting* a meal, he now *becomes* a meal!

Now, you loved him enough to do every possible thing for him, *except to let him become a fox*. Because of this kind of love you expressed to him, he was totally destroyed. The same thing can happen to a child. Many times, an only child is spoiled. Why! You have two adults making all the decisions for one child. Consequently, the child is spoiled, overprotected. He has too many decisions made for him. As a result, when he grows up he finds it very difficult to make decisions. Many times, a male who has been overprotected in this manner marries a fairly dominant female. Guess what happens? She takes up where Mom left off. The male forces her into the role of making decisions that he should be making. As soon as she makes them, he condemns her for doing so, and puts her down because she makes the decisions. Yet, he refuses to make decisions because he doesn't have the confidence to do so.

For the child who has been overprotected, there is a real conflict of emotions. The thoughts of the mind and the feelings are often in radical disagreement. I myself grew up with severe inferiority feelings, and I did not know why I had them. I had conflicts within myself that could be traced back to overprotection. There were things I knew I could do as a child; such as riding a bike. Other kids my age could ride one, and I was physically as large as they were. I knew *intellectually* I could ride a bike, and yet I *felt* like I could not do so. When a child is not permitted to confirm in his *experience* something he knows he can do in his *mind,* he may *know* he can, and *feel* that he can't!

Later, when jobs were given to me in the aerospace industry— layout jobs for which I was unprepared both educationally and experientially—the first thing that came into my mind was, "I can't do it!" Sometimes I would fight myself for hours or days before being able to begin a new assignment. I just felt like I *couldn't do it!* As the terminal date for the job approached, it was obvious that I had to get started. Usually, I would start quite late, which meant that I had to work about twice as fast as other people to get the same job done. Now, those who aren't neurotic won't understand this, but there were times after I had successfully completed a job that I *still* felt that I couldn't do it. My feelings and my mind did not agree.

Where there has been overprotection, where a child has not been allowed to confirm at the proper time that he can make a decision and live or die with it, he suffers. If he is never able to make mistakes as a child, and learn from his mistakes, *he doesn't learn the decision-making process*. His feelings may then be at variance with the *facts* for the rest of his life. Overprotection, then, is a subtle form of rejection. The parents are saying, "I love you, I love you, I love you!" They truly *do* love; yet, they do not love the child enough to let him become a *person*.

Many times such parents are loving their child to get love back for themselves, and that really is *exploitation,* selfish love. There are situations when a couple has two children, and the oldest one may be killed. They then say, "That is not going to happen to the other child. He can't do many things, because he might get killed. We would be then childless." There are many reasons why children are overprotected.

These are some of the subtle ways that rejection takes place. There are many people, however, who were overprotected by their parents and have never recognized it as rejection. Such persons may find it very difficult to admit that their parents showed rejection through overprotection. We consider it almost an act of treason to say, "My parents rejected me." However, much rejection takes place in that way. There is no intent on the part of the parents to reject, but it is perceived as such on the part of the child. When we see this in counseling, we do not put down the parents. Nor do we say, "Your parents did this to you, so you have every right to be neurotic!" Instead, we can say, "You are an adult now. You can see how Jesus Christ can meet your needs. Get your acceptance needs met in Him. Whether you ever get them met by your parents, whether they ever love and accept you in the proper way or not, you can find acceptance in Christ's love." Once they can understand that, they can then forgive their parents for the first time. With many people, who have been overprotected, they did not recognize the rejection. They simply did not want to be around their parents, and had hostile feelings. Not knowing why, they did not know what to forgive their parents for, or what to forgive *themselves* for. They did not know what had happened. Understanding the situation can cause them to forgive their parents for what they did, possibly in all innocence. They can then show love to their parents that they had never before been able to show. Overprotection, then, is a subtle form of rejection.

Thus far, we have described parents as doing the lion's share of the rejection. This isn't always true. Some of the most damaging rejections of childhood can take place on the school ground. For instance, consider a physically flawed child who has a birthmark or a hair lip or something similar. The parents may handle this very well, and not treat the child any differently than they would their other children. But when that child goes to school, he would rather be in a closet than in a classroom because of the cruelty that other children show!

However, parents obviously have more chances to communicate rejection, simply because they are with a child more than anyone else. Let us assume that parents knowingly or unknowingly *did* reject, *didn't* meet their child's needs for love and acceptance in some way. It is very natural that the child should then reject the parents. Many times these children, even when adults, identify God with their parents. This may especially be true of their father and The Father. They may then reject God *before* He has a chance to reject *them*. If the only thing a man understands is rejection, as a result he will reject his wife. The children get rejected, and other people come into their share of rejection; this is all the person understands. Consequently, rejection gets passed on as a way of life. Of course, other people always get blamed for doing something worthy of the rejecting.

I want now to look at some of the emotional results of rejection. To repeat, it makes a lot of difference whether these things happen to us at age two or twenty-two. The age the mother is when a child is born also makes a lot of difference. If the mother was twenty-two, twenty-five or thirty, that is one thing. If Mom was forty, forty-five or fifty that is another thing! In my experience, I have found that few people plan children after age forty. Usually, the child finds out that he was not planned. By eavesdropping, he may hear that he was a "tag-along," "second family," a "caboose," an "accident," or a "change-of-life baby," or some such thing. If he isn't told that, usually as he gets a little older he figures it out. The parents may want to prevent his feeling that they didn't want him, so they are always saying, "I love you! I love you! I love you!" He is hearing that with his mind, but underneath he is getting the message: "I hate you! I hate you! I hate you!"

Now, if you want a child to become schizophrenic this is the way to do it: Tell him you love him, but show him you hate him. You will put him in such a double bind that he can't think his way out of it. Then, his mind and his emotions will not agree. He will be debilitated.

Let us consider next the feelings that take place within the rejected person: First, we have *feelings of worthlessness*. If a child is not given a sense of worth, a feeling that he can do things well, it is only natural that he should feel worthless. Feelings of worthlessness typify the person who has been severely rejected. As we have already seen, many people begin to wish they had never been born. They are trapped with existence, they do not *want* to "kill their earth-suit" they are wearing; but they wish they had not been born. Then, they feel, they would not have been faced with the decisions of life.

Second, there are those *feelings of inferiority* that many people have, without knowing where they came from. One feels inferior and does not know *why* he feels that way. For example, as a child I used to feel that everyone in the classroom knew more than I did—and yet I expected to make better grades than they, *and usually did*. You say, "That is neurotic!" Yes, that is exactly what it is. But that is the way I felt. I had decided that I really was inferior.

Third, *a person can be unable to express feelings*. As I review this list, you may see that you have a couple of these symptoms floating around inside yourself. You are not likely to let others know how you are feeling, because they might hate you as badly as you hate yourself! You may lose what little acceptance you have. We then put on a "front," act the way others expect us to act, say what they want us to say, and try to get some acceptance. Yet inside ourselves, we know that this "front" is not *really* who we are. As a result, people accept what we say (everybody likes a show!), but we know our actions do not represent the real persons we are. Even though others accept what they see, as far as I am concerned it is a hollow victory. Others still do not know who I really *am!* We play those games all the time. We do not receive acceptance that means anything, and we are unable to become real persons, because we are sure people would not love us if they knew the bad feelings we have inside of us.

Fourth, *depression begins to develop.* My favorite definition for depression is *"an internal temper tantrum."* Children get on the floor and kick, scream, yell, and turn blue in the face. Uusually, we adults get a little bit more sophisticated about throwing our tantrums. For example, some husbands swash their fists through the plaster wall, and make a big hole. They then hang a picture over the hole to cover it up, because they are too lazy to fix it. Some wives throw cups at their husband's heads or through the window. Physical tantrums are sometimes *thrown!*

Other people throw *mental* tantrums. They can do so through fantasy, through flights from reality. Still other people throw emotional tantrums, otherwise known as *depression.* Depression is throwing a fit *inside yourself* or internalizing hostility.

Fifth, a person may employ emotional insulation. A person who has been hurt by other people does something to protect himself against further hurt, usually in the form of building walls about himself so other people can't get in to hurt him. A person who has been divorced may think: "I will *never* get married again. I will never take the chance of having that kind of pain another time." This is emotional insulation . . . building walls to keep other people out. As a result, it *does* keep other people from hurting us. We won't let them get *close* to us. But it also has another effect! People also can't get in to *love* us. By isolating ourselves, our walls of insulation keep others from coming in to us. That insulation also keeps us from reaching out to other people. We *isolate* ourselves, as we *insulate* ourselves from further hurt.

Sixth, *the person becomes subjective.* Life is lived on the level of the emotional plane. Illogical, the self-absorbed person is controlled by all these feelings within. To others who do not have those feelings, the conduct of the person seems very illogical. It is illogical. The person is operating on the basis of the *subjective* level, the *feeling* level, not the *logical* level.

Seventh, *the person becomes introspective.* A person who has all of this going on inside often turns inward, trying to see what is going on. He tries to sort out the garbage inside. He tries to change things, tries to figure out what happened. He usually goes in circles, trying to deal with guilt. In this case, I am not talking about *real* guilt, I am talking about *emotional* guilt, or *false* guilt.

A child who has been rejected, who has been told or feels he is not wanted, feels guilty. He feels guilt for simply existing. He may feel guilty for just *being a person* all the rest of his life. If he doesn't know where the guilt is coming from, he may think there must be some *sin* he has committed. Yet, after he has dealt with all known sin and *still* feels guilty, what does he do? It may be sin and/or psychological problems from his parents that has caused his condition, not his own. He feels guilty for just being a person! No amount of confession will ever solve that, because it isn't *his* sin at the root. There is a scriptural answer for his problem, but it is not *confession* he needs. When you confess someone else's sin it is not likely to do you any good. Such a person is introspectively trying to find in himself the reason for the guilt they feel. It will not work.

Eighth, *perfectionism develops*. Some older children get the idea that if they do everything perfectly, they might get some love and acceptance from their parents. They become perfectionists, trying to earn love from Mom or Dad, or both. Usually they never quite achieve their goal, because Dad and Mom always have the standards too high. As soon as they almost achieve them, Dad or Mom *raise* the standards. Then, even when they *do* reach the standards, it doesn't help. They then feel no better about themselves, because the parents have accepted their *performance*, not their *person*. All they have gained is a *performance-based acceptance,* or *conditional love.*

Ninth, the person exerts *little self-discipline*. The child has been told endlessly how, when, what, and where to perform. Overprotection has caused too many decisions to be made for him. When he reaches adult life, there is a little self-discipline, because he never had the childhood opportunities to be self-governing. This adult will always expect someone to tell him what to do, even though he will probably reject the person for doing so.

Tenth, *there develops irresponsibility—the inability to accept responsibility*. Many people in churches, for example, would like to take responsibility for some type of ministry. Yet, with *all* these turbulent feelings inside, there is no way they can take on responsibility. They live with fear of failure. They would rather *not* try and *not* fail, than to *try* and fail. Then, not only would they be a failure in their *own* eyes, but also in the eyes of other people. Consequently, they dodge responsibility.

Eleventh, *worries, doubts, and fears develop*.

Twelfth, *self-condemnation grows*. A person who has been condemned by other people goes into a program of condemning himself, of putting himself down. For instance, a lady might be a seamstress. She makes a beautiful garment. A friend sees it and says, "Did you make that? Oh, it is beautiful!" The seamstress says, "No, this is wrong with it. That is wrong with it." She will try to find something wrong with her work. Her attitude toward her work must agree with the way she feels about herself. Another example is the man who begins to remodel a house. He works hard at it, but when he is done, he is plagued by all the mistakes. He can't admit he did a good job. He has to find something wrong with it.

Thirteenth, there develops *self-hatred*. A person who feels hated from other people winds up hating himself. So many of the people who come to us for counseling hate themselves! Yet, the Word of God says that we should love our neighbor the way we love ourselves. If most of the people with whom I counsel loved *me* the way they love *themselves*, I'd head for the back door! They are killing themselves, and they might do the same thing to me. Usually, those people treat other people better than they do themselves. As I said, the bottom line here is guilt. And these guilt feelings are not caused by sin within their lives. They are caused by rejection.

Fourteenth, the summary of it all becomes *self-rejection*. The person who has been rejected by others, especially when it has happened at an early age, rejects himself.

Fifteenth, that rejection causes him in turn to *reject other people*. Here are just some of the attitudes that a person could have toward his parents who have rejected him:

He might resent them. You can't get some Christians to admit that they hate their parents, because the Bible says that is a "no-no." But if you can word it just right, you can probably get them to admit that they *resent* their parents just a little bit! I have heard some adults say, "I like to go home and visit my parents; but, after I am there a day or two, I am ready to leave." They love their parents but *they can't stand to be with them!* Of course, that is a little bit illogical.

He might feel bitter toward his parents. Most of us have been teenagers at one time or another! Sometimes adolescents clam up and refuse to talk. Have you ever seen a teenager do that? You ask him what is wrong and he says, "Nothing!" It is obvious there *is* something wrong, but he clams up and won't let you inside. This person has rejected you and is keeping you out. Some husbands and wives keep the old "Clam-Up Game" going on all the time. They reject each other without words. Or, one person may reject the other with words or with blows; the other rejects without words. It all depends on how big a coward or how brave a person is in the process of showing rejection.

He might rebel against the authority of the parents. Teenage rebellion is a *reaction* to rejection. When a teenager rebels, the parents many times say, "I have done *everything* for this child. How can he do this to me!" In counseling, I sometimes wonder who the parents are more concerned about: the child or themselves.

Then, there is *ambivalence:* "I love my parents for what they have done *for* me, and I hate them for what they did *to* me." This is the result of overprotection.

Finally, *he might distrust them.* There are, then, many reactions we see toward parents who reject their children.

The person who has been rejected in a family situation, then, will show rejection to his mate and his children. A person who has never received love in a meaningful way finds it almost impossible to show love. Many times children and mates are just tolerated. I have heard couples call their children, "house apes," and "rug rats," and other choice terms like that. They put a roof over their head, food in their stomachs, clothes on their backs, and that is about all the children get. Otherwise, the household is a pretty sterile atmosphere. Lot of times punishment is given out, simply to get the hostility out of the parent and on to the child—not to cleanse the conscience of the child. And many times, then, the punishment is more than the crime deserves and rejection takes place. You can spare the rod and spoil the child or you can use the rod and destroy the child depending on the motivation for the discipline and the love in which the punishment is meted out.

Some parents have little time with the children out of necessity! The father might be a long-haul truck driver and be gone five nights out of seven. In the time that he is home he has to work on the house and do other chores. The children get very little time with Dad. Sometimes father is a minister or missionary. He is so busy doing the Father's business that he never has much time to do *father's* business. Some children are rejected because the church many times expects the pastor to spend every waking moment in his work at church. Many pastors, that I deal with, feel guilty if they take one day off or one night off. As a result, they lose themselves in their work and lose their children in the process. Many times a congregation almost forces the pastor into that situation unless he is strong enough to say, "No."

Consider all these patterns.

Verbal acceptance and emotional rejection: "I love you with my mouth, but I hate you with feelings inside." After a child who has not been shown love has his own family, he may say: "I didn't get *any* love and acceptance when I was growing up, and I intend to show my kids *lots* of love and acceptance."

When he has children of his own, guess what he does? He just fawns over them, does *everything* for them . . . *and overprotects them!* Then, the child who has been overprotected grows up, has children, and says: "I'm not going to do that to *my* kids!" When his first child gets to be six years old, he says: "Go out and get yourself a paper route, because I am not going to do all your work for you!" Generation by generation, the pendulum can swing to either extreme. There can be too *little* guidance, which is as bad as too *much*.

I worked with one man who recalled that his mother let him go down the river on a raft by himself when he was only eight years of age. He could have gotten the idea that she wouldn't have cared if he had fallen overboard! You see, too *little* guidance also meets the qualifications for becoming rejection.

Then, there is physical abuse—the problem of the battered child. Statistics show that most children are battered by parents who were themselves battered. They hate their own parents for beating up on them. They are so torn up within that when their own child does something wrong, they slap their child around.

Refusal to communicate—the "clam-up routine"—is another pattern of rejection. Many things can be communicated by *lack* of communication. Or, parents may make it evident that other things or people are more important than children. Or, children can get the idea that *when they grow up* they will be "people," too. They are made to feel that Dad and Mom are interested in *people,* not children. Until they grow up, they can't expect to receive acceptance from their parents. However, when they do grow up, they don't know *how* to be "people," because Mom and Dad did not *let* them be "people" as they grew up.

Another pattern is intensive rejection of people who are identified with rejecting parents. For example, if my mother rejected me, either subtly or in obvious ways, I might decide that no female will ever do that to me again. Then, when I get married, I might act towards my wife in the way I might have acted toward my mother if I had been able to do it.

People will often enter marriage with a determination that they will not let that kind of transference happen; nevertheless, it takes place. Probably you have heard the story about the young fellow that got married. As he drove his bride away on their honeymoon, the horse drawing their buggy stumbled. The groom said to the horse: "That's once!" They went a little farther, and the horse stumbled again. He said to the horse, "That's twice!" The third time he stumbled, the young groom took out a gun and killed the horse. His bride said: "Dear, aren't you being a little *mean?*" He said to her: "That's once!"

Our attitudes and reactions toward God may be much like our attitudes toward our parents. Refusal to come under the parents' authority may result in refusal to come under God's authority. For this reason alone, children should learn obedience in the home. If children rebel against parents, they will rebel against civil authority, and they will rebel against God.

Rejection may also cause an inability to *trust* God. If a person can't trust an earthly father, how can he trust an invisible God? Many people who come for counseling think God is "up there" with a black snake whip, ready to punish them as soon s they step out of line. They see God as a tyrant, not a loving Father. They readily understand how he can condemn such a worm as they are, but they cannot understand his love and acceptance. They have had plenty of condemnation, and so they accept a condemning God. They transfer their father's behavior to God, and then reject God for being like Dad. If Dad happened to be an "absentee father," they may feel that God is also an "absentee," and become an atheist. Or, if their father died when they were a year or two old, they may feel that God will also forsake them. As a result, they can't trust God too much. They will have very little fellowship and communion with a God who is not trusted.

Rejection causes people to be unable to accept love, because they have never been given love in a meaningful way. They can't handle love. Yet, we are designed to need love and acceptance. Such a person seeks after love; when he gets it, he doesn't know what to do with it, and has to turn it off. It is sort of like a dog chasing a car: Can you imagine what the dog would *do* with it if he finally *caught* it? People seeking love may be like that! When they get it, they do something to get the loving person to reject them. They are "programmed" to see rejection in everything and everyone; if they don't get rejection, they will force it, so that they will know how to behave. It is hard for them to meet someone who just keeps on loving! It is hard to hurt someone when all they are doing is loving you.

Another pattern of handling rejection is the person who tries too hard to please. They say "Yes" even before they are asked a question. Still another pattern is for the person to refuse to say what others want them to say, because they feel to do so would be to demean themselves. They have a chip on both shoulders, and they can't say, "I'm wrong; I'm sorry." A final pattern people use is to cling like a leech to any person who finally does accept them. When some people finally find love and acceptance, they have no desire to turn loose of it. Sometimes the person who has given the love feels he has to drag the person along with every step he takes. In reality, the person who is "leeching on" is rejecting the one showing love by demanding all of his time.

Summary:

The "rejection syndrome" began in the Garden of Eve when Adam rejected God. Adam's rebelliousness (and his nature) was passed on to Cain who rather soundly rejected Abel. This pattern of rejecting and being rejected has been operating since that time. The understanding of the syndrome is not sufficient to reverse it in ourselves or in others. The antidote to rejection is acceptance and the only person in whom we can find unconditional acceptance is the Lord Jesus Christ.

It is only as we understand our *true* identity as believers through our union with Christ in death, resurrection, ascension and sealing in heavenly places that we can, by faith, appropriate our acceptance in Christ.

ACCEPTANCE

Oh, to know acceptance
 In a feeling sort of way;
To be known for what I am—
 Not what I do or say
It's nice to be loved and wanted
 For the person I seem to be,
But my heart cries out to be loved
 For the person who is really me!

To be able to drop all the fronts
 And share with another my fears,
Would bring such relief to my soul,
 Though accompanied by many tears.
When I find this can be done
 Without the pain of rejection,
Then will my joy be complete
 And feelings toward self know correction.

The path to feeling acceptance of God
 Is paved with acceptance on Earth;
Being valued by others I love
 Enhances my own feeling of worth.
Oh, the release and freedom he gives
 As I behold his wonderful face—
As Jesus makes real my acceptance in him,
 And I learn the true meaning of grace.

A pity it is that so late we find
 His love need not be earned;
As we yield to him all manner of strife
 A precious truth has been learned.
Then, as we share with others who search
 For love, acceptance, and rest;
They'll find in us the Savior's love.
 And experience the end of their quest.

C. R. SOLOMON